Children's Social Consciousness
and the Development
of Social Responsibility

SUNY Series, Democracy and Education
Edited by George H. Wood

Children's Social Consciousness and the Development of Social Responsibility

Sheldon Berman

STATE UNIVERSITY OF NEW YORK PRESS

Published by
State University of New York Press, Albany

© 1997 State University of New York

For information, address State University of New York Press,
State University Plaza, Albany, N.Y., 12246

Production by Cathleen Collins
Marketing by Theresa Abad Swierzowski

Library of Congress Cataloging in Publication Data

Berman, Sheldon, 1949–
    Children's social consciousness and the development of social
responsibility / Sheldon Berman.
        p.   cm. — (SUNY series, democracy and education)
    Includes bibliographical references and index.
    ISBN 0-7914-3197-5 (alk. paper). — ISBN 0-7914-3198-3 (pb : alk.
paper)
    1. Socialization.   2. Social values—Study and teaching—United
States.   3. Citizenship—Study and teaching—United States.
4. Social skills—Study and teaching—United States.   I. Title.
II. Series.
LC192.4.B47   1997
370.11'5—dc20   96-14444
                                                                        CIP

10 9 8 7 6 5 4 3 2 1

This book is dedicated to my parents, Morton and Eva, who survived the pain of the depression and the Holocaust and still found it in their hearts to care about the welfare of others.

Contents

Acknowledgments

The research and writing of this book has been both an arduous challenge and a joyful exploration of insight and expression. From its inception it took several years to complete. Along the way I have had the support and encouragement of many people. Without them this work would have been impossible.

I would like to express my heartfelt thanks first to my primary advisor, Donald Oliver, who saw this work through its many transitions and drafts, and to Joe Maxwell, who read this work and all the drafts that preceeded it with an eye for detail and an understanding of what it would take to argue for a new theoretical framework. I would also like to thank Vito Perrone and Sara Lawrence Lightfoot, who were valued readers and thoughtful respondents.

There were also those at the Harvard Graduate School of Education and elsewhere who deeply influenced my thinking about social responsibility. Uppermost among these were Lawrence Kohlberg and Carol Gilligan. I owe a great deal to my experience in working with a number of the just communities Larry was studying and to the incisive questions and different voice that Carol articulated in my courses and teaching fellowships with her. I am also grateful to Eric Schaps and Victor Battistich of the Developmental Studies Center, Tom Lickona of the State University of New York at Cortland, Clark Power of the University of Notre Dame, and Henry Giroux of Miami University with whom I've conferred on ideas and questions. There are also colleagues with whom I've shared ideas for this book and who helped me think through ways of understanding social responsibility. These include Larry Dieringer, Fred Gross, Keith Grove, Todd Jennings, Seth Kreisberg, Dick Mayo-Smith, Kathryn Portnow,

Dennis Shirley, Roberta Snow, David Svendsen, Gene Thompson-Grove, Eleanora Villegas-Reimers, and George Wood.

The writing of a book is personally and financially demanding. More than anyone else, I owe the completion of this work to Sarah Haavind, my wife, who supported our family for a year so that I could work on it full time, who read draft after draft and provided thoughtful advice, and who kept my spirits up by believing in the important contribution this work could make. I am also deeply grateful for the unquestioning support my parents offered throughout.

Finally, I want to thank the many teachers and administrators with whom I've worked in ESR and the ELNA Project. Although there are too many to list, this work was inspired by their courage, vision, and commitment. In the moments that were most difficult, I was able to think of them and know that, in some small way, this work was meant to honor and support their efforts.

CHAPTER 1

"I care about the world.
But I don't think it concerns me,
even though it does."

When I was ten years old, I remember watching "Harvest of Shame," the Edward R. Murrow television special about hunger in America. Something happened as I watched. I'm sure I had heard about hunger, discrimination, and injustice before. Issues of civil rights had been in the news. The topic of discrimination, especially against Jews and African Americans, had come up in family conversations. But this time something jelled. I felt pain at the suffering I observed. And I was angry. How could people let others suffer like this? This was an intolerable injustice that we—American citizens and our government—should be trying to correct. Although there were other moments of social and political awareness earlier, this one had a distinctly different quality. What jelled was the link between a social problem and its potential solution. I felt personally compelled to respond to the suffering I observed, and I realized that the solution also had to include collective political action.

There were many such moments to follow throughout my childhood and adolescence. The world became more problematic as issues of civil rights, nuclear war, ecological destruction, and military intervention set the social and political stage around me. Questions emerged. What was my place in this world? What could I do to help? Would anyone listen to my opinions and ideas? Would anyone in government pay attention to what I thought? How do I deal with the wide differences in beliefs and opinions that people have? Why aren't we doing more as a country to

1

solve our problems? Inspired by the hope of the Kennedy years and then angered by the ethics of the Nixon years, I found that there was a political background to the day-to-day life of school and play.

However, there wasn't a forum for me to bring these issues into the open. My family talked some about politics. My parents watched the news every night. They voted in every election. In spite of their strong pro-union and pro-Democratic Party stands, we were not an activist family. In fact, "don't get involved" and "look out for yourself" were dominant themes. Issues of political conflict and controversy were not present in school until late in my school years and then only in the form of academic discussion and debate. The deeper questions, the feelings, the desire to do something about problems were not dealt with. Sometimes my friends and I talked about social and political issues but not often. We talked more about presidential candidates because we felt we would eventually have a say in who was elected. There were no other available avenues for action apparent to us. Political reality was distant from our grasp but everpresent as an almost surreal backdrop to our daily existence.

I was never able to fully confront those deeper issues as a young person although I continued to try to make sense of my place in the social and political world. I continued to feel pain at the suffering of others and anger at injustice. And I continued to try to find paths in life that let me make a difference. My first year out of college I tried working on political issues in Washington. I felt alienated by what I saw—a climate that encouraged an egocentric hunger for power and status rather than collective action to correct the ills and heal the pain in the world. I retreated to the woods of Maine to reflect and figure out another path. Ultimately, I entered teaching because I felt that it was a humane and ethical way to make a difference in the world. I could help young people search for answers to their questions about the world around them and help them find avenues for action that gave them meaning and fulfillment.

In many ways I feel lucky. In spite of the seeming inaccessibility of the political arena, I was able to find an entry point and a way of living and working that were meaningful in both personal and political terms. Yet many young people are not so lucky. In fact, most stand at a great distance from the political arena, drawing a boundary around themselves that, at once, protects them from its buffeting questions and paralyzes them into inaction. At an early age they begin to live as if that social and political arena were detached from their daily lives. As one twelve year old said to me in an interview, "I care about the world. But I don't think it concerns me, even though it does" (Berman, 1990, p. 6).

In the early 1980s Arthur Levine, then President of Bradford College, interviewed freshmen on a number of college campuses. He found that students expressed strong optimism about their own personal futures but were pessimistic about the future of the country and the world. But even more striking, they seemed to see little relationship between the two. He reports the following conversation as typical of what he heard:

Interviewer:	Will the United States be a better or worse place to live in the next ten years?
Student:	The U.S. will definitely be a worse place in which to live.
Interviewer:	Then you must be pessimistic about the future?
Student:	No, I'm optimistic.
Interviewer:	Why?
Student:	Because I have a high grade point average and I'm going to get a good job, make a lot of money, and live in a nice house. (1983, p. 4)

Levine concludes that "there is a sense among today's students that they are passengers on a sinking ship, a Titanic if you will, called the United States or the world. Fatalism and fear of becoming one of the victims is widespread. And there is a growing belief among young people that if they are being forced to ride on a doomed vessel, they owe it to themselves to make the trip as lavish as possible and go first class" (p. 4).

The self-concern and political disengagement of today's young people has been reported in a number of studies. The Committee for the Study of the American Electorate reported a steady decline in the eighteen- to twenty-four-year-old vote and found this group to be the only category of newly enfranchised in our history whose voting patterns have shown a decline since enfranchisement. The rate of decline in voting among this age group is two and a half times that for the general population.

A 1990 study of fifty years of public opinion data by the Times Mirror Center for the People and the Press concluded that this generation "knows less, cares less . . . votes less and is less critical of its leaders and institutions than young people in the past" (p. 1). "The surveys conducted by Times Mirror reveal a younger generation with less curiosity about news of all sorts, and one with an especially small appetite for the most serious and complicated of issues" (p. 9). The study also found that young people were less informed about government, politics, and contemporary issues. "Over most of the past five decades, younger members of the public have been at least as well informed as older people. In 1990 that is no longer the case. Times Mirror's research finds that young people were 20 percent less likely than middle-aged and older people to give the correct answer to 74 questions on current events" (p. 1). Times Mirror concludes that the low levels of political knowledge and political commitment among the younger generation makes them an "easy target" for those seeking to manipulate public opinion (p. 28).

These results were echoed in another study commissioned by People For the American Way (Hart Research, 1989), which interviewed over 1,000 adolescents. The researchers concluded that America's youth are alarmingly ill-prepared to keep democracy alive in the 1990s and beyond. "Today's students show little grasp of the responsibilities that accompany the freedoms of citizenship, and they find politics and government remote from their lives and concerns. Sixty percent said they knew just 'some' or 'very little' about how government works, and slightly fewer (53 percent) said they trust Washington to do what is right only 'some' or 'none of the time.' Seventy percent agreed that 'sometimes politics and government seem so complicated that a person like me can't really understand what's going on' " (Fowler, 1990, p. 11).

The National Assessment of Education Progress conducted evaluations of civics achievement among thirteen- and seventeen-year-old students in 1975–76, 1981–82, and 1987–88. None of the NAEP studies reported positive results of students' civic competence. The most recent report, issued in 1990, attempted to compare the data from the three assessments and found that although the scores for the thirteen-year-olds were relatively stable, the scores for the seventeen-year-olds showed a marked decline. "As anticipated, the depth and breadth of students' performance in each content area grew as they progressed through school. However, even by the twelfth grade, students' civic achievement remained quite limited in many respects. Most students performed poorly on items that referred to technical vocabulary, detailed political processes, or the historical and intellectual traditions of our government" (Anderson et al., 1990, p. 67).

These studies reveal a problem that has been getting progressively more serious. Most of the studies frame their conclusions in terms of the threat that this lack of knowledge, interest, and engagement has on the vitality and viability of our democracy. Our democracy is, in fact, at risk. Democratic participation continues to decline and cynicism about our political institutions and leaders continues to increase. Most people, and especially young people, believe that their voices will not be heard and that their participation will be ineffectual. Leading democratic theorists—Barber, Boyte, Pateman, Dahl—argue that democracy functions well only when citizens voluntarily enter our political life and collective decision-making processes. There is disagreement among theorists about whether there is the need for broad participation or more narrowly defined participation, but all agree that some political involvement and a basic understanding of political institutions are critical to preserving democracy and preventing the concentration of power in the hands of the few.

Yet there is another less focused upon but even more critical factor that undergirds the workings of a democracy—a sense of community and a notion of the collective good. Democracy is simply a way for people of divergent perspectives to make collective decisions. The sense of community humanizes this process by adding care, mutual respect, social solidarity, and interest in the common good. In spite of past presidential rhetoric about a "kinder and gentler America," we are living in a culture of separation rather than cohesion (Bellah et al., 1985). The pervasive ethic of individualism, the increase of social divisiveness and violence, and the fragmentation of the family and community have undermined our ability to bridge our differences and build a meaningful national community (Bellah et al., 1985, 1991). When one takes a deeper look at the studies of young people (Anderson et al., 1990; Dynneson & Gross, 1991; Fowler, 1990; Hart Research, 1989; Moore, Lare, & Wagner, 1985; Sigel & Hoskin, 1981; Washburn, 1986), one finds that they do not see community participation as necessary for good citizenship, that they speak of their personal rights but not of the common good, that their notions of democracy are vague at best and often border on advertising slogans, that nationalism and authoritarian values are often preferable to democratic values, and that the only way they plan on participating in public decision making is through voting. At a time when our nation and our planet are faced with serious social, political, and ecological problems that demand both thoughtful collective decision making and persistent collective action, we are faced with a new generation of citizens less informed, less interested in public affairs, and less inclined to participate.

There is, however, some brighter news in two recent studies. The Independent Sector's study (Hodgkinson & Weitzman, 1992) of volunteering and giving found a significant rise in volunteer behavior among thirteen- through seventeen-year-olds, although very few participated in political activity. In addition, the Higher Education Research Institute's study (Astin, 1992) of over 200,000 college freshmen found increases in students indicating that influencing social values, promoting racial understanding, and being involved in environmental cleanup were important personal goals. Many communities and schools have initiated community service programs that have attracted the interest and enthusiasm of young people. Jennings and Niemi (1981) and Sears (1990) note that young people are influenced by the historic period they live in. These researchers identified small period effects. Yet we may be seeing a renewal of social and political interest among young people brought about by the changing political climate and the efforts of educators to bring the concepts of service and political involvement into the curriculum and program of the school. This renewal is far from pervasive, and it is still too early to claim a turnaround in young people's attitudes.

Researchers have placed the burden of responsibility for the lack of social and political interest and participation among young people on a number of sources. Our current social and political problems are more complex and intractable than problems of the past. There are few simple and readily available solutions to the problems of pollution, poverty, the national debt, and the distribution of wealth and power. In addition, our political process has become more contentious and distasteful. People hold out less hope for our ability to develop effective, mutually acceptable policies and programs. But the institution that receives the most criticism is our schools. In part this criticism is misdirected. It is easier to displace our frustration with the political process on children and schools rather than to assume responsibility for our failure to create workable solutions to problems. Whether it is our failure to compete effectively in the international economy or to redress issues of poverty, racism, and violence, it seems that instead of closely examining our current social policies and institutions we look to the schools as the vehicle for change.

Yet the schools shoulder a part of the responsibility. Historically, the schools have been a primary vehicle for citizenship development (Butts, 1980). The founders of our democracy "talked about education as a bulwark for liberty, equality, popular consent, and devotion to the public good, goals that took precedence over the uses of knowledge for self-improvement or occupational preparation. Over and over, leaders of the time, both liberal and conservative, asserted their faith that the welfare of the Republic rested upon an educated citizenry and that free, common, public schools would be the best means of educating the citizenry in the cohesive civic values, knowledge, and obligations required of everyone in a democratic republican society" (Butts, p. 54). Jefferson expressed this most clearly in 1779 in his proposed law to establish public schools in Virginia.

> In every government on earth is some trace of human weakness, some germ of corruption, and degeneracy, which cunning will discover, and wickedness insensibly open, cultivate and improve. Every government degenerates when trusted to the rulers of the people alone. The people themselves therefore are its only safe depositories. And to render even them safe their minds must be improved to a certain degree. This indeed is not all that is necessary, though it be essentially necessary. An amendment of our constitution must come here in aid of public education. The influence over government must be shared among all people. (cited in Butts, p. 55 from Thomas Jefferson, *Notes on the State of Virginia*, 2nd American ed. (Philadelphia: 1794), pp. 215–16)

These sentiments were echoed by Horace Mann and other leaders in the movement to establish public education. In fact, the basic purpose of universal literacy was its value in producing informed citizens. Citizenship was seen as the fundamental purpose, the "basic," upon which the curriculum rested.

We have repeatedly looked to our schools' efforts in social responsibility, citizenship education, or civic competence in times of perceived national crisis. Throughout the first half of the eighteenth century, the schools were the means for developing a civic culture and national pride. In the late nineteenth and early twentieth centuries, the waves of immigration created fears of national disunity and schools were asked to be the vehicle for political enculturation and unification. The progressive movement in education of the first half of the twentieth century called for a renewal of democracy with civic instruction as a primary element. In the 1950s, the schools were seen as the vehicle for a national competition with the Soviet Union not only in space and military technology but also in political ideology. Out of the Vietnam era and the first national assessment of civic competence in the mid-1970s came another call for improved civic instruction. In each case citizenship education was defined differently and the proposed reforms took a different shape. For the most part, these citizenship education efforts were nationalistic and conservative in orientation (Butts, 1980). Yet underlying each was the belief that the school played a pivotal role in facilitating our experiment in democratic governance. "Public education does not refer merely to a kind of education that serves a public. Rather, it expresses the idea of something to be formed—a public—through communicative practices in which all can participate" (Giarelli, 1988, p. 58).

Even among its strongest advocates, however, there has been dissatisfaction with our practice of citizenship education (Butts, 1980; Massialas, 1972; Mehlinger, 1977; Newmann, 1975; Shaver, 1977). Shaver, a past president of the National Council for the Social Studies, writes, "Despite the conscientious efforts of many educators, citizenship education is in disarray. There is little evidence to indicate that the school's citizenship education efforts have affected generally the quantity or quality of adult citizen participation, and social studies programs and school environments often appear to be inconsistent with the demands of 'adult citizenship' " (1977, p. vii). In looking at how the school addresses issues of care and community, social psychologist Urie Bronfenbrenner writes,

> [I]n the United States it is now possible for a person eighteen years of age to graduate from high school without ever having had to do a piece of work on which somebody else truly depended. . . . It is now possible for a person eighteen years of age, female as well as male, to graduate from high school, college, or university without ever having cared for, or even held, a baby; without ever having looked after someone who was old, ill, or lonely; or without ever having comforted or assisted another human being who really needed help. . . . No society can long sustain itself unless its members have learned the sensitivities, motivations, and skills involved in assisting and caring for other human beings. Yet the school, which is the setting carrying primary responsibility for preparing young people for effective participation in adult life, does not, at least in American society, give high priority to providing opportunities in which such learning could take place. (1979, p. 53)

Since the end of World War II, many educators, political scientists, and psychologists have studied the development of young people's ethical thinking, political understandings, and prosocial behavior, and the role schools play in this development, in order to improve our efforts in citizenship development. Some have produced theoretical frameworks and pedagogical recommendations to guide teachers, curriculum developers, and administrators. Others have studied young people's understanding of social and political reality and offered developmental sequences. And others have pursued empirical research on the effectiveness of classroom practices and school organization and climate. Their work, however, has appeared in such disparate fields as political socialization, moral development, prosocial behavior, citizenship education, and psychosocial development. There has been little communication or collaboration among these fields. Yet, when the work in these various fields is taken together, it provides important new insights into the development of social consciousness and social responsibility in young people and effective classroom and school practice. It gives us a clearer handle on what responsibility the school can assume and how it can effectively assume it. If we want to revitalize public participation among young people, it is important to take a close look at what we know about the processes by which young people develop a sense of social responsibility and the educational practices that support this development.

However, in order to give coherence to the disparate research data in citizenship education, political socialization, prosocial behavior, moral development, and psychosocial development, a new theoretical framework is required that uses social consciousness and social responsibility as central organizing constructs. This new framework treats the development of one's relationship with the political and social world and one's personal investment in the well-being of others and the planet as a central concern. The data that come out of these disparate fields on the development of political consciousness, social understanding, political interest and participation, prosocial attitudes and behavior, moral reasoning and moral action, and democratic values then contribute to this broader understanding. In fact, when synthesized within this framework, the empirical data illuminate specific developmental patterns, basic motivational factors and processes, and particularly effective educational interventions that had previously remained isolated or obfuscated by the research boundaries maintained by each of the fields.

The theoretical framework that I want to explicate from an examination of this research builds on, but often stands in contrast to, much of the independent work done in these disparate fields. For example, it becomes clear that moral sensibilities emerge far earlier than many moral development theorists suggest, that activism is more grounded in one's sense of connectedness, one's identification with morality, and one's sense of larger meaning and purpose than in the factors that political socialization theorists propose, and that perspective taking and conflict management are more central to the development of social consciousness and social responsibility than the prescriptive recommendations of citizenship educators indicate. The theoretical framework provided by the construct of social responsibility not only pulls together the fragmented understandings and recommendations from these fields but suggests a more adequate and holistic way of looking at both development and educational practice.

This book, then, is an effort to synthesize the research in these diverse fields, explicate a new theoretical framework, and answer the questions: What are the processes by which young people develop a sense of social responsibility? And, what are classroom and school practices that effectively support this development? In answering these questions, I hope we can begin to build the base of knowledge and research in the field of social responsibility development and use that knowledge to guide our future efforts.

CHAPTER 2

The Development
of Social Responsibility

Dear Teacher:

I am a survivor of a concentration camp. My eyes saw what no man should witness: Gas chambers built by learned engineers. Infants killed by trained nurses. Women and babies shot and burned by high school and college graduates.

So, I am suspicious of education. My request is: Help your students become human. Your efforts must never produce learned monsters, skilled psychopaths, educated Eichmanns. Reading, writing, and arithmetic are important only if they serve to make our children more human.

—Author unknown; in Haim Ginnott,
Teacher and Child, cited in
Bardige, 1988, p. 87.

The Meaning of Social Responsibility

I have been using the terms *citizenship education* and *social responsibility* somewhat interchangeably. Although social responsibility includes citizenship education, it is more encompassing. Over the past ten years, social responsibility has emerged as a new field of study that encompasses both developing students' social skills and enabling students to be active and responsible members of the larger social and political community.

11

Social responsibility is, in fact, a reconceptualization and expansion of previous work in citizenship education. Educators and researchers have realized that citizenship or civic education may be too limiting of a concept if we are trying to encourage young people to assume responsible roles in the social and political world. Although interpretations vary, citizenship or civic education generally "involves learning and instruction related to the development of citizen competence" (Remy, 1980a, p. 1) and "concerns the rights, responsibilities, and tasks associated with governing the various groups to which a person belongs" (p. 62). This focus on civic competencies and knowledge is also embedded in the definition of civic education used in the most recent national assessment of educational progress. "Civic education helps prepare students to participate intelligently in public affairs by giving them the understandings they need to make sense of civic issues. By studying the intricate structure of American government and politics, students can learn how to contribute to national, state, and local decision making. More broadly, civic education helps students appreciate the principles, such as individual liberty, justice, tolerance, equality, and responsibility, that are central to American democracy and are constantly being challenged in modern society" (Anderson et al., 1990, p. 6). In the field of curriculum, the social studies program has borne the major responsibility for developing citizenship skills.

Social responsibility, on the other hand, focuses on the nature of a person's relationship with others and with the larger social and political world. It has been defined as "the personal investment in the well-being of others and the planet" (Berman, 1990, p. 2). For the past ten years, I have led workshops and taught courses for educators in the development of social responsibility. At the beginning of each course I ask the participants to write about someone whom they consider to be socially responsible. As a group we generate the characteristics that they consider central to social responsibility. Invariably, these groups say that the individual cares for and about others; has ethical standards he or she uses in making judgments; is open to the viewpoints of others; is responsive to the needs of others; is altruistic; is politically conscious, informed, and involved; is concerned about the welfare of the community as a whole; and acts with integrity.

The portrait they paint is echoed in the prosocial and moral development literature. Social responsibility has a number of dimensions. First, socially responsible people understand that the individual is rooted within a larger social network, within interlocking communities that range from the local to the global (Bronfenbrenner, 1979). They are conscious of the ways one is influenced by and influences the social and political world. And they experience a sense of connectedness and interdependence with others. The boundaries of their identity are not drawn tightly around themselves. These boundaries have, in Jean Houston's phrase, "leaky margins." Others and the world as a whole are part of the self. Oliner and Oliner (1988), in their study of rescuers of Jews during the Holocaust, describe this type of person as extensive where "ego boundaries were sufficiently broadened so that other people were experienced as part of the self" (p. 183).

Second, relationships with others, and with society, are framed by the ethical considerations of justice and care. These two moral voices, as Gilligan (1982, 1988a, 1990) labels them, draw attention to the vulnerability of people to both oppression and abandonment—"vulnerabilities which are built into the human life cycle and constitute grounds for moral concern" (1988a, p. iii). These voices are complementary but address different concerns. The justice voice addresses claims of inequality and is often framed in terms of rules, principles, and obligations. The care voice, on the other hand, is sensitive to suffering and is often framed in terms of compassion and response to those in need. Justice offers protection in the face of oppression. Care offers protection against abandonment in the face of pain. These two voices emerged in her study of students at the Emma Willard school. She found that responsibility held different meanings for some students.

> When asked "What does responsibility mean to you?" a high school student replied: "Responsibility means making a commitment and then sticking to it." This response confirms the common understanding of responsibility as personal commitment and contractual obligation. A different conception of the self and of morality appears, however, in another student's reply: "Responsibility is when you are aware of others and you are aware of their feelings. . . . Responsibility is taking charge of yourself by looking at others around you and seeing what they need and seeing what you need . . . and taking the initiative." In this construction, responsibility means acting responsively in relationships, and the self—as a moral agent—taking the initiative to gain awareness and respond to the perception of need. (1988c, p. 7)

Johnston (1988) found that most young people, and adults, are aware of both moral voices although each person expresses a preference for one or the other. However, social responsibility involves balancing both. In caring for the well-being of others and the welfare of the community as a whole, one is concerned about both oppression and abandonment.

Third, social responsibility involves acting with integrity. Kohlberg and Candee (1984a) argue that "as a personality attribute, responsibility denotes first a concern for, and acceptance of, the consequences of one's actions. Second, it denotes a consistency between what one says one should or would do and what one actually does. It is dependability or follow-through in action of one's verbal moral commitments and judgments" (p. 56). And this follow-through means that one sees one's daily actions within a larger social context, knows that one's actions have social and political implications, and lives in ways that are consistent with one's values.

Eisenberg and Mussen (1989), in writing about prosocial development, point out that the norm of social responsibility "prescribes that we should assist others who depend on us and need help" (p. 5). When internalized, assisting others becomes an end in itself, and we act on behalf of others, not for material gain or social approval but for the personal rewards that come from doing what is right.

Social and political consciousness, a sense of connectedness, acting on ethical considerations, prosocial behavior, integrity of action, and active participation are all components of social responsibility.

Educationally, teaching social responsibility incorporates the development of social skills, ethics, and character. Although it also includes developing political knowledge and skills, it gives primary attention to the way we live with others and our responsibility for furthering the common good. Therefore, unlike citizenship education, social responsibility cuts across the curriculum and the culture and organization of the school. It adds to the commonly accepted notions of citizenship education the concepts that young people must be able to work with and care for others, that classrooms and schools need to embody and nurture a sense of responsibility through their organization and governance, and that these themes can be integrated into all areas of the curriculum. What students can come to understand is that we make a significant difference in our relationships with friends, in our work, in raising children, in our role as consumers, not only by our political understandings, positions, and actions but by how we live—the consciousness and integrity we bring to our actions and the care we take with others.

Yet if we are to nurture the complex collection of attributes that make up social responsibility, we must begin by understanding how they develop in children.

Models of Development

Researchers have created models of development to explain how internal and external forces interact in the development of childrens' social, political, cognitive, and moral abilities. The early political socialization and prosocial development research focused on how children's attitudes and behavior were enculturated by social forces. Parents, schools, peers, and the media were seen as the predominant forces that influenced the child's conceptions of the social and political world. Much of this early research was an effort to distinguish which of these influences was predominant. The major models in moral and cognitive development, in contrast, emphasized the natural maturation in "stages" of cognitive and moral abilities.

Neither of these models proved sufficient. On the one hand, children's conceptions were more independent of socialization forces for the influence of these external forces to be an adequate explanation. As Connell (1971) found in his interviews, seven- to eleven-year-olds "selectively appropriate the material provided by schools, by mass media, by parents, and build of them individual structures. . . . [T]he children are active, enterprising beings, making a way in the world, interested in what is around them and concerned to know and understand their world. Few of them will . . . actively seek out political information, but almost all will be interested in it when it comes their way and will make some attempt to place it and place themselves with regard to it" (p. 233). Many other researchers have reached similar conclusions (Damon, 1977; Renshon, 1977; Stevens, 1982; Weinreich-Haste, 1983; Williams & Minns, 1986). For example, Williams and Minns, in their study of fifth and sixth graders, found that these children did not just accept information and opinions of significant political authorities. They made their own credibility determinations about both the "authority" and his or her viewpoint. They used this credibility determination in making their own judgments. The impact of socialization forces, then, is significantly moderated as children make sense of the world around them in their own terms.

On the other hand, the early development of children's perspective-taking abilities, moral reasoning, political understanding, and abstract thinking did not match the classical cognitive developmental frameworks of Piaget (1932/1965) or Kohlberg (1984). Stevens, who also interviewed seven- to eleven-year-olds, was surprised at these children's ability to think abstractly and, even, theoretically. He concludes that "there appear to be aspects of children's political concepts which, on the evidence of this study, are not accounted for by Piaget's model" (p. 169). Moore, Lare, and Wagner (1985) found the same thing in their interviews with five- to ten-year-olds. "The pattern of our data leads us to believe that knowledge about contemporary public issues is more likely to result from social learning than from cognitive development" (p. 58). After observing two- and three-year-olds' moral and prosocial behavior, Dunn (1988) points out that "in theories of moral development concerned with the ability of individuals to articulate judgments in relation to hypothetical dilemmas . . . , our two- and three-year-olds would have no place" (p. 169). And after reviewing the literature on early social development, Bruner and Haste (1987) indicate that "all this casts doubts on Piaget's picture of the child as egocentric" (p. 12).

Bandura (1991), Bronfenbrenner (1979), Bruner and Haste (1987), Connell (1971), Kurtines and Gewirtz (1987), Moore, Lare, and Wagner (1985), Renshon (1977), and others argue for a new model that integrates both theories. What has emerged in the developmental literature is a mixing of the two models into an interactional model. Moore and his colleagues state that "our conclusion . . . is that both models are useful, indeed, complementary, for explaining growth in political understanding. Inherited dispositions, influencing the pattern of maturational development, and social experiences, involving both the interpersonal and institutional environments, interact to shape the contours as well as the rate of political learning" (p. 223). Development is fostered by the interaction between a child who is cognitively maturing and actively constructing meaning from his or her experiences and the contextual forces of parents, school, the media, and the culture. Development is bidirectional in that the child influences and changes the environment as well. Bronfenbrenner situates the child within multiple contexts extending far beyond the child's immediate environment into settings in which the child is not even present. In his conception, the person is nested within a complex set of interconnected systems, each inside the next, like Russian nesting dolls. Kurtines and Gewirtz argue that moral development is an interactive process and that research should focus on the interactive process between the person and the social context rather than simply what is going on in the minds of children.

With this shift to an interactional model, context has become an important factor in development. Kurtines and Gewirtz (1987), in reviewing the research in moral development and social interaction, argue that development is not an internal process but one coordinated with social contexts. Minuchin and Shapiro (1983) integrate context, interaction, and self into a systems paradigm where "no unit is considered separable from its context, and no part of a system is either the inevitable source of influence or the sole recipient of impact. . . . Behavior cannot be separated from the context in which it occurs . . . it is neither totally specific to the setting nor totally an expression of enduring personality traits. People bring a repertoire of possibilities into new situations, and both contribute and adapt to the new patterns that are formed. The teacher and children in a fourth-grade classroom, for instance, bring their past into the classroom, but together they create a new system that stabilizes over time and defines the ways in which different members will behave in that particular setting" (pp. 200–1). Turiel, Smetana, and Killen (1991) report that context determines whether young children will exhibit moral sensibilities or be able to resolve differences. Haan, Aerts, and Cooper (1985) found that such situational variables as the degree of moral stress strongly influence moral judgments. Bronfenbrenner (1979) has built context into the very core of his ecological approach to development and labels it "development-in-context." "Lying at the very core of an ecological orientation and distinguishing it most sharply from prevailing approaches to the study of human development is the concern with the progressive accommodation between a growing human organism and its immediate environment, *and* the way in which this relation is mediated by forces emanating from more remote regions in the larger physical and social milieu" (p. 13). Giroux (1983b) argues that the person must be situated within the historical, political, and ideological context as well, so that the accepted and hidden become explicit and the relations among knowledge, power, ideology, class, and economics are examined.

Bruner and Haste (1987) succinctly summarize this transition to a new understanding of development.

A quiet revolution has taken place in developmental psychology in the last decade. It is not only that we have begun to think again of the child as a *social being*—one who plays and talks with others, learns through interactions with parents and teachers—but because we have come once more to appreciate that through such social life, the child acquires a framework for interpreting experience, and learns how to negotiate meaning in a manner congruent with the requirements of the culture. 'Making sense' is a social process;

it is an activity that is always situated within a cultural and historical context. (p. 1)

The definition of development changes within this new framework. "Development is defined as the person's evolving conception of the ecological environment, and his relation to it, as well as the person's growing capacity to discover, sustain, or alter its properties" (Bronfenbrenner, 1979, p. 9).

As a result of this shift in definition and conception of development, meaning-making, social discourse, and environmental context become important areas of insight in exploring the social and political development of young people. Yet, this interactional approach to development remains inadequate as a model of social and political development and of the development of social responsibility. Not only are people making sense of their environment and developing within the context of an interactive social process but there is an emotional and affiliative process going on as well. People are not only interacting with the social and political environment, they are in relationship with that environment in much the same way that they are in relationship with their family and friends. Furthermore, the way they give meaning to this relationship determines the nature of their participation in the social and political world. I've deliberately chosen the term *relationship* because, like a relationship with another person, our relationship with society includes such powerful factors as emotion, influence, and vulnerability. It is a relationship that involves connectedness, efficacy, and meaning, or, in some cases, a lack of all three. Development is marked by the ongoing renegotiation of that relationship.

The term *relationship* shifts the context of our thinking beyond individual maturation and environmental context to the meaning that people derive from their interactions and the receptivity of the environment to the individual. As others have noted, people don't make moral decisions in isolation, especially not decisions that relate to larger social and political issues. These decisions emerge directly from people's relationship to society—from what they interpret as the dominant morality in the political culture and from their perception of their ability to influence that culture.

Over the past six years, I've been exploring how people view their relationship to society. Because it is difficult for many people to describe verbally their relationship to society, I've asked people first to *draw* the way they see their own relationship to society before they attempt to describe it. I've now collected pencil, crayon, or marking pen drawings from elementary school children, from high school and college students, and from adults who represent a wide range of lifestyles and viewpoints. Like Coles's (1986a, 1986b) research on the moral and political life of children, these drawings usually reveal complex feelings toward society— sometimes a rich mosaic of interconnectedness, sometimes the painful expression of alienation and powerlessness, and sometimes the struggle to reconcile both hope and pain. The drawings reveal that children are well aware of the world around them and see their relationship to society in very different ways (Berman, 1990).

Although researchers have not specifically conceived of development in relationship terms, many have referred to this quality in the moral, political, and social development they studied. Hess and Torney (1967) note the reciprocity inherent in citizenship:

> Citizenship is not only a matter of legal status. It is also a pattern of interaction between the individual and the political system. The relative roles played by the citizen and the government and other features of the system are reciprocal. For example, the small child believes that it is his obligation to obey laws, and he usually believes that in return the policeman will protect him. Political socialization can be regarded as the process by which reciprocal relationships such as this are developed. . . . This process is viewed not as one which involves the acquisition of traits or opinions, but rather the development of relationships between the individual and the institutions. In this complex process, the individual acquires images of institutions and persons and complementary attitudes about himself and how he should behave. . . . (pp. 17, 212)

Sigel and Hoskin (1981), in their study of political knowledge, interest, and participation among 1,000 Pennsylvania high school seniors, note the affiliative, emotional nature of participation. "What is important is not the form involvement takes but that the individual considers himself to be part of the body politic, that it is not a remote and irrelevant entity but one which is relevant to daily life and long-range security. Political involvement is the very opposite of political isolation; it signifies a sense of identification with the polity. Identifying with the polity and caring for it are not, however, synonymous with accepting the polity uncritically. The politically involved person can be highly critical and oriented to change, or he can be highly supportive of, and resistant to changes in, the existing system" (pp. 41–42).

Weinreich-Haste (1984) suggests that people develop social meaning systems based on an implicit theory of society, of what holds society together, and of the individual's role and meaning within the society. "These social meaning systems are the stories that people make up to explain the social and physical world" (p. 332). In fact, she contends that Kohlberg's stages represent increasingly complex understandings of the social system rather than morality. This theory of society is a key element in the formation of one's relationship to society and influences whether and how the person participates in political decision making.

Adelson (1972) reports something quite similar. He describes a variety of consistent "motifs" that dominate the political thought of certain adolescents and represent an implicit theory of how society works. "There is, for example, a politics of dependency, . . . in which the imagined and described political world is organized around the idea of government as a succoring parent and the citizen as a receptive child. There is a politics of envy, of resentment, dominated by the conviction that the high and mighty unjustly retain the world's resources for themselves. And there is a politics of power, in which we can discern a preoccupation with domination and control. These themes—guilt, dependency, envy, power, and no doubt others—seem to emerge from an interaction between salient values in the child's milieu and certain dispositions in personality. When felt strongly enough they order the political perceptions and provide a framework for the organization of ideology" (p. 125).

Although Youniss (1987) does not extend his developmental analysis to the political or societal realm, he argues that relatedness and relationship are critical factors in social and moral development. The child does not move toward autonomy as the epitome of development but rather remains in relationships that are renegotiated as he or she develops. "The individual does not then simply drop relationship to become a separate entity but remains in relationship albeit in multiple as well as transformed ways" (p. 145). It is the sustaining of relationships that fosters positive development. Adelson (1972) found this desire for relatedness within the political arena in the adolescents he interviewed. He calls it a politics of togetherness without conformity. ". . . what mattered to the American [adolescent] was the citizen's connection to the community. . . . The ideal of government is social harmony, the reduction of frictions so that people can live together amicably" (p. 140).

Gilligan, whose work rests on the relational nature of development, indicates that "moral immaturity may consist not in an absence of general moral knowledge but in an absence of the attachments necessary for making moral notions moral insights" (Gilligan & Wiggins, 1988, p. 134). She believes that moral development begins in and proceeds through relationships and that the child's cognitive and affective development must be seen as the dynamic effects of the child's relational life. Although she focuses primarily on morality in the personal rather than the public arena, she contends that our traditional view of development has mistakenly interpreted adolescents' renegotiation of relationship as the drive toward autonomy rather than the drive to maintain attachment.

We are in a continually evolving relationship with the political and social world. As Weinreich-Haste suggests, this relationship is often implicit and unacknowledged. Yet it frames our participation or nonparticipation. It gives us a sense of affiliation or alienation. And it is a critical factor in the development of social responsibility. It has not, however, framed our research efforts in social, political, or moral development. Research has examined various aspects of development but has not explored it holistically.

The research in political socialization, moral development, prosocial behavior, and psychosocial development gives us some insight into the constituent aspects of this relationship—the early emergence of social understanding, the development of political consciousness, the development of moral courage and action, and the emergence of a socially situated identity. From these we can begin to get a sense of both the substance and the process by which this relationship evolves. Yet the picture is not a complete one, and further research is needed to more fully understand the nature and evolution of this relationship.

The Early Emergence of Social Understanding

There has been a commonly accepted view in the fields of political socialization, moral development, and elementary education that children prior to age ten are egocentric, unable to take the perspective of others, morally immature, uninterested and unaware of the social and political world, and unable to think in sophisticated ways about social issues or political conflict. Recent research challenges these notions. Children's awareness of the social and political world emerges far earlier, and their social and moral abilities are far more advanced than we have thought.

Social understanding and social responsibility are built on children's desire to understand and feel effective in the social world, to initiate and maintain connection with others, and to reach out to those in distress. Reseachers have found that such basic components of social responsibility as empathy, moral sensibilities, the understanding of social conventions, and political awareness emerge prior to the age of eight.

The initial signs of empathy begin at a very young age. By seven or eight months of age children tune into the emotional expressions of adults and begin to respond to the feeling states of others (Dunn, 1988). By the time they are two they exhibit such prosocial behavior as sharing, helping, protecting, and nurturing (Dunn, 1988; Radke-Yarrow & Zahn-Waxler, 1984; Rheingold & Emery, 1986; Rheingold & Hay, 1980; Rheingold, Hay, & West, 1976; Zahn-Waxler & Radke-Yarrow, 1982; Zahn-Waxler, Radke-Yarrow, & King, 1979). Children at this age can also be observed role-taking (Light, 1987) and, by the age of four or five, some can differentiate points of view (Zahn-Waxler, Radke-Yarrow, & Brady-Smith, 1977). Zahn-Waxler, Radke-Yarrow, and Brady-Smith (1977) gave 108 children ages three through seven perceptual and conceptual perspective-taking tasks and found that "the ability of preschool-age children to differentiate their own and others' perspectives on a variety of tasks of simple construction provides further evidence that perspective-taking abilities are present and prominent earlier in life than had been previously hypothesized" (p. 88).

Dunn (1988), in a longitudinal, observational study of children from fourteen to thirty-six months found that during this twenty-two month period children grow in their understanding of others' feelings, increase their sensitivity to the goals and intentions of others, begin to understand social rules, and begin to talk about mental states and to reflect on other minds. "These developments in the ability to conceive of other minds in the second half of the third year have such profound consequences for children's understanding of their social world and their communication that a reasonable case can be made for designating this a new 'stage' in children's social understanding" (pp. 173–74).

Hoffman (1991) charts four developmental levels of empathy starting in infancy. The first is global empathy in which an infant witnesses distress or picks up distress cues and experiences unpleasant feelings in themselves. The second is egocentric empathy, which begins at about one year of age. The child becomes aware of another in distress and projects onto the other person what his or her own feelings would be. Somewhere between ages two and three children begin experiencing empathy for another's feelings.

Here children understand that the other's experience is different from their own and they respond to the other person's experience. Finally, by late childhood, children can begin empathizing with another's life condition rather than just immediate distress. They can also empathize with an entire group or class of people.

The early emergence of empathy may be linked to the early development of moral sensibilities. Dunn suggests that "[Children's] responsivity to the feeling states of others shows us that the foundations for the moral virtues of caring, considerateness, and kindness are well laid by three years" (p. 170). Hoffman (1984), in his own studies of the early development of empathy and morality, has noted that because they bridge the gap between egoism and morality, "empathy and guilt may thus be quintessential moral motives, for they may transform another's pain into one's own discomfort and make one feel partly responsible for the other's plight whether or not one has actually done anything to cause it" (p. 289).

A number of other researchers have noted that moral sensibilities emerge at a young age (Kagan, 1987; Killen, 1991; Lamb, 1991). In a yearlong longitudinal, observational study of infants in their second year, Lamb found early use of moral language. These children were aware of transgressing, of "uh oh's," of flawed objects, and of achievement standards. They used moral language of good and bad and pointed out danger. She noted that "morally related events have special salience for children in the middle of the second year" (1991, p. 181). Dunn found an even more elaborated moral awareness in two- and three-year-olds:

> [T]he evidence from the observations shows that children from 18 months on understand how to hurt, comfort, or exacerbate another's pain; they understand the consequences of their hurtful actions for others and something of what is allowed or disapproved behavior in their family world; they anticipate the response of adults to their own and to others' misdeeds; they differentiate between transgressions of various kinds. They comment and ask about the causes of others' actions and feelings. . . . [O]ur observations show that by two and a half to three years of age, children demonstrate a practical knowledge of the idea of responsibility, of excuses of intent and incapacity, of how rules apply differently to different family members and how they can be questioned, of how transgressions can be justified. They have begun to understand something of the authority relations within the family and

to comment on the behavior of others in moral terms. Moral understanding depends in part upon a child's general knowledge about the social world; what our observations show is that children even in their second and third years have a far subtler comprehension of their social world than we have given them credit for. (pp. 169–70)

Haan (1991) presented moral dilemmas to four-year-olds, high school students, and college students. She found that the four-year-olds had the capacity to operate at morally sensitive levels. "Four-year-olds did not consistently act as one would expect if they were either cognitively egocentric or morally selfish. . . . They were able to adjust their conduct and comments so as to accommodate the wishes and needs of the other child, and they showed an incidence of moral concern that was not radically different from that of the university students" (Haan et al., 1985, pp. 299–300). Damon's (1977, 1983) research on the development of conceptions of distributive justice in children four to ten years of age showed that they form increased understanding of benevolence, equality, and reciprocity. Anderson and Butzin (1978), in three studies of judgments of deservingness and fair shares with four- to eight-year-olds, found that even the youngest children had a well-developed sense of equity. Eisenberg and Mussen (1989) report that by the age of eight or nine, children can articulate and explain to others the norm of responsibility, that is, the moral prescription to respond to someone in need.

Haan, Aerts, and Cooper (1985), in their reformulation of moral development theory, argue that young children are moral actors and that moral negotiation begins at a very early age. "The usual and the cognitive supposition that young children are morally deficient and always self-serving seems simplistic and possibly not correct. However, young children are especially vulnerable to stress, so they need optimal conditions to give evidence of their moral understanding. Their moral failures may be due to limited resources rather than incapacity. The point is that from the early months of infancy, social life requires and fosters interchange that rapidly becomes morally bilateral and reciprocal, and infants are not without moral power in these circumstances" (p. 65). Dunn (1988) agrees and notes that, in her study, concern for oneself did not necessarily imply opposition to the interests of others. Damon (1983) also concurs, finding much of the writing in child development underestimates children's abilities.

Interestingly, many who have written extensively on children's moral judgment have overlooked children's fairness exchanges. These theorists have placed the developmental roots of morality in a childhood stage of unilateral obedience to adult authority, as if justice were a notion understood only by the adult. Such writings do tell us something about the nature of early adult-child relations. . . . But in overlooking children's rich and active understanding of fairness, kindness, and other prosocial notions, they have not only failed to locate the origins of morality but have inaccurately conveyed the nature of children's social behavior—particularly children's peer-oriented behavior. (pp. 133–34)

In addition, children between the ages of two and three begin to understand social rules and convention (Dunn, 1988; Turiel, 1983). Dunn finds that "what should not pass unnoticed is the nature of the rules they articulate and use. The bases for their excuses, justifications, and jokes include not only the idiosyncratic practices of a particular family, but some of the key principles of the wider culture outside the family: principles of possession, positive justice, excuses on grounds of incapacity or lack of intention, even gender-role division of labor. . . . From the basis of our observations, we can say that some of these principles are understood not in a highly context-specific way but much more broadly. The three-year-old's sense of possession rights or of the significance of sharing is certainly not limited to himself and his immediate family or peers" (p. 172).

Even at this age children know that moral transgressions are more serious than transgressions of social conventions (Nucci, 1982; Smetana, 1981, 1989). Moral transgressions involve issues of justice or care, such as lying or hitting. Transgressions of social conventions involve violations of social rules, such as manners and customs. When asked if an action would be right if there were no rule against it, most of the toddlers and preschool children in Smetana's studies indicated that a moral transgression was wrong even if there were no rule. On the other hand, a transgression of social convention was often considered acceptable if a rule didn't exist. When asked for justification of these choices children were again able to differentiate between the two. The children's reasons for moral behavior were given in terms of the effects the actions had on the rights or well-being of others. But childrens' reasons for judging conventional behavior were given in terms of their relation to the social order, social expectations, social institutions, and contextual or culturally specific standards of behavior.

Katz's (1983) review of the literature on the origins of gender and racial attitudes shows that children develop initial attitudes by the age of three or four. By the age of seven to nine, there is a good deal of constancy in these attitudes.

Even children's awareness of the political world begins to emerge earlier than previously thought. Coles (1967, 1986a, 1986b), in his portraits of children's political and moral awareness, highlights the depth and richness of their perceptions and courage.

> When I leave Belfast or Johannesburg, Rio de Janeiro or Managua, Quebec, Thailand's refugee camps, Warsaw, *and* when I leave the American homes where I've been lucky to be able to sit and drink coffee and watch television and eat snacks and play games with boys and girls and listen to them trying to make sense of this world, and watch them doing so with crayons and paints and big or small pieces of paper—in all those moments a political morality is never too distant. These children realize that what their countries or other countries do may well affect how, or indeed whether, they will live. Hendrick, well fed, destined for college and a comfortable life, worries that a nuclear warhead can kill everyone, everything. Other children, chronically malnourished and with little hope of even a minimally secure life, worry that a government seemingly indifferent to them will turn actively hostile, send out the police with orders to shoot and shoot and shoot. Anyone who doubts the capacity of children for this kind of political and moral consciousness ought to visit an *elementary* school in Soweto, or simply stand high on a favela and ask children about the city they prowl by day or night—"so that," as one child told me, "there will be another tomorrow." I hear that statement and take note of its quality of terse, sad, eloquence. *He* is telling me about death as a fact, a constant, immanent likelihood—and not because he has been reading the nineteenth- and twentieth-century existentialists. Death by nuclear bombs, death by starvation—death either way, these children know, is death by wrongdoing. The nations of the world should beware, should do better, Hendrick said, and so have injunctions to that effect also been uttered by countless black children segregated in Soweto. Occasionally the indignation of those young political moralists spill out—hence the dozens and dozens of black children who were killed in 1976 when they spoke

their minds and marched together down their dusty unpaved streets. (pp. 302–3)

In another effort to assess the development of young children's political awareness, Moore, Lare, and Wagner (1985) interviewed a group of 243 suburban California children each year from kindergarten through fourth grade. They found that by the time the children entered kindergarten they had a surprisingly sophisticated sense of our legal system. Almost half could explain the function of laws, courts, and police. Over one-third could identify the president although few had any real idea of what the presidency was about. Between 10 and 20 percent had heard of such complex contemporary issues as Watergate, Vietnam, impeachment, and the energy crisis, with over two-thirds being able to accurately comment on the energy crisis. "It appears that at least one kindergarten child in ten, and perhaps as many as one in six is able to grasp key elements in these basic processes of democratic government" (p. 52). Easton and Dennis (1969), who did one of the early political socialization surveys that involved 12,000 second through eighth graders, comment that "the discovery that during the early grades the child acquires the capacity to orient himself to objects far beyond the family, in the national sector of society, is a finding of decisive significance. . . ." (pp. 393–94).

In an effort to assess children's conceptions of public needs Moore, Lare, and Wagner asked kindergarteners, "If you were the boss of the whole country, what would you do to help people?" Almost two-thirds gave a substantive answer to this question and could identify "an impressive array of public needs" (p. 55). The researchers note that children not only knew about public needs but showed a surprising degree of compassion and concern in their answers. These were comfortable, suburban children, protected from many of the harsh realities experienced by the children Coles interviewed. Yet some of these five-year-olds were aware of hunger, homelessness, war, and ecological damage.

In contrast to earlier political socialization studies that suggested that children at this age had only intuitive, fragmented, and inconsistent views of the political world (Connell, 1971; Furth, 1980; Stevens, 1982), Moore, Lare, and Wagner found consistency in children's viewpoints. Even those who had little understanding of the political world and identified Jesus or God as running the country maintained a great degree of consistency in their answers. Knutson (1974) and Stevens (1982) found this consistency among eight- and nine-year-olds. Stevens notes that "some children, at the age of nine, were able to construct the possibility of alternative social and political arrangements to their present ways of life, and to justify these alternatives according to certain principles" (p. 169). This coherence in viewpoint is evident, as well, in the children Coles interviewed. Knutson labels it a prepolitical ideology that children formulate and use as a schema to assess and make sense of new information.

In essence, what this research tells us is that children begin negotiating their relationship with the social and political world at a very early age. The child perceives the world around him or her and attempts to make both cognitive and moral sense of it. This relationship is built on what appears to be an innate capacity for empathy and moral sensibility and a desire to make sense of the world, to connect with others, to feel efficacious.

One of the reasons we are now able to see these early developments in young children is that our research methods have changed. The initial work in political socialization (Connell, 1971; Easton & Dennis, 1969; Greenstein, 1965; Hess & Torney, 1967; Jennings & Niemi, 1974; Sigel & Hoskin, 1981) rested on large-scale, structured interviews or questionnaire surveys of children using a cross-sectional research design. The research focused more on the outcomes of political learning—knowledge, interest, efficacy, and participation—than on how children experience and make sense of our political and social environment. In aggregating development, the researchers lost both the idiosyncratic nature of political development and the meaning children give to their experience (Knutson, 1974). Palonsky (1987), in his critique of this type of research, notes that "they [the researchers] assume that if investigators periodically and unobtrusively drop into the lives of children, accurate measurements can be made reflecting the extent to which children have acquired the knowledge, goals and attitudes that society has prescribed for them" (p. 501). Instead, these methods lend themselves to confirming the researchers' hypotheses because the interviews and surveys are structured around the researchers' agenda rather than the child's. Even Moore, Lare, and Wagner's interviews suffer from this problem. Although their work is longitudinal and gives us a much better sense of the child's growing awareness over time, the questions are tightly structured and limit the opportunity for some unexpected or new understandings to arise.

Alternatively, some of the political socialization and moral development researchers used interviews based on Piagetian problem-posing methods (Furth, 1980; Kohlberg, 1984; Stevens, 1982). This research is problematic for the same reasons. A real context for the child's thoughts and actions is missing, and the focus remains on the researcher's interests rather than the child's experience and understandings. Bronfenbrenner (1979) calls it "the science of the strange behavior of children in strange situations with strange adults for the briefest possible periods of time" (p. 19). This does not mean that this research is valueless. This work broke the ground and raised the questions that moved us forward in our understanding of child development. This work also revealed important insights about children's knowledge, interest, and efficacy. What it does mean is that the conclusions reached in the early work must be held tentatively, until we are able to confirm or disconfirm them in studies using naturalistic and longitudinal research methods.

The research that is revealing a greater depth in children's social understanding and abilities has been observational research in the context of the child's daily life. It has also been longitudinal, allowing the researcher to get to know the child and his or her development. In a natural context and over time, researchers have been able to see young children exhibit behaviors that rarely are observed in the strange environments of the laboratory. These behaviors often demonstrate children's abilities and understandings that they are not yet able to articulate in interviews or in response to survey questions (Light, 1987).

Patterns of Development: Political Consciousness

In spite of the limitations of the early political socialization research in its research design and its developmental models, there are enough studies from varying perspectives to give us some general notions of the development of political consciousness in young people in Western, industrialized societies.

There is a strong similarity among these studies (Connell, 1971; Easton & Dennis, 1969; Furth, 1980; Hess & Torney, 1967; Jennings & Niemi, 1974; Stevens, 1982; Moore et al., 1985) in the developmental path that they chart for young people. The political understanding of children under the age of seven is often portrayed as vague, fragmented, or intuitive, although Moore, Lare, and Wagner found this age group to be far more knowledgeable and coherent than previous studies had. Some children this age are aware of some political authorities, national symbols, govern-mental institutions, and even public issues. Many are aware of parts of the legal system. They know that there is a political world, but it is often simply a world of important people. They know that elections have something to do with putting these people in office, but many aren't sure what the link is. The more politically aware second graders can distinguish between the president and the presidency as an institution and offer qualified responses to questions about political figures (Moore et al., 1985). By the age of seven, most children have "made cognitive contact with the political world" (Stevens, p. 149).

Children's first conceptions of politics, however, are affective rather than cognitive (Greenstein, 1965; Hess & Torney, 1967; Stevens, 1982). Evaluative judgments of political leaders, symbols, and institutions come before the child has any real knowledge about these leaders, symbols, or institutions. Most often these evaluations are positive, although this finding comes from studies of predominantly white, middle-class youth. These children tend to see leaders as benevolent. They tend to identify with a territorial entity, often the nation. They tend to feel positive about and take pride in national symbols. They tend to see the system operating in the ideal rather than the real. Later, as they begin to understand our political system, there is an attachment to a "unified chain of command" (Merelman, 1990) as children project their acceptance of the authority structures of home and school onto political authority. Their image of authority is personal. For example, when talking about law, they talk about policemen, judges, and criminals, and when talking about the government, they talk about their mayor or the president. This affective and affiliative component of childrens' political conceptions begins to frame the way they see their relationship to the political and social world.

Between the ages of seven and ten, there is a rapid growth of political knowledge and understanding. In one of the first political socialization studies, Hess and Torney (1967) found this period to be the one that produced the greatest growth in political understanding. Moore, Lare, and Wagner (1985) found that 20 percent of the children they interviewed made their greatest gains in political understanding during second grade. Thirty percent made their greatest gains in third grade. And 30 percent made their greatest gains in fourth grade. "This longitudinal analysis of when children had their greatest gain in political knowledge suggests that during the early elementary grades, some children are open to significant increases in political understanding each year" (p. 118).

Connell, in his interviews with seven- to eleven-year-olds, noted that cognitive development moves in leaps of conception. Children acquire a general concept and fill in the details later. Moore, Lare, and Wagner (1985) also found this to be the case. Particular concepts act as cognitive organizers and help children make sense of new information and develop new understandings. Those children who had acquired an understanding of these organizers were significantly more knowledgeable than those who had not.

By the age of nine children have acquired much of the adult political language and show evidence of thinking about social ideas and ideals (Stevens, 1982). Children begin to see politics as problematic and conflictual (Connell, 1971) and can construct alternative social and political arrangements (Stevens, 1982). Children shift in their understanding of authority and differentiate between personal authority of political leaders and the authority vested in institutions (Connell, 1971; Easton & Dennis, 1969). They are able to be critical of leaders and institutions (Stevens, 1982). They understand the role of elections (Moore et al., 1985) and demonstrate a prepolitical ideology (Knutson, 1974). This is a time when children are able to identify the concrete features of the political landscape. Connell labeled this period "role development" because children are able to pool together the pieces of information they have gathered into more coherent conceptions of political roles. Furth (1980) described this period as one of part-systems understanding in which children begin to understand that there is a system of interrelationship involved in politics. They are able to get perspective on themselves (Dunn, 1988), think about their thinking, and search for logical and factual coherence (Furth, 1980). Although a sense of efficacy may emerge at an earlier point, by this time children have developed a sense of efficacy or, in some cases, a lack of efficacy (Hess & Torney, 1967). Their language reveals feelings of involvement and participation. "Working back from the nature of the children's statements to the feelings of involvement that prompted them reveals an attitude that approaches society and its problems in a spirit of participation. The 'ours' is definitive, applicable to country, government, debts, money and problems, the use of 'us' and 'we' almost tribal in its assumption of close-knit interests" (Stevens, p. 175).

The period between ages ten and twelve is characterized by a systematic sense of political order (Connell, 1971) and the development of more complex political concepts (Stevens, 1982). Torney, Oppenheim, and Farnen (1975) indicate that children begin this period with a sheltered view of the political system that emphasizes the harmonizing or cohesive elements of the system and end it with a sophisticated or realistic view that includes the divisive elements. In Furth's (1980) view this is a time of serious understanding. Children are better able to work with logical and abstract thinking. They begin to work with concepts of power and conflict. At the end of this time they understand the function and structure of government and are able to think in terms of specific policy alternatives (Connell, 1971). They also develop well-defined sentiments and opinions about political issues and political figures (Easton & Dennis, 1969). Many of the early political socialization researchers were so struck by the depth of political knowledge, understandings, and attitudes that they concluded that the bulk of socialization took place during the elementary years (Easton & Dennis, 1969; Hess & Torney, 1967; Jennings & Niemi, 1974). Easton and Dennis conclude that "by the time children leave elementary school they have assembled a formidable array of basic political orientations" (p. 5).

Adolescence is identified by political socialization researchers as a time when a political outlook based on a set of values and on ideological thinking begins to emerge (Adelson, 1972; Connell, 1971; Merelman, 1969; Merelman, 1971). Based on interviews with 450 adolescents, ages eleven through eighteen in the United States, West Germany, and Great Britain, Adelson indicates that

> [T]he years of early adolescence, twelve to sixteen, are a watershed era in the emergence of political thought. Ordinarily the youngster begins adolescence incapable of complex political discourse—that is, mute on many issues, and when not mute, then simplistic, primitive, subject to fancies, unable to enter fully the realm of political ideas. By the time this period is at an end, a dramatic change is evident; the youngster's grasp of the political world is now recognizably adult. His mind moves with some agility within the terrain of political concepts; he has achieved abstractness, complexity, and even some delicacy in his sense of political textures; he is on the threshold of ideology, struggling to formulate a morally coherent view of how society is and might and should be arranged. (p. 106)

There are four major shifts that researchers have identified during these years (Adelson, 1972; Sigel & Hoskin, 1981). First, adolescents move from a focus on concrete information and personalized attribution of responsibility to abstract conceptions of systems, ideologies, institutions, and values. They think in terms of such principles as individual freedom, civil liberties, majority rule, and social justice. They think conditionally using "if" and "it depends." A sense of history and future emerges as well.

Second, adolescents move from authoritarian values to democratic tolerance. At the beginning adolescents tend to be preoccupied with human wickedness and believe in the goodness and justice of authority to control it. There is strong regard for law and strong punishments recommended for those who break the law. There is rigidity in their thinking. "What it amounts to is that at the onset of adolescence the child cannot think of human actions as provisional, tentative, empirical. He has little sense that social and political decisions are responsive to trial and error. He does not see the realm of government as subject to invention, and thus to experiment, to tinkering, to trying out" (Adelson, p. 119). This attitude shifts during adolescence to one that is more open to change and more tolerant of alternatives. Absolutist, either/or thinking becomes more flexible with the ability to see conflicting principles, systemic causes, and cost-benefit analyses. Weinreich-Haste (1986) points out that this movement from authoritarian to democratic values is also present in Kohlberg's stages of moral development that young people move through during this period.

Third, adolescents move from a preideological position to what Adelson (1972) calls "a weak ideological position" of roughly consistent attitudes organized in reference to a set of political principles. Although preadolescents may use ideological phrases, they do not really grasp their full meaning or implications. "The steady advance of the sense of principle is one of the most impressive phenomena of adolescent political thought" (Adelson, p. 121). Merelman (1985), in his study of adolescent activists and non-activists, found that the activists had a more well-defined value structure or ideological awareness that organized their political thinking than nonactivists. However, this does not mean that the adolescent is idealist or utopian. Although one can find idealism and utopianism in adolescents, skepticism, caution, and realism are more common (Adelson, 1972; Sigel & Hoskin, 1981). In fact, Torney, Oppenheim, and Farnen (1975) found a high degree of political cynicism among the seventeen-year-olds in the ten democratic countries they surveyed. Moore, who continued to interview through twelfth grade the group of students he had studied with Lare and Wagner, also reported a sharp rise in cynicism among high school students (personal communication, 1992). The collective language of 'us' and 'we' of the nine-year-old had changed to the distanced language of 'they' and 'them' of the older adolescent.

Finally, there is a shift from an individualistic orientation to being able to consider the needs of the community as an organized whole (Adelson & O'Neil, 1966; Torney, Oppenheim, & Farnen, 1975). At the beginning of adolescence, the young person sees the benefits of a policy primarily on an individual basis. During adolescence there is a growth of a sense of community. "Regardless of nationality, the adolescents in our sample develop, by the age of eighteen, a perspective which allows them to judge public policy by viewing it from the standpoint of public interest" (Gallatin & Adelson, 1970). This development may be culturally determined, however. Bettelheim (1985) and Brabeck (1989) found that children in collectivist cultures have an early sense of community and are able to view issues and decisions in terms of community interest or the common good.

Individual Differences

Although researchers have observed this developmental sequence in young people, it has not meant that young people are politically knowledgeable, interested, or efficacious. In fact, the opposite is too often the case. Although younger children are generally eager to learn about the social and political world, this world is distant and often inaccessible to them. It is a world of abstractions rather than experiences. Moore, Lare, and Wagner (1985) report that "the salience of politics and government in the lives of elementary children remains quite low" (p. 137). In their interviews with 1,000 Pennsylvania high school seniors, Sigel and Hoskin (1981) found "that politics is not salient for most people, especially adolescents, . . . their main concerns are private rather than public or political" (p. 38). Not one of the students they interviewed wanted to be president or enter a political career. Over half the students possessed an inadequate comprehension of democracy. "When government and politics were mentioned at all, they were mentioned only as possible frustraters of private goals. There would be too much pollution to assure health and nothing would be done about it. High taxes would keep them from acquiring all the goods they desired. Unemployment might force them on the public payroll" (pp. 37–38). In addition, both Sigel and Hoskin (1981) and Sears (1972) found that although young people might have knowledge of abstract democratic principles, this does not mean that they can or do apply these principles in actual decision-making situations. Sigel and Hoskin conclude that "it seems ominous that almost two out of three young people lack the interest and enthusiasm to become actively engaged in the political world around them" (pp. 171–72). Hodgkinson and Weitzman (1992) analyzed data collected by the Gallup organization on volunteering and giving among twelve- to seventeen-year-olds. Their definition of volunteering was broad and included such informal activity as helping one's neighbor and babysitting for free. Although over 60 percent of the 1,404 teenagers interviewed had participated in some volunteer activity, only 2 percent volunteered for political organizations or causes and only 8 percent participated in work that was of public and societal benefit. The interviews were done after major attention had been given to problems of environmental damage and the percent of students involved in environmental activities increased from under 8 percent in 1989 to over 18 percent in 1991. Because the interviewees could select multiple responses, these percentages are not cumulative and may actually reflect a smaller number of young people involved in volunteering in the social and political arena.

Theorists explain these findings by pointing to the child's distance from politics (Connell, 1971; Stevens, 1982), the structural barriers to political participation (Sigel & Hoskin, 1981), or the difficulty young people have in dealing with the highly contentious atmosphere of politics (Merelman, 1985). Yet, the distance from politics may be more a function of the failure of parents and schools to bring children into direct contact with the political system in a way that nurtures a positive and efficacious relationship. And the cynicism of adolescents may be a result of their realistic assessment of the difficulties of producing political change, especially after being presented with overly idealized images of our political process by texts, teachers, and political figures. Seligman (1991), in his work on learned optimism and learned helplessness, notes that if a person believes that they have little control over or influence on circumstances and are helpless to make a difference in the world, they become unable to act and give up trying.

The development of knowledge, interest, and efficacy is also not uniform among children. There are significant variations based on gender, race, and socioeconomic status. Most of the political socialization studies have found gender differences (Connell, 1971; Easton & Dennis, 1969; Greenstein, 1965; Hess & Torney, 1967; Jennings & Niemi, 1981; Moore et al., 1985; Sigel & Hoskin, 1981). In general, boys express a greater knowledge, interest, and sense of efficacy than girls and do so at earlier ages. Moore, Lare, and Wagner (1985) found that politics was more salient for boys than girls even among five-year-olds. Jennings and Niemi (1981) concluded that "on average, young adult women continued to differ from young men in ways consistent with traditional stereotypes. Sex differences were most consistent in the areas of psychological involvement, resources, and participation. . . . On every measure of psychological involvement, females were disadvantaged compared to males. Women's feelings of internal political efficacy were lower than those of men" (pp. 303–4). Hess and Torney (1967) found that boys tend to be more critical of the system, girls more trusting of political figures and the goodness of the system. To explain the differences, most researchers point to the traditional sex-role stereotyping in the culture. Moore, Lare, and Wagner indicate that in spite of the advances the women's movement has made there are few women in politics and few politically involved women discussed in elementary or secondary textbooks.

However, there may be another element involved. Eisenberg and Mussen (1989), in their review of the prosocial behavior literature, report that most studies of prosocial behavior find no gender differences and those that do tend to favor girls. Therefore, it may not be that girls have less of an interest in addressing common needs but, instead, that their voices are silenced by the contentiousness and human disconnectedness of our current political process and the ways this process is presented to them by parents, teachers, and the media. Gilligan (1982) points out that women tend to see situations in more complex terms and try to address the needs of all those in the situation. What is important to them is to maintain connection with others and to resolve conflicts consensually. Current patterns of political behavior are diametrically opposed to maintaining connection and finding solutions that meet common needs. Political behavior has been highly competitive, antagonistic, and demeaning of individuals involved. Belenky, Clinchy, Goldberger, and Tarule (1986) studied the silencing of women's voices and point out that silence is created by conflict, isolation, and disconnection. Lyons, Saltonstall, and Hanmer (1990), in their study of leadership among adolescent girls, found that these leaders were more concerned with their constituencies than with their roles and that listening to others was a central component of leadership. They point out that the vulnerability of this type of leadership is that it is often inconsistent with girls' images of the political process, which is characterized by the failure to listen and to work with others. One student leader they interviewed stated this succinctly. "I decided that I really don't like the politics of the school, or maybe politics in general.

I have never been involved in politics, so I don't know, but it's just, everything is so harsh, and people's feelings just, they don't get considered. . . ." (p. 189). Henry Giroux notes that "feminists as diverse as Nell Noddings and Jean Grimshaw have argued that the dominant conception of rationality and morality, with its instrumental logic of efficiency and self-interest, undermines a public morality in which it is considered obligatory to care for others and to alleviate needless forms of suffering and pain" (1988, p. 94). Sex-role stereotyping, the lack of political role models, and the contentiousness of the political process may all be barriers to women's participation in the political process.

Fewer researchers have found racial differences partially because many of the studies have been of Anglo-Americans. In general, however, African Americans and Hispanic Americans have been found to be less politically aware and interested (Moore et al., 1985). Liebschutz and Niemi (1974) point out that political alienation among African-American children grows with age. This is an area that needs significant additional research. We have little idea of how children of different ethnic and racial groups view the political culture, how efficacious they feel compared to people of the dominant culture, and how, and if, they see themselves participating in the political process.

Class differences have been more fully explicated. In general, children from lower socioeconomic status homes feel less efficacious, express less interest, and are less inclined to participate (Greenstein, 1965; Hess & Torney, 1967; M. K. Jennings, 1974; Sigel & Hoskin, 1981; Merelman, 1986). Greenstein found that children from a family with a higher socioeconomic status made more independent and critical judgments while children from homes with a lower socioeconomic status were more compliant with political authority. Dowse and Hughes (1971) and Stevens (1982) found that there was significantly less discussion of political issues in lower socioeconomic status homes. The lower levels of participation and efficacy echo the research done with adults. Almond and Verba (1963), Verba, Nie, and Kim (1978), Acock and Scott (1980), and Conway (1990) found that education and socioeconomic status were the clearest predictors of political participation. The more demanding this participation was in terms of visibility and time, the more powerfully class played a role in participation. This class distinction does not carry over to prosocial behavior (Eisenberg & Mussen, 1989). In fact, "parental income has generally been found to have little effect on donations" given by children (Midlarsky, 1984, p. 298). Lower income families, in general, give a higher proportion to charity than middle- or upper-income families (Hodgkinson & Weitzman, 1992).

Verba, Nie, and Kim (1978) note that this differential in interest and participation exacerbates social class inequalities. They point to an apparent paradox in the United States:

> That social class was at once so unimportant and so important in American politics. On the one hand, the United States is a society in which social class is not an important ingredient of political competition: The American working class has never manifested a strong sense of class consciousness as has the working class in other nations, nor are political parties specifically organized around a particular social class. At the same time, the class basis of political activity is very strong—the participant population is heavily biased in the direction of those who are more affluent and better educated—more so than in other nations. Our explanation of this seeming contradiction was that the very absence of class as a basis of politics in an ideational or organizational sense meant that class would play a key role in relation to individual political activity. In the absence of *explicit* contestation on the basis of social class the haves in society came to play an inordinate role in political life. (p. 307)

The sense of powerlessness often experienced by lower socioeconomic class families in the economic arena extends itself to their political participation as well.

Conclusion

In essence, what we see in the many studies of political development is the early engagement—especially on an affective level—in the social and political arena. Elementary age children develop an increasing ability to apprehend this world and, if engaged as Coles's interviewees were, can feel passionate about its dangers and its potential. Adolescents are not only trying to make moral and cognitive sense of the social and political world, they are attempting to make sense of their place in it. What we also see is that the social and political inequalities relating to gender, race, and class have already made an impact on children's ability to enter and feel a part of the social and political world.

Throughout their childhood and adolescence, young people are formulating a theory of how their society works and negotiating their relationship with society. This relationship often remains implicit, visible only in off-hand comments expressing their attitudes and judgments about the world around them. Children, in essence, feel their way into the world. The degree of connectedness that they experience determines their sense of efficacy and their interest in participation. The research reported here indicates that in spite of the stereotype of children as egocentric, children care about the welfare of others and care about issues of fairness on both a personal and social level. Social consciousness and social responsibility are not behaviors that we need to instill in young people but rather they are behaviors that we need to recognize emerging in them.

These studies have not fully tapped the richness of children's personal meanings and sense of relatedness that could give us a better understanding of how they experience their relationship to the social and political world. That will have to await further research. In spite of the wealth of information this research provides, it is limited. Most of the research is framed in terms of socialization theory or cognitive developmental theory and pays little attention to the child's interaction with their social and political context. With the exception of Moore, Lare, and Wagner's work, none of the researchers spent any significant time with children. And even Moore, Lare, and Wagner's work suffers from a lack of open-ended questions where children could begin to relate their own meanings and interpretations. Coles's work comes closest to this, yet he is reluctant to outline developmental sequences. Research modeled on the recent work done in prosocial behavior would be of great value to enhancing our understanding of children's development of political consciousness.

As thin as this research is, we are still able to see the outline of an evolving cognitive and emotional relationship. We are also able to see that there is a far greater potential for nurturing political and social development. Our conception of the child as egocentric, morally immature, uninterested in the social and political world, and unable to understand it has effectively deprived young people of the kind of contact they need to make society and politics salient. Young people's distance from politics and their lack of interest may be an effect of our misconceptions, our ignorance of their potential, and our protectiveness.

CHAPTER 3

From Consciousness to Activism

To enter history, each generation of youth must find an identity consonant with its own childhood and consonant with an ideological promise in the perceptible historical process. But in youth the tables of childhood dependence begin slowly to turn: no longer is it merely for the old to teach the young the meaning of life, whether individual or collective. It is the young who, by their responses and actions, tell the old whether life as represented by the old and as presented to the young has meaning; and it is the young who carry in them the power to confirm those who confirm them and, joining the issues, to renew and to regenerate, or to reform and to rebel. (Erikson, 1965, p. 24)

Whoever saves one life, it is as though he saves the whole universe. (From the inscription on the medal awarded by Yad Vashem to Holocaust rescuers, Oliner & Oliner, 1988, p. 232.)

Efficacy and Activism

The studies reported so far have focused on the cognitive and affective aspects of young people's political and social development. Yet a number of researchers have tried to understand the sources of moral and political behavior. Many have examined this in terms of the relationship between the individual's sense of efficacy and their political participation. Efficacy is the belief that a person has the ability to influence the social and political environment. Dunn (1988) contends that what motivates social development in infants is their interest in developing a sense of efficacy or control over social situations. Dweck's (Dweck & Goetz, 1983; Dweck & Licht, 1980) work on learned helplessness reveals that when students identify lack of ability, something they cannot control, rather than lack of effort, something they can control, as the reason for their failure, their competence diminishes. Attributing failure to ability can even cause them to fail on problems they were previously successful in solving. However, if failure is attributed to effort rather than ability, they are able to tolerate situations of failure. This applies to social as well as academic situations. She points out that "some individuals are isolated *not* because they lack social skills or the knowledge of appropriate behavior, but because they fear or have experienced social rejection and view it as insurmountable" (1983, p. 199). Given that many young people feel the political arena is inaccessible to them, learned helplessness may be one of the reasons students withdraw from political involvement.

Many of the major political socialization studies have assumed that efficacy influences participation and have assessed young people's perceptions of their political efficacy. Efficacy is often assessed by Likert-scale, agree-disagree items that ask about a person's influence on government policy. Hess and Torney (1967) and Sigel and Hoskin (1981) used a set of five items:

> What happens in the government will happen no matter what citizens do. It is like the weather, there is nothing they can do about it.
> There are some big, powerful men in the government who are running the whole thing, and they do not care about us ordinary people.
> My family doesn't have any say about what the government does.
> I don't think people in the government care much what people like my family think.
> Citizens don't have a chance to say what they think about running the government. (Sigel & Hoskin, p. 314; Hess & Torney, p. 256)

Jennings and Niemi (1981) used a slightly different set of items:

> Voting is the only way that people like my mother and father can have any say about how the government runs things.

Voting is the only way that people like me can have any say about how the government runs things.

Sometimes politics and government seem so complicated that a person like me can't really understand what's going on.

I don't think public officials care much what people like me think.

People like me don't have any say about what government does. (Jennings & Niemi, pp. 409–10)

Moore, Lare, and Wagner (1985) broke these items into two scales. One they identified as political efficacy and it included two items:

If the government makes a mistake, should you write a letter or just forget about it?

Do you think when things in the government are wrong that people like us can do something about it?

The other they labeled a sense of governmental responsiveness. This included four items, some of which appeared on the efficacy scales of previous research:

Does the government listen to what your mom and dad say?

Would the government want to help you if you needed help?

Do the people running the government care about ordinary people like us?

Do people in the government care much about what your mom or dad think? (Moore et al., p. 253)

Button (1974) used the most extensive set of questions in assessing efficacy. She combined Sigel and Hoskin's questions with some of Jennings and Niemi's questions and added two more open-ended questions:

Voting is the only way that people like my mother and father can help run things.

Sometimes I can't understand what goes on in government.

What happens in the government will happen no matter what citizens do. It is like the weather, there is nothing they can do about it.

There are some big, powerful men in the government who are running the whole thing, and they do not care about us ordinary people.

My family doesn't have any say about what the government does.
I don't think people in the government care much what people
    like my family think.
Citizens don't have a chance to say what they think about running
    the government.
How much does the average person help decide which laws are
    made for our country?
What do you think are America's two biggest problems? Do you
    feel that you personally can do anything to help solve these
    problems? If so, what? If not, why? (Button, 1974, pp. 174–75)

Much has been made of these items in spite of the fact that they are
so limited in scope and depth and tend to overrepresent perceptions
of government responsiveness rather than perceptions of people's ability
to create change. Merelman and King (1986), in their study of student
activists, found that "the high sense of efficacy acquired early in life created
a psychological dynamic which resulted in a mutually reinforcing combination of political activism and still greater efficacy" (p. 483). Hess and Torney
reported that there was a significant growth in efficacy among third and
fourth graders and that eighth graders accepted the notion that citizens
control the government and citizen action is effective. In contrast, Sigel
and Hoskin (1981) found low levels of efficacy among their high school
seniors. Low levels of efficacy have been reported in other studies of high
school students (Moore, personal communication, 1992). Yet, we know
little about what causes this change in efficacy in the preadolescent and
adolescent years.

It has been generally accepted that efficacy leads to activism. Conway
(1991), in her study of political participation, found that "voters high in
political efficacy have regularly been 20 to 30 percent more likely to vote
than those low in political efficacy. . . ." (p. 157). Hoehn (1983), in his
interviews with eighty-seven adult activists, found that "in order to get
started in political involvement, one first has to overcome inertia and fear,
has to have a sense of personal power" (p. 98). Colby and Damon (1992),
in their study of twenty-three moral exemplars, also identify efficacy as
an important contributor to moral action.

[W]e have seen in all of our exemplars a . . . sense of personal
effectiveness, the opposite of powerlessness. The importance of
this sense of effectiveness for exceptional moral behavior has been

evident in this study and others. Put most simply, it is unlikely that people will consistently put forth the effort, and take on the risks, that moral action entails without some sense that they have the power to make a difference. (p. 144)

Oliner and Oliner (1988) make the strongest case for the link between efficacy and activism in their study of rescuers of Jews during the Holocaust. Using a measure of internal versus external locus of control (Rotter, 1966) to assess efficacy, they found that rescuers felt that they could control events and shape their own destiny while nonrescuers were often fatalistic and expressed a sense of powerlessness. They conclude that "a sense of internal control did allow more rescuers to recognize a choice where others perceived only compliance and to believe they could succeed where others foresaw only failure" (p. 178).

However, Gurin, Gurin, and Morrison (1978) point out that there are several problems with the locus of control instrument as a measure of efficacy or political involvement. As a result of a study done with a national sample of 1,297 adults, they argue that the measure could be easily misinterpreted when applied to political activism. They found that, instead of providing consistent data on a person's sense of efficacy, the questions on the locus of control instrument mix two separate and somewhat unrelated concepts. Some questions focus on "personal" efficacy, that is, the degree to which people believe they exercise control over their own lives. Other questions focus on "control ideology," that is, the degree to which people believe that the political system is responsive and just. When they broke these questions into two subscales they found that politically active conservatives had a sense of internal control on both subscales but that political activism among liberals and African Americans was unrelated to a personal sense of internal control and more strongly correlated with an external control ideology. These liberal and African-American activists believed that the political system was not just and responsive and that this limited the degree of influence people could have. This lack of control was, in fact, one of the reasons they were involved in political action. They also found that personal efficacy was more highly correlated with race and socioeconomic status than activism. They point out that having a sense of low personal control, that is, feeling that external events play a significant role in one's life, may "reflect a correct perception of a harsh environment over which they have little control" (p. 292), rather than possessing personal or cultural values that need to be altered. They conclude that the items on the internal-external locus of control scale have a conservative bias by implying an extreme sort of individualism. Given that the items about political responsiveness on Rotter's scale are similar to those on the other measures of political efficacy, this criticism may apply to those scales as well. In fact, both the locus of control and efficacy measures may not be reliable indicators of political efficacy. In contrast to what these measures assume, for some individuals, the lack of trust in the political system and the perception that the system is not responsive to the individual mobilizes, rather than depresses, political engagement.

Torney, Oppenheim, and Farnen (1975), who studied civic education in ten democracies, also report that there may be a more complex relationship between efficacy and participation. They found that individuals who support current government policies can feel efficacious because their views are already represented and may not desire to participate. Also the general level of efficacy may vary based on the current social and political environment or "period effects" (Ehman, 1980; Sears, 1990).

Eisenberg and Mussen (1989) believe that efficacy in practice, rather than in belief, is complicated. "The child must first perceive the other person's needs, interpret them accurately, and recognize that the other person can be helped. In addition, the child must feel competent in this situation, that is, capable of providing what is needed, and the cost or risk entailed in helping must not be prohibitive. . . . Unless these preconditions are met, even the child who knows the norm of social responsibility is not likely to render aid" (p. 5). The same could be said of efficacy in the social and political arena. The child must perceive a need for their help as well as feel competent in the situation, and the cost and risk must not be prohibitive. Keniston (1968) and Hoehn (1983), in their studies of activists, found that such factors as having an alternative analytical framework, models of committed individuals, immediate access to a problem, a clear role to play in its solution, the time to help, and a larger movement to be part of played a significant role in moving individuals to take political action.

The significance of efficacy in encouraging political participation is further complicated by some of the findings of studies of political activists (Hoehn, 1983; Keniston, 1968), moral exemplars (Colby & Damon, 1992), and rescuers of Jews during the Holocaust (Oliner & Oliner, 1988). Each of these researchers found that the actions of the individuals they interviewed were based only partially on their hope that they could create change. Often, these individuals acted in spite of not knowing whether they would actually make a difference. These activists, at times, "decide that success is not important—that something must be done even though there is no assurance that it will change anything" (Hoehn, p. 90). For them, the essential "rightness" of the action makes the issue of success irrelevant. This was true in Oliner and Oliner's study. They note that "even when [the rescuers'] actions might prove futile, individuals tended to believe that the principles were kept alive as long as there were people who reaffirmed them by their deeds" (p. 209). Keniston remarks that "most of those who worked in the Vietnam Summer National Office had long ago lost any illusions about the possibility of early success for the New Left. On a day-to-day level, they were instead sustained by the satisfactions they derived from their work, from their associations with their friends in it, and from the deep, if usually unstated, conviction that what they were doing was politically and ethically important" (1968, pp. 141–42). Welch (1990) labels this "an ethic of risk." Without control of the situation or the assurance of some success, people act as a statement of resistance to oppression. "With an ethic of risk, actions begin with the recognition that far too much has been lost and there are no clear means of restitution. The fundamental risk constitutive of this ethic is the decision to care and to act although there are no guarantees of success" (p. 68). Allison McCrea, one of Colby and Damon's interviewees who gave up a career in advertising to open a homeless shelter, exemplifies this ethic:

> I love the things we do. How effective are we? (Laughs.) What we do probably doesn't amount to very much of anything—in the long run. We haven't stopped homelessness, we haven't stopped hunger, we haven't stopped rotten things from happening. But that doesn't allow us the luxury of walking away from it. We are committed. Our destiny is a commitment to good and we may never achieve it. (p. 273)

Although much additional research needs to be done in order for us to fully understand the link between efficacy and action, there is enough data to argue that efficacy is one influence on active participation. In healthy personal relationships one knows that one's views are valued and that one can make a difference in the other person's life. The same is true of our relationship with society. In a healthy relationship with society one knows that one's views are valued and that one can help effect change. Yet, the studies of activists point to other deeper and clearer roots of participation that are anchored in one's sense of self as a moral being inextricably connected to others. It is from these studies of activists as well as the moral and identity development work of Kohlberg, Gilligan, and Erikson that we begin to uncover the deeper roots.

The Roots of Activism: Moral Integrity

Each of the studies of social and political activists found that the roots of activism were grounded in moral values. Hoehn's (1983) extensive interviews with eighty-seven adult activists, some of whom had been activists for decades, revealed that most became involved because they were confronted by a situation that violated their moral values. Through his in-depth interviews and observations of fourteen New Left activists, Keniston (1968) found that all were motivated by a commitment to deeply held values—"justice, decency, equality, responsibility, nonviolence, and fairness" (p. 28)—values that were often very similar to their parents' values. "[T]he crucial sustaining force in [their] commitment is probably an underlying sense of acting on one's basic principles" (p. 31). This is echoed in Todd Jennings' (1992) study of twenty-eight adult activists, in Colby and Damon's (1992) study of the lives of twenty-three moral exemplars, and in Oliner and Oliner's (1988) study of 406 rescuers. Each of the studies traces the lineage of these values to parents or significant individuals who lived and modeled these values.

Yet, in spite of these roots in a commitment to moral principles, the research in moral development has largely ignored the link between moral beliefs and social and political action and focused instead on moral reasoning and judgment about personal dilemmas. The dilemmas presented to interviewees by Kohlberg and his colleagues and the conflicts discussed by Gilligan and her colleagues are personal dilemmas and conflicts. In Kohlberg's Heinz dilemma, where a druggist is charging a price for a cancer drug that the husband of a woman dying of cancer cannot afford, the interviewers ask whether Heinz should steal the drug (Kohlberg, 1969). They don't ask about whether the economic system that provides the context for this situation is fair. They don't ask whether there are alternative legal actions that he should pursue. They don't ask whether there is an alternative system of health care that is more just. The larger questions are strikingly absent (Torney-Purta, 1983). Furthermore, "Kohlberg's pedagogy provides little or no understanding of how voice and history come together within the ongoing asymmetrical relations of power that characterize the interplay of dominant and subordinate cultures" (Giroux,

1988, p. 57). The same is true of the research on the moral voice of care (Gilligan, 1982). The interview questions pursue the deeper personal dimensions of moral conflicts and neglect the social, political, and historical context for these choices. Colby and Damon (1992) point out that Kohlberg and Gilligan share the same cognitivist assumptions and methods and overemphasize reflection over action. In fact, for most of the activists that Hoehn (1983), Oliner and Oliner (1988), and Colby and Damon (1992) interviewed the decision to act preceded conscious reflection.

A few researchers, however, have looked at the link between moral reasoning and moral action. Blasi (1980, 1983) and Kohlberg and Candee (1984a) argue that there is a direct relationship between moral reasoning and moral action. They believe that moral action is a rational response to understandings and reasons. Moral action emerges out of a moral judgment. "Without judgment, an action, no matter how beneficial, would not be moral" (Blasi, 1980, p. 4). For Kohlberg and Candee the transition from judgment to action is mediated by a judgment of responsibility, a judgment about one's accountability to perform the right action in a situation. Blasi (1983) takes this one step further and suggests that the transition from a judgment of responsibility to taking action is also supported by a desire for self-consistency or integrity. If an action is inconsistent with a judgment of responsibility then one feels guilt. "Responsibility to what one knows—about right and wrong, about others and oneself—is integrity. Integrity acquires then a more precise meaning: it is not logical consistency, nor consistency among personality traits, nor the resolution of dissonance between cognition and action, when it is dictated by the need to reduce one's anxiety; it is, instead, a responsible actualization of what one knows to be right and true. . . . Reasoning is cheap and painless, action and integrity are not. Integrity requires the development of the whole person; a concern with it tends to emphasize one's failures more than one's successes" (pp. 206–7). Because we have a responsibility for what we know, immorality is "not wanting to know, blinding oneself, acting against one's knowledge" (p. 206).

In looking at the empirical studies on the relationship between moral reasoning and such behaviors as delinquency, honesty, altruism, and resistance to conformity, Blasi (1980) concludes that at higher stages of moral reasoning, there is a greater ability to resist the pressure to conform one's judgment to others' views. Individuals at higher stages of moral reasoning also tend to be more honest and altruistic. Kohlberg and Candee (1984a) review Haan, Smith, and Block's (1968) study of college activists and nonactivists involved in the Berkeley free-speech movement and Milgram's (1974) study of individuals' obedience to authority and conclude that the higher one's stage of moral reasoning, the more likely the person is to act consistently with one's reasoning and to make a judgment of responsibility. This is also their conclusion after analyzing the reasoning of participants in the Watergate and My Lai affairs (Kohlberg & Candee, 1984b) and Candee's (1976) conclusion after looking at college students' judgment of Watergate.[1]

Haan, Smith, and Block's (1968) study was the only empirical study reviewed by Blasi that dealt with moral action in the political arena. In an attempt to relate political activism to moral judgment, Haan and her colleagues interviewed 957 college students and Peace Corps volunteers using Kohlberg's moral judgment scale along with several other psychological and social measures that included self-descriptive adjectives and perceived parental child-rearing practices. They divided the group into five types: inactives (low on volunteer work and protest activities), conventionalists (below median in volunteer work and protest activities), constructivists (high on volunteer work, low on protest), broad spectrum activists (high on both), and dissenters (high on protest, low on volunteer work). They found that the inactives, the conventionalists, and the constructivists all fell mainly at the second level in Kohlberg's stage framework, the morality of conventional role-conformity. It was the two types who had engaged in substantial protest activity, the broad spectrum activists and the dissenters, who reasoned at Kohlberg's third level of principled morality (p. 337).

One other study came to a similar conclusion. Patterson (1979) attempted to link Kohlberg's moral development framework to political thinking through the use of political dilemmas dealing with the issue of free speech. He hypothesized that the higher the stage of moral/political reasoning, the more likely it was that the respondent would be consistent in the application of the principle of free speech and the more likely the individual would be tolerant of deviant ideas. He surveyed and interviewed twenty-two fourth graders and thirty-three sixth graders in a small Midwestern university town. He presented them with political dilemmas, such as a mayor encountering community resistance to giving a demonstration permit to people wanting to protest the bad treatment of poor people. The interviewee was asked if the mayor should give them the permit. To check for consistency in the free-speech dilemmas, he then asked whether it would make a difference if the group asking for the permit were Communists. He found that, "as hypothesized, level of moral reasoning is related to the child's ability consistently to apply the principle of free speech to concrete situations" (p. 17).

In this study he also looked at the relationship of moral reasoning and political participation and found that participation in politics was highly correlated with levels of moral reasoning. "Participation in the family context and in the actual political realm is important here. Participation included such activities as working for a candidate, wearing a campaign button, searching out information about government and politics, and discussing political questions with friends and parents. Those children more likely to engage in such activities are also more likely to have reached higher stages of moral development" (p. 16).

What these studies reveal is that as the level of moral reasoning increases, people become more concerned with their integrity and act in ways that are consistent with their beliefs. They point to the importance of moral engagement and integrity in the development of a participatory relationship with the political world.

Although none of the studies of activists (Colby & Damon, 1992; Hoehn, 1983; T. Jennings, 1992; Keniston, 1968; Oliner & Oliner, 1988) use Kohlberg's framework, moral integrity emerges as one of the striking characteristics of activists. Colby and Damon (1992) describe this integrity as a unity of self and morality. Using a method of case study called assisted autobiography, they completed extensive interviews with twenty-three individuals nominated for their sustained commitment to moral ideas, their moral integrity, and their willingness to risk their self-interest for their moral values. These exemplars, nominated by twenty-two leaders in the fields of moral philosophy and moral development, ranged in age from thirty-five to eighty-six. Many had been activists for decades. They were a diverse group as well in terms of race, ethnicity, and political orientation. Yet common among all of them was a strong identification with such moral values as honesty, justice, charity, and harmony. So strong was this identification that their moral mission became their personal goal as well. The researchers comment that:

> We did not find our moral exemplars to be a suffering, grim lot. . . .
> *None saw their moral choices as an exercise in self-sacrifice.* To the
> contrary, they see their moral goals as a means of attaining their
> personal ones, and vice versa. This can only be possible when
> moral goals and personal goals are closely in synchrony, perhaps
> even identical. Our exemplars have been invulnerable to the debili-

tating psychological effects of privation because all they have needed for personal success is the productive pursuit of their moral mission. Their hopes for themselves and their own destinies are largely defined by their moral goals. In the end, it is this unity between self and morality that makes them exceptional. (pp. 300-1)

Virginia Durr, a long-term civil rights activist interviewed by Colby and Damon, describes this commitment:

I knew that the things we were working for were right. When times get bad, you only have one thing to fall back on—that you believe in what you are doing. My children, as they reached young adulthood, would sometimes say they wished I had stayed at home and baked brownies as other mothers did. But what good were brownies in a society that tolerated poverty and denied people the education that enabled them to get out of poverty? What good were brownies in a society that denied people the right to vote? (p. 123)

The activists Hoehn (1983) interviewed, although all from liberal to radical political orientations, had also been active for periods of time from several years to several decades. They had made lasting commitments to work toward a just and humane society. Some were full-time activists, community organizers, and public officials, but most were middle-class citizens deeply invested in participating on behalf of the public good. Hoehn describes the process of becoming aware and involved as an awakening-to-selfhood or I-am-me experience that integrates one's moral action with one's identity. He found that each developed a moral frame of reference "through which one intends with care toward a world perceived as intrinsically social, comprised of people (and nature) who (and which) in meaningful respects are like-me, yet not-me. To intend with care is to care about, be appreciative of, and assign priority in seeing and doing to moral dimensions of the social and natural world. It is to view the human world in moral and aesthetic terms first, not residually. It means putting the questions, 'Is it good? is it beautiful?' to the multiple contexts of one's lived engagements. Perception and interpretation of the world as a moral phenomenon is requisite to taking the responsibility that leads a person to act in behalf of the common good" (pp. 82–83). Exemplifying this unity of self and morality, one of his interviewees states that:

I couldn't shake off the notion that suffering hurts and that I'm in a position to alleviate it sometimes. I have seen suffering, and just because I would prefer not to be bothered by it, that doesn't take away my responsibilities. It doesn't take away my consciousness. I can't just say, "Well to hell with suffering, I've done my share." (p. 25)

Keniston (1968) spent the summer with a group of New Left activists who were organizing a national campaign to end the Vietnam War. This campaign was called Vietnam Summer. Although his interviewees were far younger, ranging in age from nineteen to twenty-nine, and had been deeply involved with "the Movement" for only one to three years, he found the exact same unity of self and morality. "[W]hat I observed of them in their work was consistent with what they had told me of themselves in interviews, and indeed suggested an unusual integration of private and public life" (p. 24). He goes on to note that, in spite of their age, they lived their values.

These young men and women were not possessed of any sense of destiny. But they retained from earlier life an unusual orientation to moral principle. . . . For them, more than for most of their contemporaries, it was not enough merely to 'have principles'; it was necessary to live by their principles. The increasing sense of the inadequacy of their own lives and of the options before them was therefore related to a growing feeling that the direction in which they were moving was ethically inadequate and therefore personally irrelevant. Once again, the issue of principle—and the shame that arose from failing to follow its lead—was crucial [in their becoming activists]. (pp. 99–100)

Oliner and Oliner (1988) studied 406 rescuers of Jews during the Holocaust and compared them with 126 nonrescuers who were similar in sex, age, education, and geographic location during World War II. Unlike the interviewees of the other studies, all of these rescuers had risked their lives to help others. They undertook these efforts in the context of a campaign of political and ethnic terror in which any assistance to Jews could have cost them and their family their lives. In addition, they provided assistance to this "outsider" and socially ostracized minority group for an extended period of time, sometimes as long as several years. The researchers point out that "we are looking at a particular form of altruism—marked by life-threatening risks to self and a long duration in time, extending to a 'pariah' group marked for death, and occurring in the context of a disapproving or, at most, equivocal normative social climate" (pp. 6–7). They too found that what motivated the action of many of these rescuers was a unity of self and morality.

> Because of their solid family relationships, such children tend to internalize their parents' values, increasingly incorporating standards for personal integrity and care within their own value systems. While they may articulate such standards as cognitive principles, they experience them viscerally. They provide an organizing frame-work for their life activities and assessments of right and wrong. Even minor infractions distress them, and fundamental violations threaten them with a sense of chaos. It is no accident that when the lives of outsiders are threatened, individuals with this orien-tation are more likely to initiate, or be asked for, help. More sensitive than others to violations that threaten their moral values, they may seek out opportunities to help. (p. 250)

Rescuers, in significantly higher percentages than nonrescuers, emphasized that ethical values should be applied universally and extended to all human beings. They also expressed a stronger commitment to care for others in need. Rescuers exhibited altruistic behavior prior to the war and continued it afterward. The unity of self and morality is evident in the explanations for their actions:

> The reason is that every man is equal. We all have the right to live. It was plain murder, and I couldn't stand that. I would help a Mohammedan just as well as a Jew. We have got to live as humans and not as beasts.

> I found it incomprehensible and inadmissible that for religious reasons or as a result of a religious choice, Jews would be per-secuted. It's like saving somebody who is drowning. You don't ask them what God they pray to. You just go and save them.

> I could not comprehend that innocent persons should be persecuted just because of race. We all come from the same God.

> I knew they were taking them and that they wouldn't come back. I didn't think I could live with knowing that I could have done something.

> I saw the Germans shooting people in the street, and I could not sit there doing nothing.

My husband told me that unless we helped, they would be killed. I could not stand that thought. I never would have forgiven myself. (pp. 166–68)

Hoehn, Colby and Damon, and Oliner and Oliner observed this unity of self and morality in the immediacy with which these activists responded to moral situations. Their moral character was well enough established to enable them to respond without needing extensive reflection. Hoehn observed that action often preceded any reflection when the activists he interviewed were confronted with injustice. Colby and Damon and Oliner and Oliner also found that their interviewees' acted out of an almost instinctive ethical compulsion. Colby and Damon indicate that "the sense of compulsion simply to do the right thing runs throughout our interviews" (p. 71). "Among our exemplars, we saw no 'eking out' of moral acts through intricate, tortuous cognitive processing. Instead, we saw an unhesitating will to act, a disavowal of fear and doubt, and a simplicity of moral response. Risks were ignored and consequences went unweighed" (p. 70). Oliner and Oliner comment that "this sense of internal compulsion was characteristically so strong that most rescuers reported rarely reflecting before acting. Asked how long it took them to make their first helping decision, more than 70 percent indicated 'minutes.' Asked if they consulted with anyone prior to making the decision, 80 percent responded 'no one' " (p. 169). One of their interviewees responded that "I cannot give you any reasons. It was not a question of reasoning. Let's put it this way. There were people in need and we helped them" (p. 216).

Although these studies focus their attention on young adults and adults, this unity of self and morality may be foreshadowed in younger children. In a study of students talking a course that examined the ethical and human questions arising from historical cases of genocide, Bardige (1988) found that some early adolescents responded emotionally and actively to the suffering they were studying. They were passionate in their condemnation of violence and vehement in their call for action. She indicates that when they saw another's suffering they wanted to help simply because, in the words of one student, "we should do something" (p. 95). The language in their journals, Bardige notes, "calls attention to the central moral truth of the situation—the fact that hurt is being inflicted and to the pressing need to stop it" (p. 97). Although this "face value thinking," as she labels it, is sometimes lost as students are confronted with divergent perspectives and growing intellectual complexity, it is a powerful testament to young people's potential for a moral sense of self.

Whether this characteristic is described as a unity of self and morality, a sense of self as a moral being, or moral integrity, it is a cornerstone for moral behavior. In fact, Colby and Damon (1992) conclude that "in the end, moral behavior depends on something beyond the moral beliefs in and of themselves. It depends on how and to what extent the moral concerns of individuals are important to their sense of themselves as people" (p. 307). These studies point to the major sources of this integration of self and morality as emerging from a complex set of family and situational circumstances that include family modeling of moral behavior and social and political consciousness, active participation in family decision making, modes of parental discipline that focused on reasoning and care for others, and early identification of or direct confrontation with injustice. However, there is another side of activists' moral sense of self. This side rests less with their identification with moral principles or the consistency between beliefs and actions and more with the activists' sense of self as connected to others and to the world as a whole.

The Roots of Activism: A Connected Sense of Self

Todd Jennings (1992) most clearly identifies this aspect of the activist's sense of self, yet it emerges in the interview data in all the studies. Jennings interviewed twenty-eight human-rights activists in California, thirteen of whom were volunteers and fifteen of whom were employed in human-rights organizations. He found that these activists had a "sense of self" that was defined both by their moral values and their sense of connectedness with others, especially those suffering injustice, and with the world as a whole. One of his interviewees, Diane, works to promote human rights in Central America. She explains her motivation in helping people that she barely knows by saying that "they're a part of my life, they're a part of my family" (p. 17). She goes on to explain:

> . . . in a sense nothing can happen to one person on this planet . . . that it doesn't happen to everyone. It may sound a little mystical but it still is the solution out of our enormous problems. . . . To begin to realize that we are diminished by the oppression that happens to these people because . . . we're part of humanity, and

if we become inhuman here . . . then [the] quality of life for everybody's really diminished, or the quality of our souls is diminished. (pp. 17–18)

Another interviewee, Ellen, is a lawyer who started a legal clinic servicing the needs of the homeless. She, too, acts out of a sense of deep connection to others and their suffering.

I think that if you come with a natural sensitivity to the feelings of others and if you become aware of your connection with other people, then that's where the desire [to help] springs from, that you're basically unhappy just to tend your four corners. You do have to reach out. . . . It's not just an intellectual understanding, I mean, your happiness and sense of well-being then is connected as well. That's part of the connection. It's not just an abstract, intellectual connection with others of your species. You know, there's a feeling that their quality of life and their suffering is also connected to yours. (p. 20)

Sarah, who is working with Jews to address the needs of non-Jews, describes her sense of connectedness in terms of being part of a fragile web where people share responsibility for protecting one another.

Unless we sort of realize that our lives are quite fragile and that hope is a pretty thin web and that if we don't somehow do something to be really protective of that web, which is at least extending our arms to other people . . . the only hope for human beings is the frail web of understanding of one human being for another [and] . . . we need to assert or exert ourselves so as to not rupture the web. (p. 19)

· This theme emerges in twenty-three of the twenty-eight activists as a primary motivator for action. Jennings concludes that "a response to human-rights violations and human need is practically linked to a sense of self defined through connection and affiliation with others. Consequently, advocacy behavior may be a manifestation of the need to maintain a sense of integrity between one's behavior and a 'self' understood and defined through connection with others, including those outside one's own group" (pp. 3–4).

Oliner and Oliner (1988) found that what distinguished rescuers from nonrescuers was "not their lack of concern with self, external approval, or achievement, but rather their capacity for extensive relationships—their stronger sense of attachment to others and their feelings of responsibility for the welfare of others, including those outside their immediate familial or communal circles" (pp. 249–50). They describe the rescuers as

> Already more accustomed to view social relationships in terms of generosity and care rather than reciprocity, they are less inclined to assess costs in times of grave crisis. Already more deeply and widely attached to others, they find it difficult to refrain from action. Already more inclined to include outsiders in their sphere of concern, they find no reason to exclude them in an emergency. Unable to comprehend or tolerate brutality as anything but destructive of the very fabric that gives their lives order and meaning, they react in much the same way as if caught in a flood— holding back the tide through whatever means possible. Hence, their actions appear impulsive, without due consideration of consequences. In fact, however, they are merely the extension of a characteristic style of relating developed over the years. (p. 251)

In terms very similar to the ones used by Jennings's interviewees, one of the rescuers comments that "my father said the whole world is one big chain. One little part breaks and the chain is broken and it won't work anymore" (p. 142). Another states that "I did everything from my heart—I didn't think about getting something for it. My father taught me to be this way. I still feel the same way now. I cannot refuse if somebody needs something. That's why I still help people—I'll do it until I don't have the strength to do it anymore" (p. 227). Rescuers revealed a greater sensitivity to the needs of others and commitment to care for others than nonrescuers. The researchers conclude that "for most rescuers, then, helping Jews was an expression of ethical principles that extended to all of humanity and, while often reflecting concern with equity and justice, was predominantly rooted in care" (p. 170).

Keniston found personal connection with others was central to the work and style of organization of the activists he studied. These activists committed themselves to the New Left out of identification with the victims of injustice. Whether these victims were African Americans deprived of their civil rights, Vietnamese peasants deprived of their national autonomy, or the poor in the United States deprived of basic human needs, these activists felt a sense of connection with the struggle of victims of injustice. In fact, the causes they chose were rarely concerned with improving their own conditions but rather with alleviating the oppression of others. "As a group, activists seem to possess an unusual *capacity for nurturant identification*—that is, for empathy and sympathy with the underdog, the oppressed, and the needy" (p. 309).

Their organizational structure also reflected the value they placed on personal connectedness. Keniston quotes one activist saying that "the politics came after the people. There was always a personal relationship first. And the most important thing of what you were going to do with a person was personal, not political" (pp. 26–27). They shunned bureaucratic and hierarchical structures for face-to-face, egalitarian, and collaborative ones. He concludes that "in their personal manner and values, these young men and women favor open, equal, and direct relationships with other people; they are psychologically and ideologically hostile to formally defined, inflexible roles and traditional bureaucratic patterns of power. Their organizational ideal is the face-to-face group of equals" (p. 164).

In Colby and Damon's (1992) study, the connected sense of self emerges both in the compassion and direct support these exemplars provide to those in need. But it also emerges in the collaborative network of support that sustains their commitment. Often deeply committed individuals are stereotyped as isolated moralists. Yet one of the most striking findings of their study was the collaborative nature of both their initial entry into social and political action and their continuing development as activists. They conclude that "enduring moral commitment takes years to forge, and it is not accomplished in splendid isolation but through extended, frequent communication with collaborators and supporters" (p. 168). In fact, they believe that the moral goals of these exemplars are "co-constructed" through ongoing dialogue and negotiation with collaborators, supporters, and others. Oliner and Oliner also stress the importance of a network of support. Although rescuers had to be extremely cautious in their dealings with others and secretive about their efforts, "almost all rescuers depended on informal networks to sustain them materially and emotionally" (p. 96).

This connected sense of self is, in essence, Gilligan's (1982) moral voice of care that emerges out of attachment and reaches out to respond to those in need. Gilligan and her colleagues (1988, 1990) have found that most adolescents are aware of both justice and care solutions. Preference for one voice over the other emerges in early adolescence, with boys more often basing their judgments on concerns about fairness and girls on concerns about response to hurt and the severing of connection. Yet, she argues that the goal of development is not greater differentiation but an ability to hear and sustain both voices. Neither one is sufficient. Both have vulnerabilities that necessitate hearing the other voice. The vulnerability of care solutions is that they seem naive, while the vulnerability of justice solutions is that the reliance on principles can detach one from feeling the pain of another.

Johnston (1988) found these vulnerabilities in her study of adolescent moral voice. Those who were aware of care solutions to moral dilemmas but did not choose them often claimed that these solutions were unworkable, naive, and utopian given the aggressiveness and destructiveness that they saw as part of human nature. On the other hand, for those who chose a care perspective the detachment, objectivity, and focus on standards and principles that is a valued aspect of justice reasoning is seen as having the potential for rationalizing injustice, treating others as objects, disconnecting from others, and discounting the personal impact and personal feelings involved in a conflict or dilemma. When there is an excessive focus on justice concerns "norms and rules become reified as 'self-chosen principles,' removed from the relational contexts which give them life and meaning" (Gilligan & Wiggins, 1988, p. 134). Both voices are necessary to balance the vulnerability of each.

The studies of activists reveal that many are able to hold these two moral voices in balance. They experience a deep sense of connection to others and the world as a whole. Their actions are often a response to the suffering and oppression of others. Yet they are deeply grounded as well in moral principles of justice. What maintains the balance is a strong commitment to honesty. Both Colby and Damon's and Oliner and Oliner's studies reveal that honesty was a central value for their interviewees. Keniston, too, notes that his activists were committed to an intellectual and moral honesty.

One of the results of this commitment to honesty is an openness to new perspectives and to change. Both Keniston (1968) and Colby and Damon (1992) remark, with sincere surprise, that the activists they studied were far more open then they expected and far less dogmatic. Keniston found that "as a rule, formal elaborated and dogmatic ideological considerations were seldom discussed in these interviews; they rarely formed a major part of the [activist's] presentation of himself to me" (p. 27). He quotes one of his interviewees directly addressing this lack of ideology:

> One of the things that makes it difficult for me to trace where
> I came from is the fact that I don't have an ideology. If I did, if

I knew precisely, I mean if I had clear political goals—well, I have something of an analysis of why certain things happen, and why certain things must happen. But it's not very tightly formulated and I'm very flexible about it. If I did have a rigid view, I would be better able to look back and say, 'This is where this and that came from.' . . . But I think it's better this way. It's more real . . . it forces you to bring yourself together more. . . . (p. 27)

In fact, most of these activists used the term *ideology* pejoratively. "[I]n underlining the connection between the personal and the political, they spoke with some pride, as if to contrast arid ideological positions with honest personal views. Ideology to them seemed to suggest dogmatism, doctrinaire rigidity, lack of responsiveness to people and events, and, ultimately, the misuse of intellect" (p. 180).

Although Colby and Damon's (1992) moral exemplars have strong and stable moral principles, they are also flexible, open, and changing.

[P]erhaps their most intriguing common characteristic was the paradoxical mix of lasting commitment and sustained capacity for change. . . . Even as the exemplars' grip on their core ideals remained unwavering, they continued to reexamine their most fundamental attitudes and choices at frequent intervals. Many of them expanded the nature and extent of their engagements, many took on unexpected challenges, and many dramatically altered their beliefs, conduct, or life conditions on short notice. All the while, the exemplars remained true to their overarching original values, which endured the flux of frequent change and growth, and in a fundamental sense contributed to the shape of that change and growth. (pp. 184–85)

Colby and Damon note that all through adulthood these activists balanced stability and change. They continued to grow in insight, capability, and sensitivity. The researchers credit this to their open-mindedness and personal honesty as well as to their ability to be open to the perspectives of others and to be changed by these perspectives. In fact, they believe that it is through their open, reciprocal, truthful, and self-reflective communication that these individuals "keep themselves developmentally alive" (p. 197). They point out that when people are deeply committed to honesty and are persistent in truth-seeking, as these exemplars are, then other values and beliefs are forced to change. Core values such as justice and nonviolence can coexist with these changes, but they are applied differently as the individual grows. "A stable belief in honesty thus injects a vital dynamism in all other belief systems, possibly leading to their revision or, in some cases, even their overthrow" (p. 77).

Therefore, what is revealed in these studies of activists is that the roots of activism are not only grounded in moral principles but in a deep sense of connection to others and the world around them. Maintaining an integration of the moral voices of justice and care fosters a humility about one's rightness and an openness to new perspectives. Maintaining collaborative connections with others also fosters continued moral growth. These studies, however, point to one additional motivator of activism—the need for a sense of meaning and a sense of place within a larger context.

The Roots of Activism: Meaning and Place

The roots of political and social activism are also grounded in the human need for meaning. In his discussion of the development of humanitarian concern, Robert White (1981) points out that we have a need for "fellowship in the human community." We have a desire to be bigger than ourselves, not egotistically, but in an expansive and compassionate way. He notes that this desire to contribute to the welfare of others and society has a long history in psychological literature. Adler (1927) describes a natural tendency to outgrow egotism and the urge for superiority and develop a sense of human solidarity. Angyal (1941), too, sees the trend away from egotism and superiority and writes that the individual longs "to become an organic part of something that he conceives as greater than himself . . . to be in harmony with super-individual units, the social world, nature, God, ethical world order, or whatever the person's formulation of it may be" (p. 172). Allport (1961) and Sullivan (1953) identify the growth of an interest in extending oneself beyond the self and making the interests of another as important as one's own. In Erikson's (1958, 1963, 1964, 1968) work the same theme appears in his formation of identity and his concept of generativity.

Erikson (1958, 1968) contends that one of the tasks of adolescence is to find one's own place in the world, to find the intersection of one's personal history with history itself. "I have called the major crisis of adolescence the *identity crisis*; it occurs in that period of the life cycle when each youth must forge for himself some central perspective and direction, some working unity, out of the effective remnants of his childhood and the hopes of his anticipated adulthood; he must detect some meaningful resemblance between what he has come to see in himself and what his sharpened awareness tells him others judge and expect him to be" (Erikson, 1958, p. 14). Central to the formation of a positive identity is the acceptance of an ideological outlook. "The adolescent mind becomes a more explicitly ideological one, by which we mean one searching for some inspiring unification of tradition or anticipated techniques, ideas, and ideals. And, indeed, it is the ideological potential of a society which speaks most clearly to the adolescent who is so eager to be affirmed by peers, to be confirmed by teachers, and to be inspired by worth-while 'ways of life'" (Erikson, 1968, p. 130).

Identity and ideology are two aspects of the same process. Identification with ideology helps define a meaningful direction and something to which one can commit oneself. "Adolescent development comprises a new set of identification processes, both with significant persons and with ideological forces, which give importance to individual life by relating it to a living community and to ongoing history, and by counterpointing the newly won individual identity with some communal solidarity. In youth, then, the life history intersects with history: here individuals are confirmed in their identities, societies regenerated in their life style" (1965, p. 23). Erikson, in essence, believes that we have a deep human need for a way of organizing both our personal and our social reality into a larger whole that can give us meaning and direction.

The desire to feel connected to a larger sense of purpose emerges even more significantly in the stage following identity formation, generativity. Generativity embodies the care of others, "the concern for establishing and guiding the next generation" (Erikson, 1968, p. 138). Browning (1973) builds on Erikson's notions of generativity. He believes that "generativity sums up that in man [sic] which is most basic and most primitive. But it also points toward that which is the end and goal of existence. . . . Generativity is not only the instinctive source behind biological procreation and care; it is also the ground for man's higher attempts to create a total environment ecologically supportive of the general health—not only of family and tribe, but of the entire human species" (p. 146).

Each stage in Erikson's ladder of psychosocial development embodies the crises of the other stages and therefore the desire to meaningfully contribute appears in all of them. In the first stage of trust vs. mistrust, the individual is confronted with the generative challenge of developing a basic trust in the world and hope for the future. The generative task of the second stage, autonomy vs. shame, is experiencing a reciprocity between personal power and the powers of the social world. In the third stage, initiative vs. guilt, the generative challenge is to feel purposeful and feel that one's efforts are socially valued. In stage four, industry vs. inferiority, the individual struggles to develop competence in entering the wider public arena and to develop the ability to make a meaningful contribution to the larger common good. The generative task of stage five, identity vs. identity confusion, is to link one's personal history to history, to make a commitment to a general set of values that fosters the common good. The sixth stage, intimacy vs. isolation, involves the ability to develop a shared commitment without the loss of a sense of individual identity (Browning, 1973). Generativity, the care for the well-being of others and for society, is the primary task of the seventh stage. In Erikson's last stage of integrity, one asks oneself, "What have I left behind?" He says, "Man [sic] as a psychosocial creature will face, toward the end of his life, a new edition of an identity crisis which we may state in the words 'I am what survives of me' " (1968, p. 141). The quality that forms the thread throughout this development is care for the well-being of others and for the world as a whole (Erikson, 1964). Whether or not these issues develop in the order Erikson has charted, each of these issues emerges in the political socialization literature as negotiations between the individual and the political world. In fact, these are issues—trust, hope, efficacy, appreciation, competence, meaning, affiliation, integrity—that the activists interviewed by Hoehn (1983), Keniston (1968), Colby and Damon (1992), and Jennings (1992) describe as continuing struggles in their participation in the political world. The nature of our social and political world sustains these challenges.

In Browning's view, generativity has two tasks. One is caring about what one leaves behind. The second is restraining one's capacity for unlimited propagation, invention, and expansion. "The real problem with man's [sic] Promethean will . . . is not that he aspires to do too much, but aspires to do more than he is able or willing to care for" (1973, p. 164). This has become an increasingly problematic issue for our culture. "For modern man [sic], his generativity has degenerated into mere creativeness, experimentation, and inventiveness; it has become torn apart from that deeper capacity for care which completes and limits the truly generative impulse. Modern man [sic] appears to be generative because he creates so much; in reality his problem is his nongenerative mentality which is seen in the fact that he cares so poorly for that which he creates" (p. 164).

The psychosocial approach represented in the work of Erikson and Browning has been most directly applied to political participation by Keniston (1960, 1968). Keniston's (1960) first study explored the sources and dynamics of political alienation. Twelve subjects, all male Harvard students, were selected from a group of 3,000 who took a series of tests to determine alienation. This group was followed for three years through interviews, journals, and autobiographies. In a highly personal mosaic that he prepares from this data, Keniston explores both the personal and the societal sources of their alienation. Although he does not frame his discussion with Erikson's stages, his in-depth analysis of family dynamics, his application of Freudian theory, the identity formation terminology, and his focus on the historical and social circumstances share Erikson's orientation. Like Erikson, Keniston sees our relatedness to history and the development of historical meaning as central to our identity.

> Man's [sic] relationship to time and to history is of central importance to him. The basic events of human life occur within a context of subjective time that helps determine and sets limits on his feelings about all specific events in the past, present, and the future. Behind this sense of time lies the universal need for historical relatedness, manifest partly as a desire to understand where one comes from and where one is going, partly as a more concrete need to define one's relationship to one's own individual and familial past and future, partly as a need to feel oneself part of a group and a universe with an intelligible past related to a comprehensive future. A man's sense of his own place in time, and of his place in a society and world located in history, is central to his definition of himself. . . . (p. 237)

Keniston's research finds the central themes of alienated development resting initially in the dynamics of family life during childhood. But Keniston, like Erikson, situates these individuals in their historical circumstances. He contends that "alienation is a response *of* individuals especially sensitized to reject American culture by their early development, a development which in part reflects their families' efforts to solve dilemmas built into American life; and it is in part a response *to* social stresses, historical losses, and collective estrangements in our shared experience" (p. 391). "Every individual is in this sense his society writ small—though he is more than this, and though there are many scripts for the transliteration of society to personality" (p. 382). The social causes of alienation that Keniston identifies are the chronic social change present in American society, the complex and fragmented nature of our culture, the disorganization of the American family, and an intellectual climate that undermines positive values and substitutes immediate experience and materialism. Each of these contributes to the individual's loss of meaning and place in the larger society. Bellah and his colleagues (1985, 1991) and Seligman (1991) add to this list the excessive individualism that has dominated our culture. They argue that individualism separates individuals from their context and deprives them of a larger sense of connection and meaning.

Keniston's (1968) research with 1960s New Left activists reveals that these activists, in contrast to the alienated youth of his earlier study, derived a deep sense of meaning from their activism. They identified with the New Left movement because it echoed so many of the values they grew to believe in during their childhood. Not only did the movement embody their values but it proposed that American society set about implementing them. It presented them with the opportunity to work together with others toward a shared vision of a just, free, peaceful, and participatory society. "[The activist's] estrangement from the mainstream is countered by his feeling of engagement with the Movement. His earlier feeling of stagnation is replaced by a greater sense of being in motion, his feeling of aimlessness by a new sense of direction, and, perhaps most important, his feeling of lonely isolation by a new solidarity with others moving and searching in the same ways. Little by little, there developed a feeling of being part of something bigger than oneself, something linked not only to one's individual life but to the broader social and historical scene. By identifying with others, by coming to feel responsible with them for doing something about the perceived inequities of our society, these young men and women came to feel more a part of the world in which they lived" (pp. 143–44). In this way, the movement met the need for a sense of belonging to something meaningful and for giving one's time and energy to something beyond oneself.

Colby and Damon (1992) describe the moral exemplars they studied in very similar terms. Given that they focused on older adults, many of whom were older than fifty, the sense of meaning is attached less to identity and more to generativity and care. Their sense of meaning came from seeing themselves as contributors to a set of ideals that would make the world a better place. Their attention was not on themselves but on a larger goal. A large number, especially those who were involved in charity to the poor, had strong religious beliefs that gave them this sense of meaning.

"We believe it is accurate to say that, among the twenty-three exemplars, there was a common sense of faith in the human potential to realize its ideals. Although the substance of the faith and its ideals was too varied and too elusive to be captured in a final generalization, it can perhaps best be described as an intimation of transcendence: a faith in something above and beyond the self. The final paradox of our study is that the exemplars' unity of self was realized through their faith in a meaning greater than the self" (p. 311).

For many of the exemplars, especially those whose meaning comes from their religious beliefs, there is a basic faith in the goodness of each person in spite of the negative or destructive behaviors they exhibit. Their work takes on meaning as a vehicle for bringing out this goodness in others. Luisa Coll, one interviewee, puts it this way:

> And I can see Jesus on the cross saying "Forgive them, for they know not what they do." Because we don't know. We really don't. We're so ignorant. So many times, we just act things out because we have been programmed that way. But if they are given a chance—and I have learned to give second and third and fourth chances. And I have been rewarded in those instances by the people that I have been willing to give a second and a third and a fourth chance to. And they have proven that yes, once they are really able to tap into that goodness in themselves and to find that self-image based on the love that God has for us, and that he didn't create junk . . . that he created goodness in all of us. Those persons are doing perfectly well now. (p. 276)

Often the activists whose meaning came from religious beliefs focused their efforts on helping others directly through charity. Colby and Damon argue the apolitical nature of their work is due to the inability of their religious framework to provide a way of understanding secular politics or one's own political action in a religiously meaningful manner.

However, like Keniston's activists, being part of a movement or an organization, either secular or religious, enhanced this sense of meaning and placed it within a larger context. One activist who quit her career in advertising to start a shelter for the homeless expressed how being part of a larger struggle sustained her through the years of challenges, setbacks, and, at times, achievements:

> I have enormous faith that somehow it's going to be OK. I also know that I am a part of a struggle. I am not *the* struggle, I am

not leading any struggle. I am there. And I have been there for a long time, and I'm going to be there for the rest of my life. So I have no unrealistic expectations. Therefore, I'm not going to get fatigued. (p. 88)

As individuals who had been active in social and political causes for long periods of time, it was this sense of meaning that sustained them over the long term. It was this sense of meaning that provided the scaffolding to support the growth of their moral integrity. "It is this faith, this hope, this meaning that provides the glue joining all the self's systems of action and reflection. This is what held the exemplars together during all the trials, the successes and failures, . . . that would test the strength and endurance of their commitments. . . . It is, in short, what made the center hold throughout all the decades of the exemplars' uniquely consequential lives" (p. 311).

These studies show that the roots of activism also lie in the desire for a sense of meaning that takes one beyond oneself. To be bigger than oneself, to feel one is contributing to the welfare of others and society, not only motivates action but sustains it over the long term.

Although moral integrity, a connected sense of self, and the desire for meaning are the roots of activism common to many of the activists in these studies, activists are a diverse group and their motivations reflect this diversity. Some are more focused on moral integrity, others on connection with and care for others, and others on the historical meaning of their efforts. Oliner and Oliner (1988) identify three motivational patterns similar to the ones I have identified and found that rescuers were influenced to a varying degree by each of these. Some were more empathically oriented and responded to events that aroused their empathy. Others were oriented to ethical principles and responded to events that they interpreted as violating their principles. And others were "normocentrically" oriented, that is oriented to a social reference group, religious affiliation, national identification, or movement whose values and ideals one supports. Although Oliner and Oliner describe normocentric motivation as emerging from feelings of obligation to a highly valued social group, individuals who are normocentrically oriented see their actions fitting into a larger context of meaning and purpose provided by the goals and values of this group. Some rescuers were primarily oriented to one of these motivational orientations, others mixed two or all three of them. The researchers conclude that "the variation in motivations leading to rescue behavior highlights the important point that the paths to virtue are neither uniform nor standardized. Rather, they represent alternative pathways through which individuals are equipped and disposed to interpret events of moral significance. Different rescuers found different meanings in what was happening to Jews, but once their plight was understood through the prism of the individual's orientation, the necessity to act became compelling" (pp. 220–21).

The Emergence of Activism

Efficacy, moral integrity, a connected sense of self, and the desire for meaning come together as the roots of activism in individuals. Yet these individuals were not always activists. In examining the history behind their moral commitment, the studies of activists reveal a relatively common pattern.

The first characteristic common to the background of these activists is that there was a continuity of values between their parents and themselves. Keniston (1968) found that, in opposition to previous assumptions about New Left activists, becoming committed to the New Left involved "*no fundamental change in core values*" (p. 113) from their family's values. Keniston points to many continuities between these students' current values and their backgrounds. They were brought up to believe "that prejudice, hatred, and discrimination are wrong, that suffering should be alleviated, that all men [sic] should have equal opportunities and an equal say in the decisions affecting their lives, that peace and justice should be sought after, that violence should be minimized, and that men [sic] should seek to relate to each other in a humane, open, direct, and personal way" (pp. 116–17).

> Somehow these parents communicated, often without saying outright, that human behavior was to be judged primarily in terms of general ethical principles; that right conduct was to be deduced from general maxims concerning human kindness, honesty, decency, and responsibility; that what mattered most was the ability to act in conformity with such principles. Whether the principles were religious or secular, the atmosphere within these . . . families during their early years was one in which ethical principles occupied the highest position. (p. 66)

None of them questioned the rightness of these principles. There was a strong identification with that aspect of their parents that was idealistic, effective, and actively principled. But the strongest continuity was their concern about aggression, hostility, and violence, which began in their earliest memories. "The only startling fact is that [these activists] take these values seriously and propose that American society and the world set about implementing them" (p. 116).

There was an early awareness of social and political events, often stimulated by the family's interest and open discussion of these events. Keniston asked these activists about some of their earliest memories. "In these recollections, two crucial themes stand out. First, these earliest memories are to an unusual degree connected to the broader social and historical scene: the end of the war, a well-publicized riot, the interviewee's favored social position. This sensitivity to the social scene recurs throughout these young radicals' lives. Second, the issue of violence, external and internal, runs through these early memories: the outer violence of the atomic bomb, the threatening crowd, or the 'gruesome fights' in the schoolyard; the inner violence of fear-filled anger and jealous rage. This issue, too, persists" (pp. 50–51).

Oliner and Oliner (1988) observed a very similar pattern. Parents modeled caring behavior and communicated caring and egalitarian values. "Rescuers brought to the war a greater receptivity to others' needs because they had learned from their parents that others were very important. . . . [W]ords and phrases characterizing care—the need to be helpful, hospitable, concerned, and loving—were voiced significantly more often by rescuers [than nonrescuers] as they recalled the values they learned from their parents or other most influential person" (pp. 161–64). In talking about their parents, these rescuers clearly note the importance they gave to tolerance, equality, and caring for others:

> He taught me never to forget where you come from; to always appreciate anything from anybody. He impressed on me never to forget that when you work for yourself and have people under you, don't look down on them. Be honest and straightforward. See other people as your friends. All people are people. (p. 143)

> My grandfather was the most religious man I knew. I had more respect for him than for the minister. He practiced what he

preached. He visited the sick; he went to the church to get money for poor people. That's the kind of character he was. (p. 144)

She taught me to be responsible, honest, to respect older people, to respect all people—not to tease or criticize people of other religions. She taught me to be good.

He taught me to love my neighbor—to consider him my equal whatever his nationality or religion. He taught me especially to be tolerant.

I learned to live honestly, to study well in school, to respect others, and to have compassion and generosity toward those who were less well treated by life.

I learned to be good to one's neighbor, honesty, scruples—to be responsible, concerned, and considerate. To work—and work hard. But also to help—to the point of leaving one's work to help one's neighbor.

To be good and caring, to love people. Mother always said to remember to do some good for someone at least once a day. (pp. 164–65)

They taught me discipline, tolerance, and serving other people when they needed something. It was a general feeling. If somebody was ill or in need, my parents would always help. We were taught to help in whatever way we could. Consideration and tolerance were very important in our family. My mother and father both stressed those feelings. My father would not judge people who lived or felt differently than he did. That point was always made to us. (p. 220)

Rescuers' parents not only lived these values but expected their children to live them as well. When confronted with injustice, the rescuers' response was natural and immediate.

Although Hoehn (1983) does not explicitly explore the family background of his interviewees, the influence of family values emerges in the interviews. One of his interviewees describes this parental influence:

It's not a very hard transition to translate what I saw my parents doing and forcing us to do (which I resented as a child) into the obvious. When I saw other people who needed help, then it was a natural thing to try to better the situation too. . . . It's because of the way my mother lived her life in my presence when I was a child that I could easily become conscious of suffering on the part of others. She was aware of suffering, and she did what she could to alleviate it on a one-to-one basis. And she used all the family facilities to do that with. (p. 24)

Two other studies of altruistic behavior affirm the importance of parental modeling. Rosenhan (1972) did extensive interviews with the forty-six "freedom riders" who participated in the civil rights movement of the 1950s and 1960s in order to explore the differences between fully committed and partially committed participants. The fully committed participants had an extended commitment of up to a year at great personal sacrifice and risk. The partially committed freedom riders took one or two freedom rides at moderate sacrifice and risk. He found that the critical difference was parental modeling and nurturance. Although his interviews showed that both groups of freedom riders were equally strong advocates for equality, the parents of the fully committed activists had been models of both altruism and political activism. Rosenhan reported that one of the civil rights workers in his study remembered being carried on his father's shoulders to protest the Sacco and Vanzetti trials, another remembered his father going to fight on the Republican side in the Spanish Civil War, another one's mother devoted herself completely to Christian education, and a fourth remembered his father being so outraged at Nazi atrocities that he insisted on serving in the military in spite of being overage and physically disqualified. In contrast the parents of the partially committed activists had strong moral and prosocial values but did not practice them. They reported being told one thing but observing their parents practice another. In addition, the fully committed activists had more positive and sustained relationships with their parents that continued into adulthood than the partially committed.

Clary and Miller (1986) attempted to replicate Rosenhan's study with 162 crisis counseling volunteers. This study is significantly weaker in that the commitment demonstrated by the fully committed was the completion of a six-month agreement to staff the crisis phone lines once a week for four hours. Using a questionnaire that focused on parental influence, empathy, and motivation, they found that the most significant difference between the fully committed and the partially committed was parental nurturance and modeling of altruistic behavior. As a result of this parenting, the fully committed were more autonomous, not needing extrinsic rewards to encourage their efforts. However, they found that the partially committed volunteers would maintain a high level of commitment when part of a highly cohesive, self-rewarding group.

Colby and Damon (1992), too, found that many of the exemplars' parents modeled values for their children, especially honesty and commitment to stand up for what one believes. One of the interviewees, Jack Coleman, described how his parents modeled altruism and respect for the dignity of each person that he came to prize as well:

> My mother was not an educated person, but she was just an amazing woman in terms of the respect that she had for every single human being she met, up to the point where that person put on airs and pretended to be something he or she wasn't. Then, I'm sorry to say, she was unforgiving. So if you were the garbage-man and you did your job well and you didn't go around griping about the thing all the time, then that's fine. If you were the mayor and you went about your job in what, for her, were ethical ways and realized that you were very, very privileged and used your privilege to help other people, then that was just fine with her. And that's a large part of it. Decency has been, I think, for me, this respect for all human beings [that I got from her].

> A very good example [of the altruism of my father] was in the middle of the depression, I remember one night we were listening to the radio just before Christmas and there was a story on about a woman who had come into town with her money to go Christmas shopping and somebody stole her purse. And I remember [the] impact it had and I also vaguely remember my father getting up and going out. I found out years later, when I worked for the radio station for a brief period, that my father had come into the station that night and had given her the money. (pp. 141–42)

In spite of parents' influence emerging in their interviews, Colby and Damon are less inclined then the others to place primary importance on family background. "[W]e start with the realization that many people raised in secure, warm, and ordered family environments do not acquire this quality [of dedication]. We also start with the belief that some unusually dedicated people come from backgrounds quite the opposite. For all these reasons, we are skeptical about analyses that reduce extraordinary moral commitment either to social factors such as family background or to personal ones such as the tendency to have close relationships" (pp. 7-8). Instead, they place a greater emphasis on the ongoing social interaction with collaborators, colleagues, and opponents as a primary means for deepening one's commitment. They believe that family background supports the development of an inclination toward activism but is not the sole source. In fact, the variability in parental influence is evident in all the studies. Not all parental relationships were healthy and not all parents modeled prosocial behavior. Clary and Miller (1986) found that 30 percent of those with low nurturant and less altruistic parents still completed their commitment to the crisis counseling center. Parenting was not uniform in Keniston's, Hoehn's, or Oliner and Oliner's studies. Factors other than parenting play a critical role as well.

A second step in the development of activism is the influence of individuals other than parents. Often these individuals are themselves activists who represent an ideal or who engage the incipient activist's thinking and move him or her to take the next step. Colby and Damon point to the strong and continuing influence of communication with collaborators and colleagues. Hoehn and Keniston find that modeling often came from other activists who provided patterns of performance for them to emulate and evocative images that inspired their imagination. The qualities that these activists most admired were "commitment, human warmth, and intellectual relevance" (p. 136). Keniston notes that these role models communicated a "charisma of commitment" that impressed and inspired them to make a corresponding commitment to their own values. Oliner and Oliner note the importance of informal networks of support in helping rescuers initiate and sustain their efforts. Clary and Miller's study demonstrates the powerful influence of committed collaborators on the partially committed activist. Although these studies identify the importance of other role models, none explore the role that educators and schooling play in the development of activism.

A third step in the development toward activism is the confrontation with injustice. Keniston (1968) reports that "as relatively empathic and compassionate young men and women, when concretely confronted with the toll of American society, they quickly lost their 'intellectual remoteness and feeling of objectivity,' and felt 'personally responsible' for doing something to change things" (p. 126). Hoehn (1983) notes that "many of the awareness-shaping encounters in the interviews came through confrontations with human suffering. Sometimes it was the suffering of other people; sometimes it was the suffering of those interviewed" (p. 15).

The activation experience for many of Oliner and Oliner's (1988) rescuers was observing the oppression and misery Jews were experiencing. "It took a catalyst to translate predispositions into action—an external event that challenged rescuers' highest values" (p. 187). Colby and Damon (1992) also point out that confrontations with injustice crystallize and strengthen the moral exemplars' activism. These exemplars were outraged at injustice. Many of them saw poverty as an unacceptable state of existence for any member of the human race. Others considered peace to be a self-evident moral concern for anyone committed to respecting life. Others found it absolutely unacceptable that individuals in a country committed to freedom and equality were discriminated against and prevented from having access to their rights. One of their interviewees, Virginia Durr, described how having to pay her poll tax retroactively to her twenty-first birthday in order to vote outraged her and led her to realize that this was an insurmountable obstacle for many women, African Americans, and poor whites. "It made me perfectly furious . . . [and] got me stirred up on the right to vote" (p. 128). Another interviewee who worked to support political refugees from Central America talked about the importance of seeing injustice in moving her toward activism:

> [W]orking in the fields of America and understanding the whole immigration program back then when I was only twelve years old and seeing the injustices that were committed against my own people, and how they were treated . . . you know, I just couldn't sit back and fold my arms and be part of the upwardly mobile community. And I felt very committed, from a very early age, to do something to help my people. (p. 281)

In each of these studies the activists' identification with a victim is a critical component of this confrontation with injustice. As Colby and Damon's exemplars became more aware of the victims' circumstances, their commitment deepened. Hoehn found that "in some ways the most significant others in the awareness and activation experiences are the victims. It is the plight of a victim, whether oneself or someone else, which often triggers an awakening experience. The potential activist responds to the situation of the victim. Responsibility is as much a response to persons who suffer as it is some quality of personality shaped by one's prior experiences. Instead of blaming the victim, the activist identifies with her" (p. 125).

The other steps are situational. Keniston found that confrontation with the failures of our system was supported by finding models of committed individuals, a role the person could play, an alternative ideology and vision of the future, and a movement to be part of. Hoehn found that, prior to becoming aware, these activists discovered the contrast between two disjunctive realities and bonded with someone who gave them access to an alternative worldview. Situational factors such as immediate access to the problem and having the time to take the time played an important role when the confrontation with injustice occurred. Colby and Damon place a strong emphasis on the ongoing social communication and support of collaborators and colleagues. In contrast, Oliner and Oliner found that situational factors played only a minor role in distinguishing rescuers from nonrescuers. They examined such factors as knowledge and comprehension of the need, judgment of risk, available material resources, and a precipitating occasion and found little difference between rescuers and nonrescuers.

The developmental path of these activists, then, began in their early childhood and continued well into their older years. The awakening to awareness and the emergence of activism is a slow process that may complete itself in early adulthood or much later. And there are many contributors to developmental progress, from the early experience of one's family's values to confrontations with injustice to the continuing growth stimulated by social communication.

Conclusion

The studies of activism delve deeply into the life experience and background of activists. They are filled with the personal insight and experience of individuals who have committed themselves to helping others. They add depth and the richness of human experience to the more particularistic vision of political involvement portrayed in political socialization literature. They tell us something about the importance of family background. They place the individual within the context of social and political circumstance. And they reveal the important role that efficacy, moral integrity, a connected sense of self, and the desire for meaning and place play in activism.

Yet this research is not free from problems. As Gilligan (1982) points out, Erikson derived his theory from primarily male experience, thereby equating identity with autonomy rather than connection. Keniston's studies confront the same problem for he relies on a predominantly male sample and a highly privileged one at that. Hoehn's population is broader in age, sex, and socioeconomic background but is uniform in its predominantly liberal or radical political attitudes, which are also his own. Jennings also uses a predominantly white, middle-class sample with a liberal orientation. Oliner and Oliner have a much broader and more thorough study, as do Colby and Damon. Yet in each of these works, as with Coles's (1967, 1986a, 1986b) work, one finds the passion of the theorist interwoven into the analysis.

In spite of these drawbacks, examining the lives of long-term committed individuals is an extremely valuable source of insight into the development of activism. As Colby and Damon point out, however, it is easy to place these individuals on the pedestal of exceptionality (pp. 301–3) and see their moral commitment as something beyond what the average person can aspire to. Colby and Damon argue that most incidents of moral commitment are so common that they often go unnoticed—a mother holding the hand of a child as they cross the street, a teacher sacrificing her own time to help a student, a person telling a painful truth to a friend. The same is true for socially responsible action within the political arena. The socially responsible person is often stereotyped as the committed activist. Yet there are political implications in each of our daily acts that do not entail protest or direct participation on political or social campaigns, actions as simple as selecting products that are environmentally safe, choosing foods that have not been treated with pesticides, modeling for one's children a moral and political consciousness, trying to confront prejudice in one's workplace. In what Colby and Damon describe as morally neutral occupations, what is important is that the person realize the potential their role offers for ethical behavior and for helping others (p. 140). The difference between the average person and these activists is not one of kind but of degree. Colby and Damon conclude that "the parallels between these ordinary examples of morality and the extraordinary actions that we have studied in this book are striking" (p. 303). Oliner and Oliner concur. They note that "rescuers are not saints but ordinary people who nonetheless were capable of overcoming their human frailties by virtue of their caring capacities" (p. 239). Evidence of moral integrity, a connected sense of self, and the desire for making a contribution are in each person as is the potential for their enhancement.

What keeps many from more fully participating in extensive moral or political activity is the stereotype of self-sacrifice and pain involved in such activity. Colby and Damon did not find the individuals they studied to be either suffering or grim. In fact, they found them to be quite joyous and fulfilled. They also found them to be open and continually growing. Keniston and Hoehn report that the activists they studied were also fully engaged and fulfilled by their efforts. Oliner and Oliner note the pride and continuing personal value that rescuers derived from their actions. There is a sustaining and growth-enhancing power that emerges from activism that is rarely observed in the publicity around political and social issues. Welch (1990) argues that in spite of the lack of guarantees of success, the necessity of recognizing the depth and persistence of injustice, and the daring that political action often requires, political and social action "enables deep joy" (p. 68). This joy comes from living in such a way as to promote good in the world, being fully present in one's efforts, and experiencing a sense of connection with others, with a struggle, and with the welfare of the planet as a whole.

Throughout these portraits of activists the issue of one's relationship with society is apparent. The individual is continually negotiating a sense of meaning, place, and commitment. Are there larger purposes that my actions can serve? Do I have a meaningful place in the social and political world? Are there values that I can make a commitment to and people I can stand with? Am I capable of contributing something useful to others and will they welcome and appreciate it? Will my efforts actually make a difference? Do I have the courage to act without any guarantees of success? Often action comes before there are clear answers to these questions and serves as a vehicle for finding answers. The unity of self and morality, a connected sense of self, and the identification of a meaningful contribution are brought together in our sense of connection with the social and political world around us. They are embodied in the integrity we exhibit and the care we offer in our daily actions. This connected relationship with society emerges over time and through ongoing dialogue with others. Family and important role models play a critical role in its development. Direct experience with human suffering or injustice helps crystalize it. It is expressed in a deep sense of connection and interdependence with humanity and one's environment, as one of Hoehn's interviewees describes:

> I've been talking a lot about my own increasing freedom as a person, maybe not enough about the sense of ties with other people that went along with that. The sense of belonging in a real sense to all kinds of humanity and having those terribly important human ties that makes me part of all aspects of society.

And somehow that all comes together. My personal sense of freedom is tied in also to that sense of belonging and being responsible for, being a part of, all those other parts of humanity that I had really been ignorant of before. Somehow that goes together and I'm not sure just how, the sense of all of us being a piece. (p. 79)

The implications of these studies for education are profound. The research indicates that interest in participation and actual activism are stimulated, not so much by the traditional theoretical constructs of efficacy and locus of control but by much deeper sources—the unity of one's sense of self and one's morality, the sense of connectedness to others, and the sense of meaning that one derives from contributing to something larger than oneself. This understanding dramatically shifts our focus away from concepts of internal confidence to concern with the nature of one's relationship with others and with the social and political world. It shifts our attention away from the development of self-esteem to the development of a sense of meaning, place, and commitment. It shifts our educational emphasis away from talking about morality, democracy, and politics to living morality, democracy, and politics and having educators model prosocial action, moral commitment, and political involvement. It means lifting the veil we place between young people and the social and political world around them and allowing them to confront injustices and to help those in need. But more than anything else it means acknowledging the value of our connectedness with others and the world as a whole and nuturing a meaningful, active, and long-lasting connection with that world.

Many young people do not experience a positive, empowered, and connected relationship with society. Most, in fact, distance themselves from this arena. If we are to help young people gain the confidence and skills that enable them to participate in our democratic society, we will need to acknowledge their capacity for social and political engagement and examine the processes and interventions that can help nurture those capacities. That is the task of the rest of this book.

* * * * *

Note

1. Research using Kohlberg's developmental framework and research methods has been seriously questioned in recent years. His six-stage

hierarchy has been criticized for focusing on only one dimension of morality, for relying on hypothetical dilemmas rather than real-life material, for not distinguishing between the moral and conventional components of a moral conflict, and for having gender and culture bias. But the most significant criticism in applying the stage framework to political activity is that there may be a liberal bias in the stages.

From a radical perspective, Sullivan (1977), Broughton (1986), and Giroux (1988) point out that the liberal ideological bias inherent in Kohlberg's theory obscures a serious critique of liberalism and preserves the status quo. Broughton contends that "moral stage theory thereby achieves a simultaneous psychologization and depoliticization of liberalism and its problems. Attention is drawn away from liberalism as a 'ruling consciousness,' as a system of social policy, as a political apparatus for the practice of governing, managing and controlling society, and as a form of nationalism ordering the global relationships of states. Liberalism is reduced to a 'liberal ideology' that is based on scientific fact and can be improved, perhaps even perfected, by developmental and social psychologists. Ideology itself is given a rational basis, so that the less rational competing ideologies can be subordinated to the dominant form. Once established as supremely reasonable, liberal ideology's historical function of legitimizing entrenched authority is simultaneously concealed and rendered inconceivable" (p. 379). Giroux concurs with this assessment and adds that, in Kohlberg's framework, the very definition of justice becomes "merely the application of procedural rules to varying contexts" rather than "an attempt to understand how moral sensibilities are formed amid human suffering and the struggle for liberation and freedom" (p. 93). Giroux proposes an ethic of risk and resistance in which justice "is not organized around an appeal to abstract principles but is rooted in a substantive project of transforming those concrete social and political structures that deny dignity, hope, and power to vast numbers of people" (p. 93). This radical critique has its own bias, however. Its analysis favors challenging and replacing the existing system rather than working within it.

From a different perspective, Emler, Renwick, and Malone (1983) contend that the liberal bias places liberal radicalism at a higher stage than conservatism. In a study of college students from different political perspectives they found that the majority of right-wing or conservative students were stage four reasoners while the majority of left-wing or radical students were at stage five. This was also found in another study of college students by Fishkin, Keniston, and MacKinnon (1973). However, Emler, Renwick, and Malone took an additional step. Students were asked to respond twice, once from their own perspective and once from the point of view of either a conservative or a radical. They found that right-wing and moderate students could significantly increase their principled-reasoning scores if they responded as a liberal. They suggest that this finding calls into question one of the basic assumptions in Kohlberg's theory, that people cannot generally use reasoning of a stage higher than their own. They conclude that the conventional reasoner-principled reasoner distinction is not one of development but one of political ideology and that there is no substantive moral difference between stages four and five.

The liberalism or radicalism that Emler, Renwick, and Malone talk about is different than the liberalism that Sullivan, Broughton, and Giroux are discussing. Sullivan, Broughton, and Giroux's liberalism includes both modern liberalism and conservatism as embodiments of a rationalist perspective emerging out of Enlightenment philosophy. Emler, Renwick, and Malone's liberalism, however, represents a modern political position.

In defending his theory from his more radical critics, Kohlberg acknowledges that the roots of his theory are in liberal ideals but that this does not mean that they promote the status quo. "Just because the Kohlberg theory of justice reasoning grows out of the liberal tradition does not mean that it will or can only be used in similar fashion" (1984, p. 336). In terms of the more conservative critique, the evidence of stage four representing conservatism and stage five representing liberalism is disputed by Rest (1983) who notes that "the correlations of moral judgment with general measures of liberalism/conservatism are inconsistent or low" (p. 601). Emler, Renwick, and Malone, in fact, used Rest's (1975) Defining Issues Test in their study. Not only is this measure only moderately correlated with Kohlberg's, it tends to be more responsive to political positions on public policy issues (Rest, 1983). Although it is important to question whether there is a liberal political bias in his theory, the data on this are mixed and still inconclusive.

I believe that there is a good deal of substance, however, to the critique that Kohlberg's notion of morality is limited to an ethic of justice (Gilligan, 1982; Giroux, 1988). A good case can be made that there are other ethics that are equally important in moral decision making. Yet, if morality is more encompassing than Kohlberg's interpretation, it still leaves a place for his conception of justice within a larger conception that includes an ethic of care, an ethic of risk and resistance (Welch, 1990), and, possibly, other ethics yet to be identified. Including other ethics also makes room for alternative philosophical perspectives, such as the liberation theology perspective embodied in the ethic of risk and resistance.

The questions raised by Emler, Renwick, and Malone (1983) go to the heart of the hierarchical nature of Kohlberg's stages. Although Gilligan (1982) also criticizes this hierarchy, she acknowledges that within the ethic of justice, the continuum that Kohlberg has charted might have some validity (personal communication, 1988). If one unhinges the stages from their hierarchy, they become differing perspectives that are appropriate in different contexts. What becomes more important than what stage a person is at is whether the person has an ability to use each of these perspectives. My reading of the data is that there is a continuum, of levels rather than stages, and that this continuum moves from being able to use a very limited number of perspectives to being able to see all six of the stage perspectives and make reasoned judgments about which is most just in the situation. To adequately assess development, it would be important to give interviewees the opportunity to articulate alternative perspectives and to explain the rationale for their choice. Gilligan and her colleagues do this in their interviews about the justice and care ethics by asking if there is another way to look at the conflict.

Reformulation of moral development theory has become common to the field. The field has moved in a multitude of different directions since Kohlberg's death, searching for a way to reconcile the many critiques of his work with the consistent data it generated. It has moved away from assessing the development of the content or stage of a person's moral thinking to an exploration of the processes that foster development itself. There are numerous divergent and competing perspectives. Kohlberg's (1969) dilemmas and Rest's (1975) Defining Issues Test, however, still remain key instruments in research studies. Although his original theory is no longer as commonly accepted as it once was, Kohlberg's work, like Piaget's in cognitive development, has been of critical importance in getting us started on the path of exploring moral development. It is too simple and clean for the diversity of human morality, but it has given us an entry point for our research efforts and a philosophical and psychological theory against which to test our observations.

Although there are now many reformulations of moral development theory that attempt to deal with the criticisms, the consistency in data across numerous studies leads me to believe that at its heart Kohlberg's work does chart the development of reasoning about issues of justice. The stages may need to be considered more flexibly as levels, ethics other than justice may need to be included in the full consideration of morality, and, with the acknowledgment of young children's moral sensibilities, development may need to be framed in terms of the development of moral skill, but I believe that there is still a good deal of substance in his theory.

CHAPTER 4

Processes that
Promote Development

Up to this point we have looked at the content of what develops, charting paths through the development of political consciousness and social and political activism. We have also identified some of the motivation that encourages development—a desire for efficacy (Dunn, 1988), a need for meaning (Erikson, 1958, 1965, 1968), relief from empathic distress (Hoffman, 1984), reconciling cognitive disequilibrium (Kohlberg, 1984; Piaget, 1932/1965), a desire for moral integrity (Blasi, 1980, 1983; Colby & Damon, 1992), and a sense of connectedness with others (Gilligan, 1982; T. Jennings, 1992; Oliner & Oliner, 1988; Youniss, 1987). These and other research studies, however, also identify some of the specific processes that promote the development of social responsibility. In fact, it is here where the literature in political socialization, moral development, prosocial behavior, and psychosocial development overlap most significantly. There are four essential processes that support the development of social responsibility: prosocial modeling by parents, teachers, and significant individuals; cooperative and nurturant relationships with others; perspective taking and perspective-taking dialogue; and learning to manage conflicts effectively.

Modeling and Cooperative,
Nurturant Relationships with Others

The nurturance and modeling of adults, especially parents, is one of the most basic processes that fosters development of prosocial behavior, political activism, and social responsibility. Eisenberg and Mussen (1989) found that children imitate the altruistic behavior of an adult model and that this influence is long-lasting. In addition, they found a high correlation between altruism and parental identification. The more nurturant and altruistic the child perceives the parent, the more altruistic the child tends to be. Hodgkinson and Weitzman (1992), in their study of volunteering among twelve- to seventeen-year-olds, found that parent volunteering has a marked influence on the level of volunteering among teenagers. While 87 percent of teenagers whose parents participated in volunteer activities volunteered as well, less than 50 percent of those teenagers whose parents did not volunteer participated in volunteer activities. Hoffman (1984) notes that parental affection and modeling of prosocial behavior instill higher levels of empathy. This is strongly confirmed by studies of altruistic action and political activism. All the studies of activists reported in chapter 3 (Colby & Damon, 1992; Hoehn, 1983; Keniston, 1968; Oliner & Oliner, 1988) found a strong continuity in values between parents and their activist children. Keniston's (1968) study of anti–Vietnam War activists, Rosenhan's (1970) study of Freedom Riders in the South, Clary and Miller's (1986) study of crisis intervention workers, and Oliner and Oliner's (1988) study of rescuers of Jews from the Nazis directly examined parental influence and found that the most significant difference between those who were fully committed activists and others was parental modeling of caring behavior and caring values. Parents were exemplars for many of these activists. Many activists remembered incidents where parents took a stand or clearly modeled moral or prosocial behavior. Moore, Lare, and Wagner (1985) found strong parental influence on the political attitudes of the five- to ten-year-olds they studied. Merelman (1985), in his study of activist youth, noted that activists were close to their families and that their families articulated moral and participatory values. This was seen as well by Adelson (1972) in his study of adolescent political development. Those who were intensely interested in politics came from "families which are politically active and for whom politics are morally passionate" (p. 124).

There is a particular pattern of parental nurturance and modeling that is described by these researchers and others (Feshbach, 1983; Maccoby & Martin, 1983; Staub, 1988). It involves the development of caring relationships where parents reason with their children about moral and other conflicts, involve them in family decision making, behave in prosocial and socially responsible ways, and set high moral expectations. Eisenberg and Mussen (1989) point out that "when caregivers react to their children's transgressions by reasoning with them, pointing out the consequences of their actions for themselves and for others, they inevitably model consideration and concern for others and a rational, controlled orientation toward social interactions. At the same time, they inform their children about acceptable standards of behavior, arouse empathic feelings, stimulate role taking, and communicate that the children are responsible for their behavior, thus promoting the internalization of motivation for prosocial behavior" (p. 82).

Oliner and Oliner (1988) found this pattern of parenting among the rescuers they studied. Parents explained their reasoning in discipline situations. They would tell the child that he or she had made a mistake or hadn't understood a point of view and then offer help rather than punishment. Some of their interviewees described this pattern:

> She didn't hit but explained everything. Father used to shout when he was in a bad humor. Besides that, he tried to persuade people.
>
> He would talk to us—he could talk very well. And I would listen to him. I was impressed by what he said.
>
> My mother talked with me, pointed out mistakes to me.
>
> She told me when I did something wrong. She never did any punishing or scolding—she tried to make me understand with my mind what I'd done wrong.
>
> He would discipline me rationally—I am not sure that the word *discipline* applies. Moral questions, interhuman relations—he would say, 'It's this way; you are wrong when you consider it that way.' When I came home from school full of criticisms of some friend, he would bring up both sides. 'Moral education' is the best expression.
>
> He didn't beat—he used to explain. Sometimes father was upset when we didn't get good grades at school; then he tried to help. Mother sometimes spanked. (p. 182)

The researchers point out that this form of discipline communicates a message of respect and trust. Because it demonstrates a faith in the child's ability to comprehend, develop, and improve, it heightens a child's sense of personal efficacy and responsibility.

Yet the pattern of parenting they identified involved more than reasoning. It included close relationships between parent and child, the modeling of ethical principles and caring values, and the expectation that children would also act to assist others.

> It begins in close family relationships in which parents model caring behavior and communicate caring values. Parental discipline tends toward leniency; children frequently experience it as almost imperceptible. It includes a heavy dose of reasoning—explanations of why behaviors are inappropriate, often with reference to their consequences for others. Physical punishment is rare. . . . [P]arents set high standards they expect their children to meet, particularly with regard to caring for others. They implicitly or explicitly communicate the obligation to help others in a spirit of generosity, without concern for external rewards or reciprocity. Parents themselves model such behaviors, not only in relation to their children but also toward other family members and neighbors. Because they are expected to care for and about others while simultaneously being cared for, children are encouraged to develop qualities associated with caring. Dependability, responsibility, and self-reliance are valued because they facilitate taking care of oneself as well as others. . . . (pp. 249–50)

Although not all of the rescuers' parents acted in this manner and not all parent-child relationships were close ones, the parenting rescuers experienced had at least one of these characteristics and often more. Oliner and Oliner point out that this pattern of parenting and modeling allowed rescuers to develop extensive relationships with others, relationships in which their ego boundaries were broad enough to allow them to experience others as part of the self. "The family relationship became the prototype for an inclusive view of obligation toward humanity generally" (p. 183).

In contrast, the parenting nonrescuers experienced was marked by a lack of close relationship with their parents, forms of discipline that emphasized punishment, a lack of prosocial action, and an emphasis on material values and practical results. They describe nonrescuers, especially those who were bystanders and provided no assistance to others, as being "constricted persons." Constricted people are centered on themselves and their material needs. They tend to see relationships in terms of exchanges of material goods and benefits rather than in terms of connectedness or ethical responsibility. Their failure to act on behalf of others is an expression of their tendency to distance themselves from relationships that impose burdens on them. In the social and political arena they tend to define the world in terms of a hierarchy of power and feel powerless to influence change. They tend to be passive and externalize blame for their circumstances. Oliner and Oliner note that

> To them the world is controlled by external malevolent forces that make the rules. These external forces vary: They may be Nazis, Communists, the governments of their nations or other nations, atheists, Jews, 'foreigners,' or a collective unspecified 'they.' Innocent people like themselves are neither consulted by nor represented among them. They suffer while the guilty run things in their own self-interest. The forces of selfishness and immorality are all about, and people are essentially helpless in their wake. Mighty others control their destiny and make them act against their will. They are powerless pawns and the principal victims of an unjust world. The above might be understood as the defensive posture of people attempting to rationalize their wartime behaviors. Censuring and attributing guilt to others help deflect introspection; residual anxieties about actions not taken or nagging doubts about deeds done are not confronted. (p. 244)

Studies of moral development also confirm the power of parental nurturance, reasoning as a form of discipline, and modeling of caring and ethical principles. Dunn (1988) points out that the growth of social understanding starts with the child's interest in and responsiveness to the behavior and feelings of others but that it is fostered by involvement in the moral discourse of the family. Edwards (1980), in her review of the cross-cultural literature on moral development, suggests that studies within the United States, as well as several cross-cultural studies, have found a positive correlation between the level of moral judgment in children and both the affection shown by parents and the frequency of parent-child discussion of morality. She describes the kind of parental behavior that facilitates development in much the same terms as Eisenberg and Mussen do in relation to prosocial development:

> The most successful parents are expected to be those verbal and overtly rational people who encourage warm and close relations with children and who promote a "democratic" style of family life. That is, they foster discussions oriented toward reasoned

understanding of moral issues and toward a fair consideration of everyone's viewpoint. (p. 517)

The democratic style of parenting Edwards refers to emerged in Keniston's (1968) interviews also, as one woman he interviewed described:

It was all, well, it was all *very* democratic. Everybody sat down and made decisions. Only some decisions happened and other decisions didn't happen. [Laughs] Some people could work on making them happen. We talked about a lot of things, we talked about our dreams, and my mother was very progressive. . . . She read Spock all the time. And when she heard about the peace movement, that Dr. Spock is in it, she didn't think it was that bad. . . . When she was young, my mother was active in politics, although she says she was active more than she really was. Probably a lot of what I do now is because of her telling me I should be involved—she never actually *said* I should be involved, but I had a feeling she felt that way. (p. 66)

In addition, Keniston points out that activists' families emphasized responsibility and, as in the families of the rescuers Oliner and Oliner (1988) studied, provided opportunities for children to assume responsibility.

As reported in chapter 3, Hoehn (1983), Keniston (1968), and Colby and Damon (1992) found that the modeling could come from an adult other than one's parents. In general these individuals were not famous figures distant from the individual but individuals the activists knew personally. Often they had been able to observe them in their efforts and, at times, work alongside them.

The data on the influence of schools also point to the same style of interaction and modeling between adults and children. Ehman (1980), in his review of the political socialization literature, found that schools that had nurturant, open, and participatory climates encouraged greater interest in politics and a greater sense of efficacy.

Development is not only fostered by adults but by relationships with peers as well, especially where cooperation and intimacy are present. Studies of peer interaction have shown that peers can have a significant impact on moral and social development (Berkowitz & Gibbs, 1983; Berndt, 1987; Nakkula & Selman, 1991; Selman, 1980; Sullivan, 1953; Youniss, 1980). Youniss (1987) points out that cooperative relationships build mutual respect, which is a central element of morality. "The sense of solidarity, which is so central to morality, is engendered by a special dynamic in friendship" (p. 134). Cooperation and mutual trust lead to open self-expression and risk-taking, which, in turn, promote mutual respect, shared meaning, and intimacy. Youniss explains that "cooperation functions on two levels. One is cognitive in the standard sense of the use of reason to comprehend experience. In this vein, cooperation refers to joint reasoning in which participants pool ideas, exchange criticisms, work to resolve differences, and otherwise serve as validators for one another. At the second . . . level, cooperation functions in the sense of felt commitment. The basic idea here is clearly expressed in Gilligan's (1982) *ethic of caring.* This means that persons in a close relationship cooperate to help and protect each other. . . . They practice mutual aid because they care about one another" (p. 133). Berndt (1987), in a review of the literature on friendships, concludes that "the current theories and recent research converge in suggesting that conversations with friends are particularly significant for children's social and moral development" (p. 298). As mentioned in the chapter 3, Colby and Damon (1992) found that peers played a significant role in adult moral development and the deepening of commitment.

Essentially, then, development is promoted by nurturant, cooperative, inclusive, and participatory environments where relationships are valued, adults model prosocial and moral behavior, cooperative peer interaction is fostered, and young people are given a voice.

Perspective Taking and Perspective-Taking Dialogue

One of the reasons that cooperative relationships and participatory family and school environments promote social and moral development is that they represent opportunities for perspective taking and for perspective-taking dialogue.

Selman (1980) argues that perspective taking is the central dynamic in social development. He points out that "interpersonal morality is contingent upon the level of interpersonal understanding; one's moral behavior in relationship with another is dependent, in part, on how well one is capable of understanding the other—the other's needs, feelings, thoughts, motivations, etc." (Nakkula & Selman, 1991, p. 210). Selman has been using peer therapy to facilitate the social development of children who come from threatening and dysfunctional environments. These children are often self-protective in their interpersonal relationships and develop an interpersonal morality "relatively devoid of the capacity to care for an other" (ibid., p. 209). Through participation in pair-therapy sessions where children must negotiate with each other, Selman has observed that they develop through four phases of perspective taking. They move from a focus solely on themselves to one that takes either the self's or the other person's perspective, then to balancing the two perspectives through reciprocity, and finally, to balancing the perspectives through finding mutual goals. Considering another's perspective is the force that moves this development.

Perry (1970) also found that considering multiple and divergent perspectives fostered the development of ethical and intellectual development. In a study of Harvard undergraduates, Perry found that students often began their college years with an absolutist or dualistic worldview, that is, an either/or view of the world polarized between right and wrong, good and bad, and so on. They had confidence that there was a right answer to problems and that authorities held that answer. Over their college years, as they were confronted by multiple perspectives and diversity of opinion, their faith in absolute authority was shaken and their ability to appreciate alternative perspectives grew. The students progressed from either/or thinking through relativism to the point of understanding that knowledge is a human construction and changeable. In this last stage they understood that truth was contextually relative and that responsibility for commitment was inescapable. They were able to make moral commitments to a perspective and, at the same time, remain open to reflection and change.

In the field of empathy development, Hoffman (1984) and Staub (1988) found that one of the ways that empathy is nurtured in children is through parents identifying the feeling states and perspectives of others. Eisenberg and Mussen (1989) agree and point out that role taking is significantly correlated with prosocial behavior although it is not sufficient in itself to instigate prosocial actions. To promote empathy Hoffman suggests a form of discipline he calls inductive discipline. When using inductive discipline the parent directs the child's attention to the consequences of the child's actions on the feeling state of the other person rather than scolding, moralizing, instructing, or lecturing. Feshbach (1983) and Feshbach and Feshbach !1982) found that when empathy training was focused on recognition of the feelings of others, role taking, and identifying appropriate emotional responses, it increased prosocial behavior. Bettelheim (1985) also found that empathy and prosocial behavior can be nurtured by helping the child take the perspective of another. In his study of Japanese children, he points out that these children may exhibit more self-control and prosocial behavior than American children because "from a very early age the American child is told what to do, while the Japanese child is encouraged not only to consider other persons' feelings but to control himself on the basis of his own deliberations" (p. 58). For example, if a Japanese child is running through a grocery store, the parent does not tell the child that she is wrong or bad, or tell her to stop. The parent simply directs the child's attention to how the grocer feels by asking such questions as, "How do you think it makes the storekeeper feel when you run around in his store?"

A number of researchers in the field of moral development have suggested that growth in perspective taking is at the heart of Kohlberg's developmental continuum. Enright, Lapsley, Harris, and Shawver (1983) contend that what develops in Kohlberg's stages is really perspective-taking ability. Weinreich-Haste (1983) contends that what is developing is our perspective on society. And Haan, Aerts, and Cooper (1985) contend that what is developing is one's perspective-taking skill in conflict situations.

Enright, Lapsley, Harris, and Shawver (1983) think of Kohlberg's stages in terms of the growth in perspective taking. In the first stage, the person takes one perspective, that of authority. In the second stage, the person takes a self and other perspective that involves reciprocity. In the third stage, the person takes a group perspective and attempts to find resolutions that meet the needs of the group. In the fourth stage, the person takes a systems or societal perspective that has as its goal the maintenance of a functional and orderly society. In the fifth stage, the person takes the perspective of abstract principles that guide moral behavior and help create moral societies (p. 134). If we unhinge this framework from the stage hierarchy (see chapter 3, note 1), then developmental movement may not be so much from one stage to the next but to greater complexity in perspective and to the ability to use multiple perspectives.

Weinreich-Haste (1983) argues that Kohlberg's stages actually reflect the development of perspective taking as well but on a societal level. What develops is a larger conception of society, rather than the more limited notion of morality. "The two fields of research [development in political thinking and moral reasoning] are picking up the same phenomena, namely the development of a broad conception of the social world, a set of schema for making sense of relations between persons and between the individual and social institutions" (p. 347). Implicit within each stage is a theory about the desirable basis for human interaction, the resolution of conflict, and the attainment of various forms of the "good." Development in social reasoning is marked by an "increasing awareness of the wider implications of individual and social events and their consequences, and the function of rules and roles" (p. 100). She traces the conception of the good within each stage. In stage one the good is the rule. In stage two the good is instrumentally fair distribution in a world of personal and group conflict. In stage three the good is social and interpersonal harmony. In stage four the good is order rather than harmony. In stage five the individual balances four goods: the personal, the societal, the legal, and the moral. Although she stays closer to the stage theory than the others, she is outlining the development of societal perspective taking where each of the elements delineated by Enright and his colleagues is embedded in an implicit theory of society.

Haan, Aerts, and Cooper (1985) build on Kohlberg's work and develop a theory of interactional morality. They reformulate his stages into the growth of the personal ability to handle conflict. Morality in their framework is contextual and based on action rather than judgment. Because moral exchange arises out of human interdependency, people are moved to compromise even their legitimate self-interest when confronted with other's needs and claims. Through dialogue, people with moral dilemmas negotiate their moral claims so that balanced, equalized relations with others can be achieved or reestablished. Morality, for them, is "a particular kind of social agreement that equalizes people's relations with one another" (p. 11). What develops is not moral concern, but "moral skill," that is the ability to resolve moral conflicts, and this develops gradually rather than in stages. Growth is a gradual progression toward more complex, discriminating dialogical skills. "Development of moral skill occurs as forms of dialogues and solutions achieved earlier are reused, but most often revised, modified, or elaborated in new dialogues" (p. 61). Their five levels, however, parallel Kohlberg's stages. In level one the person is focused on their own self-interest and unable to see mutual interests. Conflict is seen in an oppositional, win-lose framework. In level two there is the ability to differentiate the other person's interests and to accommodate to the other's interest through compromise. There is still no ability to see mutual interests. In level three the ability to see mutual interest emerges but mutuality is seen as harmony. In level four mutual interests are seen in a larger system or structure and conflicts are resolved through accommodation of one's interests to the larger common interest. In level five self, other, and mutual interests are differentiated and coordinated. Conflicts are resolved by finding balances that are based on mutual interest. Embedded within this growth in conflict management is a growth in perspective taking very similar to the one outlined by Enright, Lapsley, Harris, and Shawver. One's perspective-taking abilities move from self or authority to self *and* other to the group to society to the coordination of these multiple perspectives.

Not only can Kohlberg's stages be seen as a continuum in the development of perspective taking but Berkowitz and Gibbs (1983) found that movement along the continuum is best facilitated by conversations that involve entertaining and working with the perspective of another. They analyzed tapes of moral discussions of students who advanced in moral stage and of those who made no change. They identified a mode of moral discussion they called transactive discussion, which is "reasoning that operates on the reasoning of another" (p. 402). In transactive discussion each person engages the reasoning of the other person with his or her own reasoning rather than making consecutive assertions. They identified eighteen types of transactive behaviors or transacts and divided them into three categories. The first is representational, where the person represents or states in a variety of ways another's reasoning but does not take or work with the other's perspective. Representational transacts include feedback requests, paraphrasing, justification requests, and juxtaposition of two positions. The second type is operational, where the person operates on or transforms another's reasoning through clarification, refinement, extension, contradiction, integration, finding common ground, or comparative critique. Third is hybrid. These are borderline between the other two and consist of completion of the other person's reasoning and a competitive paraphrase that highlights a weakness.

Using this framework, Berkowitz and Gibbs had sixty undergraduates participate in dyadic discussions of moral issues five times during a two-month period. They analyzed the dialogues for types of transacts and the percentage of statements in each of the transact categories. They broke the thirty dyads into one group of changers (16 dyads) and one group of nonchangers (14 dyads). They found that there was a significant difference in operational transacts between the groups but not representational transacts. They conclude that "significantly more transactive communication was evidenced in the moral dialogues of dyads that demonstrated significant development in moral reasoning stage from pretest to posttest.

Operational transaction seemed to be the crucial form of transactive communication, while representational transaction seemed to be relatively unrelated to the developmental impact of the moral discussion intervention. . . . We conclude that operational transaction is not only a valid measure of the developmentally relevant features of undergraduate moral dialogue, but furthermore, that it explains pretest to posttest development in a moral discussion intervention program better than the more traditional variable of relative stage mixture between discussion members" (p. 408).

Damon and Killen (1982) did a similar study with children ages five through nine and found that peer interaction "characterized by a reciprocal quality of acceptance and transformation of another's ideas" was strongly associated with stage change (p. 365). They classified children's responses into three categories as well, acceptance, rejection, and transformation. The children in the experimental group participated in triadic debate about how to fairly distribute ten candy bars among them. Those that changed least were those that were the most destructively conflictual. "Children who performed rejecting acts (disagreement, contradiction, contrary solutions) were disproportionately among those who failed to advance." They conclude that "such conflict may have *impeded* advances in children's moral reasoning" (p. 364). Those that advanced were communicating in a reciprocal manner, "either agreeing with one another's statements or . . . working constructively with them by extending, clarifying, or compromising with the other's statements" (p. 365).

Higgins (1991), in her work with just community schools, saw a very similar pattern. "We believe that developing role-taking skills and perspective taking influences students' view of themselves as moral beings and as moral agents, able to choose to act upon their ideas of what is right and good. . . . In the first year of the Bronx just community program in the Theodore Roosevelt High School, the Roosevelt Community School, the students who emerged as leaders were those who most quickly developed and used the abilities to understand the perspective of others in the group and to integrate those perspectives into their own positions and discussions of issues at hand" (pp. 136–37). In fact, Niles (1986) found that when there wasn't diversity of perspectives, moral growth was limited. Haan (1991) also confirmed this in her study of moral action, indicating that "higher moral action occurred when the young people considered all possible solutions, understood their protagonists and regulated their emotions" (p. 268).

The studies of political socialization have focused on two areas, charting the development of political knowledge, interest, and efficacy and assessing the degree of influence that social institutions have on this development. Even where researchers have articulated stages of development, they have not examined the processes that promote development other than to suggest a balance between a social-learning model and a cognitive-developmental model. However, perspective taking can be seen as instrumental in the development of political consciousness, especially when young people begin to assess alternative social arrangements and political policies. Berlak (1977) notes that " 'consciousness' is significant for political and social action because persons are less likely to remain passive victims to these forces if they gain perspective on their social lives" (p. 39). He recommends two approaches to the development of political consciousness. First is helping students take the perspective of others and, in George Herbert Mead's (1934) terms, present themselves to themselves. The second is helping students explore alternative conceptions of reality. "Developing consciousness, then, involves two related pursuits. First, increasing the capacity of persons to objectify themselves; that is, seeing themselves and the circumstances of their work and play from the perspective of others. These other perspectives include norms, traditions, world views, social values, and priorities other than one's own. Second, developing consciousness involves the exploration and pursuit of alternatives" (p. 40). Both involve perspective taking.

In Mead's (1934) framework, self-reflection is a form of perspective taking, and the three studies of the impact of self-reflection show that it can be an effective support to development. Dozier (1974), in a moral development study of sixth graders, found that activities designed to encourage self-reflection and reflection on parent attitudes and beliefs produced as significant a change in moral development as moral discussions did. Button (1974) found that self-reflection on the sources of students' political attitudes was effective in promoting attitude change. Lieberman (1991), in a study of a curriculum focused on the study of human behavior in situations of genocide, found that students' moral and personal reflection significantly enhanced their interpersonal perspective-taking skills.

Berlak's second strategy for developing political consciousness was having students examine alternatives. Merelman (1971), in a study of the development of policy thinking in eighth and twelfth graders, found developmental changes in thinking that reflect the ability to take larger social perspectives. He found that as sociocentric thinking developed young people moved from seeing political problems in the personalistic terms of the motives, intentions, or behavior of particular people to seeing these problems in the collective terms of communally defined standards and socially formed institutions.

The studies of activists reported in chapter 3 also point to the importance of perspective taking in political and moral development. Identification with the victim, understanding and appreciating the victim's perspective, is a critical component in the emergence of activism (Hoehn, 1983; Oliner & Oliner, 1988). And the combination of self-reflection, honest communication, and openness to new perspectives is a critical feature of continued moral growth (Colby & Damon, 1992).

Perspective taking and perspective-taking dialogue are linchpins in social, moral, and political development. They are also vital to the effective handling of social, moral, and political conflict. In fact, it is the combination of perspective taking and conflict that most studies point to as the moving forces in development.

Conflict and Equalizing Dialogue

Many researchers have pointed to conflict as the stimulant to perspective taking and social and moral growth. Negotiations around conflict is central to Selman's (1980) work in social development. Kohlberg's moral development theory is based on creating cognitive conflict and hearing the perspectives of moral stages higher than one's own. In his just community approach to moral development, the conflicts became negotiations around real-life differences rather than hypothetical dilemmas. Making sense of conflicting perspectives is the moving force in Perry's (1970) work as well. Hoehn (1983), Keniston (1968), Oliner and Oliner (1988), and Colby and Damon (1992) found that, for the activists they studied, confrontation with injustice produced moral awakening and moral growth. In fact, conflicting perspectives, needs, and interests are everpresent in moral questions, interpersonal and social interaction, and politics. Merelman (1985) points out that "the primary distinguishing aspect of political participation is the role's conflictual quality" (p. 43) and that being able to appreciate political conflict is critical for political efficacy and participation.

However, not all conflict is productive. Damon and Killen (1982) point out that destructive ways of handling conflict can impede social and moral development. Conflict is growth promoting under specific circumstances.

Haan, Aerts, and Cooper (1985) have done the most comprehensive study of the role conflict plays in moral development and the circumstances in which conflict promotes growth. They reformulate Kohlberg's work, focusing on moral action rather than moral reasoning. The heart of their theory is interactional. They believe that people are in conflict over their self-interest and enter into negotiations with each other to equalize the balance between competing interests. Morality is action that equalizes people's relations with one another and enhances their relationship. The moral interchange is a joint search for moral balance. "From the cognitive view, the moral actor's question is: How can *I* draw the morally correct conclusion from the principles I already possess and endorse? This self-contained process moves within a closed system. From the interactional perspective, the moral actor's question becomes: How can *we* discover a solution that will equalize and enhance our relationship and also pass scrutiny from outside neutral observers, real or imagined?" (p. 274).

Development in this conception is not of moral concern or understanding, because moral concern is present even in young children, but of skill in resolving moral conflicts. "Our social difficulties are not due to lack of moral concern, but because of lack of skill in resolving conflict and social circumstances that make quality moral action difficult to enact" (p. 217). Development is not promoted by cognitive disequilibrium but rather by social disequilibrium, that is, experiences of miscarried or failed relations with others. Although their formulation tends to equate dialogue with moral action and does not adequately address the different nature of moral interchange when there are inequalities in power, it does provide a way to study the impact of conflict on moral development.

To examine the role of conflict in moral development, they did three studies, one of four-year-olds, one of junior high and high school students, and one of young adults. In each study friendship groups played "moral games" a number of times over a period of months. These were generally social studies simulations or group values exercises that were experiential and, at times, stressful. They chose moral games because these exercises created experiential situations of moral conflict that necessitated action on the part of the participants. They point out that "this kind of opportunity for action may be as close to real life as research can practically and ethically come" (p. 81). The young adult study was the most comprehensive. It used comparison friendship groups that participated in moral dilemma discussions rather than moral games. In assessing the participants' moral scores they used both Kohlberg's framework and an interactional framework in pre- and postinterviews. They also developed an observational measure of participants' behavior that was used during each of the sessions and a measure of the style of group dynamics that evolved in each of the groups. In addition to the moral scores, they assessed the coping and defensive strategies that participants used in their interactions.

The researchers found that members of the conflict groups, those involved in moral games, gained more often than did members of the discussion groups on both Kohlberg's scale and their interactional scale. Experiential conflict was more effective in promoting moral development. But they also found that an individual's coping and defending strategies made a significant difference as did the nature of the group. Positive coping included such strategies as objectivity, intellectuality, logical analysis, tolerance of ambiguity, empathy, reviewing, concentration, and integration of feelings and ideas. Defensive strategies included self-righteousness, submission to group-think, withdrawal and isolation, intellectualization or rationalization, projection, giving up, denial, and displacement of feeling. Participants that used positive coping strategies and avoided defensive strategies gained more than others. Those participants whose moral scores declined used either self-righteous or self-effacing defensive strategies. In fact, a regression analysis showed that coping strategies had the greatest association with moral development scores. Essentially, participants who were better able to handle conflict effectively were able to learn the most from the situation.

In addition, members of those groups that were egalitarian in nature, where participants were able to speak freely and leadership was shared, made the greatest gains. Those groups that were hierarchical and dominated by particular individuals caused members to use defensive coping strategies. Members of these groups made the least gains. "We learn here that the equality of the members of these [egalitarian] groups generally allowed them to cope; the disjointed hierarchical functioning of the dominated groups forced members to use defensive strategies" (p. 138). They found that the dialogue in the egalitarian groups was closer to their conception of an equalizing, "truth-identifying" dialogue where participants seek to balance competing points of view and come to a consensus about the resolution. Effective moral dialogue, then, is characterized by "the stipulation that all can speak, none must dominate, and all may veto" (p. 350). Participants in groups where conflicts were resolved well gave sincere and accurate consideration to the issues, were sensitive to the needs and contributions of other group members, considered whether certain ways of deliberating were good ways to arrive at a solution, evaluated the practicality and reasonableness of possible solutions, and were concerned that all could agree to the proposed solutions. These strategies are not only effective for moral conflicts but form the core of the conflict resolution field in general (Fisher & Brown, 1988; Fisher, Ury & Patton, 1991).

They found similar results in their study of preschoolers and adolescents. What stands out for them as the major difference between these age groups is not their level of moral reasoning but rather the difference in skill levels in resolving conflicts. "Our study suggests that the moral concerns of preschoolers and adults are basically the same but that children gradually develop skills that enable them to act in a wider range of conflict situations" (p. 303).

Conflict, then, plays a critical role in development. Those who gained most morally in this study took the risk of exposing themselves to conflict in sincere and straightforward ways. Those who remained stable or regressed avoided entering into the conflict. They conclude that "the kind of disequilibrium that made both interactional and cognitive development possible was passionate, stressful debate, not abstracted cognitive disagreement. This disequilibrium was not simply generalized stress but was, more specifically, the stress—even the shock—of discovering that one's friends and even one's self could morally violate, easily and unthinkingly. As a result, morality comes to be seen as a delicate interchange that requires careful nourishment. And it involves the risk of self-exposing commitment; it means frequently attempting to right wrongs that people inevitably commit and frequently forgiving wrongs done to the self. Members of groups that functioned so smoothly that moral violations seldom occurred did not have these instructive experiences despite the fact that they usually acted effectively" (p. 273).

Yet it is not simply conflict that fosters development. "The two critical conditions of development seem to be a person who can deal with conflict and group functioning that allows conflict to be directly and honestly addressed" (p. 355).

Conclusion

The processes that foster development are not independent of one another. They are, in fact, inextricably linked. The environments that foster development are ones that are open, nurturant, and participatory, where people model and live prosocial values and where conflict is handled instructively and effectively. They are environments where young people

MOTIVATORS OF ACTIVISM

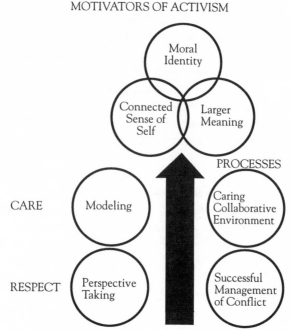

Figure 4.1. Sources of Social Responsibility

are provided opportunities for taking the perspective of others and reflecting on their own attitudes and beliefs. They are places where young people are able to learn from conflict and engage in equalizing dialogue about meaningful issues. Not only does the developmental literature provide this portrait, but, as the next chapter will show, the literature on educational interventions that support social responsibility affirms and amplifies it.

These processes are deeply relational in nature. Moral and political development is fostered by experiencing healthy relationships, caring for others, listening to and appreciating the other's perspective, and entering into dialogue with those with whom one is in conflict in order to reestablish balance in the relationship. These need to be experienced in both the interpersonal and larger social arena. As these processes reveal, development is, in fact, the growth in our ability to sustain ethical and caring relationships not only with others but with the world as a whole.

CHAPTER 5

Educational Interventions
and Social Responsibility

The school is a social institution, reflecting the culture of which
it is a part and transmitting to the young an ethos and a world
view as well as specific skills and knowledge (Minuchin & Shapiro,
1983, p. 197).

The school is a social system in itself with an explicit and implicit political
structure. It is, in essence, a microsociety, providing young people with
a specific set of social and political experiences. The classroom and the
school are social and political communities with a governance structure,
a system of justice, social conventions, moral and political dilemmas and
conflicts, and patterns of living and working with people of diverse ages,
cultures, and skills. Because the school is a context for social and political experience, it either furthers or inhibits the development of social
responsibility.

There have been numerous studies examining the impact of particular
educational interventions on political, social, and moral development.
Many of them involve the processes of modeling, providing a nurturant
environment, encouraging perspective taking, and helping students manage
conflict effectively. They show that development is influenced not only
by what is taught but by how it is taught and how the classroom and
school are structured. Collectively they point to particular ways of teaching
and particular classroom and school structures that not only help students
learn about the social and political world but nurture in them a sense
of social responsibility.

A Knowledge Base and an Ideological Framework

Ehman (1980), in an extensive review of the political socialization literature on school effects, found that the school had a strong impact on political knowledge but a weak impact on such political attitudes as efficacy, interest, tolerance, and citizenship. Given the cognitive emphasis in U.S. schools, this seems quite natural. Yet, a number of studies (Moore et al., 1985, Westholm, Lindquist & Niemi, 1990) show that young people need a knowledge base in order to develop deeper understanding.

Westholm, Lindquist, and Niemi (1990) studied the impact of civic instruction on Swedish sixteen- and eighteen-year-olds. They found that there was a strong relationship between the study of civics and history and the acquisition of political knowledge. But they also found that those students who were above a particular threshold of knowledge at the beginning of the study gained significantly more knowledge than those below this threshold. In fact, those who were below this threshold did not develop a deeper understanding of political concepts and processes.

Moore, Lare, and Wagner (1985) found a very similar pattern in a longitudinal study of children as they progressed from kindergarten to fourth grade. They found that when a child grasped particular concepts, other political information was easily acquired. "Without threshold understandings or a cognitive structure by which to interpret and make meaningful passing media references to political phenomena, children appear to gain only an 'extensive acquaintance' with what Connell calls 'the phenomenal surface of politics' " (p. 137). They describe these threshold understandings as "organizing concepts," which then provide the framework for learning additional information.

As they charted knowledge development in the first five years of school, they were able to identify several organizing concepts that supported progressive development of political understanding. During the primary grades, the key organizing concepts were an understanding of the concept of law and the process of how laws are made. They found that many primary age children are already aware of aspects of our legal system, and that understanding the scope, impact, and purpose of law was related to a growing sense of political efficacy as well as an increasing awareness of government processes.

> While the children hold a general view that the President is the
> dominant figure in the governing process, it is with the making

of laws that they first become aware of the interdependence of the three branches of government. As a child becomes familiar with the far-reaching implications of the legal system, he or she begins to appreciate the complexity of the process by which laws are made, the mechanisms used to enforce the laws, and the procedures involved in adjudicating disputes over the application of laws to particular situations. In our analysis of the young child's impressively rapid growth in legal understanding during the elementary school years, we begin to explain how this area of cognitive awareness provides an organizing framework for more rapid growth in other areas of political understanding. (p. 222)

In second and third grades the key organizing concept is elections. Understanding elections gives children the ability to focus on the political authorities in election campaigns, to retain the names of candidates, and to begin to understand political geography. In fact, understanding the electoral process correlated highly with greater political understanding in general. In the middle elementary grades, an understanding of the more particular functions of Congress allows children access to understanding legislative proposals. If they also understand the concept of taxes, then legislation becomes even more meaningful. Law, elections, and Congress form a continuum of concepts that can be meaningfully taught in the early elementary grades and seem to bear some relationship to children's cognitive development.

Children learn a great deal about the political world from current political events reported in the media and discussed by their parents. In fact, these sources of political information are more significant than their elementary school instruction. Moore (1989) found that the political environment taught children about national political symbols, policy issues, elections, and partisanship. For example, in his study with Lare and Wagner, the greatest increase in awareness of national symbols came during the bicentennial and the greatest increase in understanding of elections came during the 1976 and 1978 election campaigns. He concludes that children, especially in second, third, and fourth grades, are open to polit- ical information and able to understand age-appropriate concepts. He argues for inclusion of these organizing concepts in the curriculum in order to help students pay attention to the world of politics and make politics real in their lives.

There is little current research on organizing concepts in the upper elementary or early middle school years. Moore has continued to interview the students in his study through twelfth grade, and when he completes his analysis of this data we may have a better insight into middle school children's political lives.

The organizing concept for adolescents appears to be ideological frameworks. Merelman and King (1986) found that high school age activists are unusually efficacious and ideologically coherent. Ideological coherence provides a framework for them to organize political information. "Ideological awareness is more a motive for than a consequence of political involvement" (Merelman, 1985, p. 54). Having an ideological framework allows young people to situate conflict within a larger political context and to make it intelligible and accessible. Hoehn (1983), in his study of adult activists, found that individuals need to have an ideological framework or framework of interpretation so that they can give meaning to their social and political experience. As he points out in reference to one of his interviewees, "it is possible, like Bill, to experience discrimination, but at the time, lack a framework of interpretation to assign it any meaning other than just suffering. One can see something, but not connect that seeing to a larger pattern of meaning until later" (p. 62). Hoehn suggests that having a meaning system and framework for understanding political events allows individuals to look beyond an immediate problem, find its roots, and address it in terms of policy that affects the structural nature of the system.

Engaging young people in conversations about ideology and helping them develop ideological coherence raises concerns about our encouraging dogmatism and narrowmindedness. However, studies of activists reveal that possessing an ideological cohesiveness did not make them ideologically rigid. Merelman and King (1986) found that the students in their study were generally independent of partisan identification. "They were self-confident and policy-sensitive, yet able to evaluate political events without tying themselves tightly to specific political commitments" (p. 487). In fact, much like the older activists in Keniston's (1968) and Colby and Damon's (1992) studies discussed in chapter 3, these students remained open to change and political development as they became young adults.

Yet, researchers have found that knowledge is not sufficient if one wishes to enhance democratic values, efficacy, or participation. Teaching political concepts and knowledge has not had an impact on the development of political attitudes (Ehman, 1980; Leming, 1992). Langton and

Jennings (1968), in their interviews with over 1,600 high school seniors, reported little effect of the civics curriculum on political efficacy. In a smaller but more sophisticated panel study of the relationship between political efficacy and social studies instruction, Ehman (1972) also found that there was little observable change in attitude as a result of this instruction. Patrick (1972) studied the implementation of a revised civics curriculum that focused on understanding political behavior and political processes through an inquiry and critical thinking methodology. Although this curriculum made some impact on students' political knowledge, it had no impact on the attitudes of political tolerance, cynicism, and efficacy. Torney, Oppenheim, and Farnen (1975), in their study of civic education in ten democracies, found the same pattern among fourteen- and seventeen-year- olds. "The acquisition of knowledge does not correlate highly with support for democratic values, and even less as children get older. It is therefore unwise to assume that knowledgeable students will automatically support democratic values. Neither does knowledge of civics correlate highly with various measures of political participation" (p. 19). Ehman (1980) reviewed five other studies of the relationship between political knowledge and political attitudes and reports that "the message is clear: adding more of the typical civics and government courses to students' experience does little to modify political attitudes" (p. 106). In fact, several of these studies found a negative relationship between civics courses and democratic values. Ehman reviewed material prior to 1980, but Leming (1992) found this true of more current material. Leming reviewed post-1980 studies of the impact of contemporary issues curricula and found that few of these curricula achieved their attitudinal or behavioral goals.

There was one exception to this pattern. Langton and Jennings (1968), Ehman (1972), and Button (1974) found that social studies courses made an impact on the sense of efficacy experienced by African-American students. They hypothesize that this was the result of the difference in political information provided by the parents of these students. They suggest that the information that Anglo-American students receive at school may be redundant of what they have heard at home, while the social studies information learned at school by African-American students may be new to them and therefore more empowering.

The lack of relationship between knowledge and efficacy was not the same for early elementary children as it was for high school students. Moore, Lare, and Wagner (1985) observed that the more politically knowledgeable young children were, the more likely they were to have a strong sense of political efficacy and to become involved in political life. "The more knowledgeable a child is, the more likely he or she is to believe that government is a caring institution that will act responsively in meeting the needs of its citizens. This positive relationship between feelings about government responsiveness and political knowledge becomes stronger as the child moves through the elementary grades" (p. 204). They point out that this may be based on the misperception among these students that anyone who helps others is a government employee. It may also be the result of an overly positive portrait painted of government in the elementary grades. With a more realistic appraisal of government in the upper elementary grades their sense of efficacy may drop.

Knowledge of key organizing concepts and an ideological framework provide an important base for integrating additional political knowledge. But to encourage democratic values, efficacy, and participation we need to look elsewhere. Ehman (1980) notes that "it is not *who* teaches, nor *what* is taught, as much as *how* the teaching is carried out which makes an impact on student political orientations" (p. 108).

An Open Classroom Climate

When researchers in political socialization and moral development talk about how teaching is carried out, they point to a particular classroom climate that has proven effective across numerous studies. It is an open classroom climate that welcomes and effectively works with controversy and conflict. Ehman (1980) describes this classroom environment as one where students have an opportunity to engage freely in making suggestions for structuring the classroom and where they have opportunities to discuss all sides of controversial topics. A closed classroom climate is one where teachers use authoritarian classroom strategies, maintain singular control of the classroom and curriculum, and either avoid controversial topics or present limited perspectives on these conflicts. In his extensive review of the political socialization literature, he found that open classroom climates promoted democratic values, enhanced efficacy, and encouraged participation while closed climates promoted authoritarian values and had a negative impact on efficacy and participation. Leming (1992) found the same pattern in his review of the impact of contemporary issues curricula. He notes that "curricula that involved peer interaction, most often through group discussion and activities where students were actively involved in the collective exploration of attitudes and values in an open and democratic atmosphere, were found to be consistently effective in producing attitudinal change" (p. 148). Research in moral development also points in this direction. Although Kohlberg (1978) does not label classrooms involved in moral dilemma discussion as open or closed, the teaching strategy he recommends is very similar to an open climate. It is a classroom where an atmosphere of interchange and dialogue exists and where students are able to compare conflicting moral perspectives in a respectful and open manner.

The political socialization study that most extensively examined the issue of classroom environment was Torney, Oppenheim, and Farnen's (1975) study of ten-, fourteen-, and seventeen-year-olds in ten democracies. The major emphasis in their study was examining the relationship between civic instruction and knowledge of civic processes, democratic values, efficacy, and interest in participation. Data were collected from 30,000 students and teachers. They operationalized democratic values as freedom to criticize the government, equal rights for all citizens, tolerance for diversity, freedom of the mass media, respect for others, equality in voting, belief in the freedom of the individual, the right to vote, and the right to be represented. The results from all ten countries affirmed the importance of an open atmosphere on all the major variables.

> While the students' responses from different countries varied considerably, the underlying influencing processes were remarkably similar—despite differences in regimes, school system, social structure, and so on. . . . 'Traditional' schools with a strong emphasis on memorizing facts produced students who tended to be *less* knowledgeable and informed about politics; and students who reported frequent participation in patriotic rituals were both less knowledgeable and less democratic in their outlook. On the whole, the results showed that specific classroom practices were less important than what is often called the 'classroom climate'; more knowledgeable, less authoritarian, and more interested students came from schools where they were encouraged to have free discussion and to express their opinion in class. (p. 18)

The characteristic of classroom climate that was most significant in promoting democratic values was the open expression of student opinions. The use of printed drill in class, the stress on factual information, and the engagement of the students in various patriotic rituals had the most counter-productive effect. "The most consistent positive predictor of antiauthoritarianism in all countries was the extent to which teachers were reported to encourage the expression of opinion by students in the classroom. The extent to which patriotic ritual was practiced was a negative predictor in all countries" (Torney-Purta, 1983, p. 302).

Other political socialization studies confirm and expand on these findings. Owen and Dennis (1987) found that children in families where they were able to communicate with adults about politics and where they were encouraged to challenge opinions and cultivate their own ideas developed an increased level of tolerance for dissent. Ehman (1972), in a panel study of Detroit high school students, reported that exposure to open discussion of controversial issues enhanced political efficacy. Hoover (1967) studied the impact of controversial issues curriculum materials in an experimental high school course and reported that the systematic study of controversial issues enhanced democratic values. Button (1974) found significant change in student attitudes about democratic values, efficacy, and participation in a study of an experimental classroom process that combined self-reflection on attitudes, open discussion, and political action. Ehman (1980) concludes that "although there are a few contradictory studies, it is impressive that the evidence from a variety of studies lines up solidly in support of classroom climate as a potent correlate of student political attitudes. The different studies use different indicators of this rather vague construct, but the relationships show remarkable consistency. Open-classroom climate generally is related to higher political efficacy and trust, and lower political cynicism and alienation—to more democratic attitudes" (p. 110).

This finding is affirmed in reviews of studies of Kohlberg's dilemma discussions (Enright, Lapsley, Harris & Shawver, 1983; Lapsley, Enright & Serlin, 1989; Leming, 1981). Leming's review compares the effectiveness of Kohlberg's approach to moral education with that of the values clarification approach. He notes that the difference in these approaches is that Kohlberg's encourages internal cognitive conflict through classroom discussions of moral controversy while the values clarification model is focused primarily on explication and clarification. Kohlberg's model involves dilemma discussions that present divergent perspectives and create cognitive conflict. The teacher takes a Socratic role and provokes open-ended discussion in which students have the opportunity to outline their thinking and engage the different perspectives of other students. The aim is to support the development of more adequate forms of resolving conflicting claims of justice or human rights. He indicates that twenty-two of the twenty-seven studies of dilemma discussions show that Kohlberg's open-discussion model has a significant positive effect on moral reasoning.

Enright, Lapsley, Harris, and Shawver (1983) reviewed studies of a variety of moral development strategies: Kohlberg's model, training in communication skills, didactic courses, and the just community approach. They found that moral discussion proved significantly better than didactic approaches. In fact, the three studies of didactic approaches in civics courses (Arrendondo-Dowd, 1981; Morrison, Toews & Rest, 1980; Rest, Ahlgreen, & Mackey, 1980) found that the didactic strategy did not work to improve moral reasoning. In a 1989 update of this review, Lapsley, Enright, and Serlin provide additional confirmation of Kohlberg's approach. They add that Berkowitz and Gibbs's (1983) work on transactive dialogue and Haan, Aerts, and Cooper's (1985) work on equalizing dialogue further affirm the importance of open discussion of moral conflict in an atmosphere where divergent viewpoints are respected and worked with.

Welcoming Controversy and Conflict

Underlying the strategy of open discussion is another important intervention that promotes the development of social responsibility—the welcoming of controversy and conflict. Conflict and controversy take on a particularly important role in the development of political consciousness and efficacy. Merelman (1985) points out that conflict is a primary characteristic of political behavior but that young people's inexperience with and avoidance of conflict make political roles particularly difficult for them. "Political participants almost always engage in conflict with other persons in their society. No matter how they rationalize their efforts under the guise of public service or contribution to the common good, participants must still struggle against others of different partisan hue. In no other role that teenagers play does major conflict become legitimate" (p. 43).

In fact, as Coles's (1986b) study of the political lives of children and Merelman's (1990) examination of the role of conflict in the political socialization process indicate, childhood learning reproduces the fundamental mode of conflict in a political culture. Young children in such contested regimes as Northern Ireland or South Africa accept and integrate conflict as a fact of daily life, so much so that the task of resolving conflicts is made much more difficult. However, young children in such uncontested regimes as the United States and Great Britain marginalize and avoid conflict (Merelman, 1990). In early childhood, children develop an image of the United States as possessing an uncontested democratic order. They believe in the benevolence of leadership, identify with America as a territorial unit, and see government as having a unified chain of command with the president at its head. It is only later, in the upper elementary grades, that the hierarchy is reversed, "the people" are seen as instrumental in government, and the conflictual aspects of politics become apparent. These perceptions and beliefs tend to minimize and marginalize political conflict and promote a view of government as harmonious. As children begin to learn about the conflictual nature of politics from the media and other sources, they tend to overestimate its danger and withdraw from engaging in it. Sears (1972) found this pattern in his study of children's concepts of political conflict and power among sixth and eighth graders. He reports that the majority of sixth-grade children have already formed a coherent attitude toward conflict. Almost all of the sixth and eighth graders believed that conflict was inevitable but very few felt that this was desirable. Only 10 to 20 percent of his sample of almost 1,000 felt that arguments in government facilitate rational decision making or that partisan conflict serves a useful purpose. Only a minority felt that it was all right to criticize laws or the president.

The consequences of this marginalization are significant. On the one hand, marginalization makes it more difficult for children to be prepared to enter political life. On the other hand, it has an impact on the quality of our democratic process. "Marginalization restricts the range of discourse in democratic regimes, disparages the claims of powerless groups who turn to protest out of despair, and reinforces unwarrantedly the power of entrenched elites" (Merelman, 1990, p. 61).

The benefits of engaging in conflict in an atmosphere that is open and instructional are also significant. Haan, Aerts, and Cooper (1985), in their study of moral action discussed in chapter 4, point out that "developmental gain followed vivid, morally troubling experiences; it was not achieved if either the group and/or the individual failed to deal straightforwardly with moral conflict" (p. 354). In a series of studies examining the impact of academic conflict and controversy within cooperative, competitive, and individualistic learning environments, Johnson, Johnson, and their colleagues (Johnson & Johnson, 1985; Johnson et al., 1985; Lowry & Johnson, 1981; Smith, Johnson & Johnson, 1981; Tjosvold,

Johnson & Johnson, 1984; Tjosvold, Johnson & Lerner, 1981) found that
controversy within a cooperative learning structure promotes motivation,
the search for and exchange of information, the reevaluation of one's
position, positive attitudes about controversy, a sense of self-esteem, supportive relationships among students, as well as enjoyment of the subject
matter and the instructional experience. Conrad and Hedin (1982) studied
thirty experiential education programs. They found that the degree to
which students were directly confronted with conflicts in their experiential
setting and the degree to which problem solving was a deliberate focus
of an accompanying seminar significantly influenced a student's level of
empathy and the ability to think in more complex terms. Kohlberg,
honoring the instructional and developmental value of engagement in
conflict, moved away from dilemma discussions to the establishment of
just communities where students could engage in resolving differences over
real issues of community and school life.

Haan and her colleagues recommend that schools facilitate moral
development by giving young people real opportunities to engage in moral
conflict. "The educational intervention that logically flows from the interactional formulation is moral conflict itself. It is a full-bodied confrontation with one's own and the others' ideas, emotions, and interests within
the context of real situations" (p. 65). To implement this they offer five
guidelines:

1. Children need to argue with one another without adult control
   but with responsibility for the outcomes and with occasional
   adult guidance. Children, especially small children, need adult
   guidance because they are easily stressed and typically abandon
   dialogue and conflict by leaving the field.

2. Children need to learn, without undue anxiety, that on occasion they themselves and all others including their parents and
   teachers morally violate but that reparations can be made, and
   when they are, relations improve.

3. Children need to feel that the protection of their self-interest
   is legitimate, within the context of their recognizing and recip-
   rocating the self-interest of others.

4. Parents and teachers need to recognize that although their
   power is awesome compared to the child's, the process of proper
   moral negotiation is always among equals. Nevertheless,

between the young and adults, imbalance in conclusions is sometimes necessary and legitimate, given the young's short-sightedness and their comparative inexperience. . . .

5. Children need to understand that moral conflict is a necessary and inevitable part of life. (p. 395)

Many researchers in political socialization would affirm Haan's recommendations and apply them to the political arena. In order to foster the development of political consciousness, young people need to understand conflict and the process of its resolution within our political system as well as to experience direct engagement in political conflict. Langton and Karns (1969) argue that the more young people are politicized by their social surroundings, the more politically efficacious they will become. Merelman (1990) recommends using curriculum, at an early age, that disputes "the building blocks of marginalization, namely, the triumverate of the benevolent leader heading a single line of authority in a unified territory" (p. 61). This means introducing material and facilitating discussion that subjects leaders to close and realistic scrutiny, points out deficiencies in past leaders, and informs students of the different forms of authority in our system, of popular resistance to current political circumstances, and of the concept of federalism. Moore, Lare, and Wagner (1985) concur. "The public school classrooms have not been very effective in introducing school children to the conflicting values that lie at the heart of a democratic political process" (p. 236). They recommend that teachers should "take a more active role in promoting the elementary school child's appreciation for the competitive side of democratic politics and the benefits of diversity, pragmatism, and change" (p. 236). Something as simple as a mock election campaign had had a profound impact on the students they studied and was referred to in interviews many years later.

> By giving pupils an opportunity to participate in mock elections, examine the arguments and the evidence on opposing sides of public issues, and encourage involvement with local political figures through field trips and correspondence, the teachers of third, fourth, and fifth grades can awaken earlier an interest in and perhaps even a thirst for political competition. These steps would encourage a participatory rather than a passive role in the political process. (p. 236)

Button's (1974) study of a semester-long course that engaged students in real politically conflictual issues also affirms the importance of teaching about and working with conflict. She found that the course produced increases in students' democratic values, efficacy, and interest in participation. She concludes her study by saying that "educators should promote the belief that political and social change is necessary and good; that American society has problems (a 'reality' students are well aware of); that there are means by which citizens can work to resolve these problems; and that when the channels of political change within the system are closed to certain groups, conflict (not necessarily violent) may emerge. Conflict should be treated as creative rather than necessarily destructive, because eventually it may open up avenues of participation to those who have been excluded. Conflict is thus a vital and constructive aspect of the American political system" (p. 197).

The *Facing History and Ourselves* curriculum (Strom & Parsons, 1982) exemplifies the power of an open classroom environment that raises important moral and political conflicts. Studies of this curriculum (Bardige, 1988; Lieberman, 1981, 1991) reveal that it significantly enhances students' interpersonal perspective-taking skills, their moral reasoning abilities, their ability to think about subject matter in complex ways, and their interest in social and political participation. The curriculum is an eight- to ten-week civic education unit designed for middle and high school students. Its focus is on the study of the roots of two twentieth-century genocides, the Holocaust and the Armenian Genocide. The authors of the curriculum, Strom and Parsons, identify its goal as seeking "to foster cognitive growth and historical understanding by using content and methodology that induce conflict and continually complicate students' simple answers to complex problems" (p. 14).

Facing History and Ourselves is a courageous curriculum. It risks going deeply into a subject that confronts us with the human potential for passivity, complicity, and destructiveness by asking how genocide—the mass annihilation of people—can become state policy. It raises significant ethical questions and uses emotionally powerful material. It confronts students with the darker side of humanity and sensitizes them to injustice, inhumanity, suffering, and the abuse of power. It risks being academically challenging and morally profound in an educational climate that often avoids difficult questions and issues. Yet, through a classroom environment filled with individual and shared reflection, perspective taking, consideration of multiple points of view, and moral dialogue, it calls on the best in students' moral and intellectual sensibilities. History is personalized through accounts of Nazi supporters, Holocaust survivors, and bystanders, as well as primary source documents. Students feel and think their way through the curriculum, and through their journals, they then reflect on and reexamine these feelings and thoughts for insights about themselves. In the process of studying both a historic period and the personal and social forces that produce genocide, they confront their own potential for passivity and complicity, their own prejudices and intolerances, and their own moral commitments. Then, to prevent these emerging under-standings from being neatly left to the circumstances of the past, the curriculum applies its basic questions about prejudice, complicity, and moral commitment to present issues. In their introduction the authors acknowledge that "confronting this history will be uncomfortable. But by denying students access to this history, we fail to honor their poten-tial to confront, to cope, and to plan to make a difference, today and in their future" (p. 11).

Lieberman (1981) studied three years of the course using both a measure of students' understanding of the content and a measure of their per-spective-taking and social-reasoning abilities. He found that the experi-mental classes in all three years of the study showed significantly higher development in perspective-taking and social-reasoning abilities than the control groups. In a follow-up study (Lieberman, 1991), he examined eight geographically diverse classrooms during the 1989-1990 school year. The findings were even more significant than the ones in his earlier study. Bardige (1988) studied student journals from two eighth-grade classes. Although she was interested in examining cognitive growth, she found that students learned something of a different nature. "Rather than showing cognitive advance or restructuring, they reflected what one student called 'a sort of enmoralment,' an enhancement of moral awareness and a new commitment to moral action" (p. 92). As one student wrote, "Before I was a 'watcher,' now I'm a 'doer' " (p. 105). The students also observed that they had become more sensitive and reflective, and less hasty in their judgments. "They find that they are more aware of others' problems and of the consequences of their own actions or inaction. Many become more attuned to the evils in their world—prejudice, deception, lack of care, and violence. Many also learn to recognize the good; they express appreciation of what they have been given and see what they can contribute. . . . As students reflected in their journals on material that engaged their empathy and moral outrage or that challenged their theories about history and human nature and their sense of themselves as moral, as they saw the cost of avoiding issues or keeping silent and the possibilities for making a difference, the 'finely human' aspects of their thinking were revealed and strengthened" (pp. 92–93). These students were not only moved to understand the moral implications of their actions and failures to act but they learned how they might confront and negotiate difficult moral and political conflicts.

Bardige offers a caution, however. She found that developing complexity in thinking places some students' moral passion at risk. She traces a developmental continuum reflecting the Piagetian changes from concrete to formal operations. Students move from single perspective or "face value thinking" through "composite picture thinking" that considers both sides to "multiple lens thinking" where they possess the ability to consider situations from multiple perspectives and recognize that what people believe is affected by their circumstances. She found that face value thinkers tend to be passionate in their condemnation of violence and vehement in their call for action. Injustice must be stopped, suffering must be relieved. However, multiple lens thinkers are more cautious. With their ability to appreciate multiple perspectives and the complexity of situational circumstances, they become less sure of what action they would take and more questioning of the authenticity of what they are perceiving. She suggests that "a more 'powerful' framework, in the Piagetian sense, can also be a more dangerous one. The ability to see both sides can bring a new understanding of others and, therefore, an enhanced ability to take their needs into consideration. Yet it can also allow a concern for the rights or welfare of the victimizers to obscure the experience of the victim and the reality that the two sides are not equal. The use of multiple lenses can bring a new assumption of responsibility. But on the other hand, this ability can, as several multiple lens users pointed out in their journals, be used to rationalize inaction, evade decisions, or shrewdly manipulate others into complacency in the face of evil" (p. 108). Although the *Facing History and Ourselves* course walks this fine developmental edge, its ability to sustain students' moral focus through processes of self-reflection allows students to emerge with a greater sense of moral responsibility and a greater commitment to participate. In order to best facilitate development, however, it is important that we acknowledge this developmental vulnerability.

Gilligan (1988d; Bernstein & Gilligan, 1990; Gilligan & Wiggins, 1988), too, offers cautions about working with conflict. Her studies of adolescent girls' development reveal that there are a number of factors that make the traditional debate approach to conflict problematic for them. She points out that there are two choices in conflict situations, to leave and to protest, or, in her terms, exit and voice. Those in conflict situations make the choice to stay or leave based on whether their voice will be heard if they attempt to protest or negotiate. Yet this choice is more complex for girls who are grounded in a sense of attachment and would prefer to try to renegotiate relationships rather than abandon them. The availability of the exit option serves to silence some girls' voices and causes them to withdraw from conflict situations so as not to risk abandonment. However, in the social and political arena, as in most debate situations, exit is often seen and experienced as an easy and viable solution. The contentiousness and win-lose atmosphere that pervades most political discourse often further polarizes the parties in conflict. It serves to increase the sense of detachment they have from each other, thereby increasing the vulnerability girls may experience in entering political discussions.

In addition, she points out that the very standards that are used to evaluate solutions to conflicts are often standards of justice rather than standards of care. Standards of justice are based on principles and place a high value on objectivity and dispassion. Judgments of care, on the other hand, are contextual and place a high value on taking on and experiencing the feelings of others. She argues that "what appears as dispassion within a justice framework appears as detachment from a care perspective: the ability to stand back and look at others as if one's feelings were disconnected from their feelings and one was not affected by what happens to them" (Gilligan & Wiggins, 1988, p. 128). While detachment is valued from the justice perspective, it is a sign of moral danger from the care perspective. From the care perspective the vulnerability of justice solutions is that they place too great a faith in the infallibility of principles and risk the severing of connection between people. From the justice perspective the vulnerability of care solutions is that they are unworkable and naive. Although each perspective's vulnerability makes the use of both perspectives vital, Gilligan found that the belief that care solutions were impractical silenced the dissenting care voices. "The fact that boys who choose justice strategies but say they prefer care solutions consider care solutions to be naive and unworkable is in itself of significance. For example, in one high school, students of both sexes tended to characterize care-focused solutions or inclusive problem-solving strategies as utopian or outdated; one student linked them with impractical Sunday school teachings, another with the outworn philosophy of 'hippies.' Presumably, students in the school who voiced care strategies would encounter these reactions from their peers" (p. xxii).

Even the typical process of political debate is one that makes it more difficult for the care voice to emerge. Debates tend to set up antagonistic adversarial relationships, polarize complex issues into simple competing positions that are often articulated in simplified and dramatic terms, and institutionalize a win-lose framework for deciding who is right. Rather than focusing on listening to the other perspectives in order to find common ground and consensual solutions, the participants focus on responding in ways that diminish the other position and enhance their own. Bernstein and Gilligan (1990) found that fairness and listening are intimately related concepts for girls. The failure to listen, to enter the perspective of the other, to consider all possible ways of seeing the situation, and to seek consensus is seen, from the care perspective, as injustice. The first step toward violence is the failure to listen. "[T]he imperative to hear or respond comes to form the core of the girls' concepts of fairness, and the sense that it is only fair to hear comes to form the core of their concepts of listening" (p. 147).

Gilligan (1988d) concludes that "the preference for the neatness of exit over the messiness and heartbreak of voice, the focus on inequality rather than attachment in human relations, and the reliance on male experience in building the model of human growth have combined to silence the female voice" (p. 146). Therefore, for conflict to be a meaningful learning experience, the approach to it needs to be inclusive and respectful of both the justice and care voices. Haan, Aerts, and Cooper's (1985) work on moral conflict is instructive. In democratically managed groups where all voices were heard and the group attempted to reach consensus, both boys and girls developed skills in effectively managing moral conflicts. Johnson and Johnson's (1985) research found that conflict within a cooperative learning framework was significantly more instructive and empowering than within a debate format. The rules that they suggest students follow in order to structure cooperative consideration of a controversial issue encouraged them to listen carefully to others, consider alternative perspectives, and look for common agreements. These rules include: "(a) I am critical of ideas, not people; (b) I remember that we are all in this together; (c) I encourage everyone to participate; (d) I listen to everyone's ideas even if I do not agree; (e) I ask someone to restate what was said if I do not understand; (f) I try to understand both sides of the issue; (g) I have good reasons for changing my opinion; and (h) I first bring out all the ideas and then I put them together" (p. 243). The development noted for both boys and girls in Berkowitz and Gibbs's (1983) and Selman's (1980) work also affirms the value of listening to the other person's perspective, working with that perspective in a transactive dialogue, and pursuing inclusive solutions. The qualities of authentic dialogue provide a constructive alternative to debate (Becker et al., 1992; Chasin & Herzig, 1994). Dialogue is "simply an exchange in which people speak authentically and listen respectfully with openness to learning something new about themselves and others" (Chasin & Chasin, 1992, p. 3). The process of dialogue involves suspending one's disbelief and listening to others to learn the positive qualities in their viewpoint. It examines areas of uncertainty and complexity in the various positions. In addition, it explores both the common ground between positions and the areas of difference in order to develop mutually acceptable and inclusive solutions.

Dialogue is dramatically different from debate. Instead of framing the conflict as a competition between different perspectives, dialogue poses conflict as a problem whose complexity is revealed by the differing perspectives. Instead of polarizing the differing positions and making judgments of rightness and wrongness about various solutions, it encourages the search for common ground and consensus building. Instead of focusing on winning as the purpose, learning and enlarging one's understanding become central. And instead of silencing one or the other moral voice, it affirms the need for both ethical principles and caring response. Although debate may have an appropriate role in ferreting out the problematic aspects of each position, dialogue breaks down the barrier between positions, humanizes the people who take a different position, and uncovers common purposes. It allows people with differing positions to stay connected to each other and to grow from their difference.

My own teaching experience echoed these findings. As a social studies teacher I often taught courses on current political and social issues. At the beginning of the semester I would ask students to select current controversies they would like to know more about. We would then launch into the study of these controversies or problems. The topics ranged widely from world hunger to pollution to international conflict to political ethics.

I found, however, that after two to three weeks of studying the facts of the situation and the competing perspectives on solutions, students would say that they had had enough of the topic and wanted to move on. This happened over and over again until I realized that what they were labeling as boredom with the topic was actually despair. In the first weeks of considering each of these topics, the presentation of information led them to a deeper understanding of each problem's seriousness and the discussion of competing perspectives left them with a sense of each problem's intractability due to political contentiousness and stalemate. The latter was the most devastating for them. They could identify solutions but felt frustrated that there was no viable way to get agreement about these in the political arena.

As I realized that they were experiencing despair rather than boredom, I became aware that each unit brought them to the point of despair. Moving on to the next unit at this point only deepened their despair. Rather than empowerment, my teaching had been promoting cynicism. In the years following this realization I shifted my instructional style. I dealt directly with their feelings of despair. I went beyond the two- to three-week cycle and delved into material in greater depth so that students were better able to develop some expertise and confidence in their analysis of the problem and its potential solutions. I taught strategies for conflict resolution and engaged them in exercises that promoted dialogue and problem solving. And I provided them with opportunities for involvement and action so that they could make a difference on issues that concerned them. Managing conflictual material in this way allowed them to move beyond despair and experience a sense of social and political empowerment. It also gave them new strategies for working in the political arena that promoted dialogue rather than contentiousness. One student expressed this change clearly in the concluding entry in his journal:

> I learned to be less dogmatic about my ideas, more open to change and other opinions. It's nice now at the end of the course to feel a little less ignorant by recognizing my capacity for ignorance. But it is also not too fun to lose ignorance because ignorance was bliss. I think because the issues are so complicated that just learning about it is important. In class we were asking what can we do about it [nuclear weapons] and what should be our next step. Well, I think education in itself is pretty good because instead of just picking a Republican ticket or a Democratic ticket or choosing a specific issue and fighting for that we are constantly reevaluating our ideas and helping people reevaluate their ideas too—just sharing all the ideas.

When taken together learning to manage political conflict, practicing dialogue rather than debate, and taking action in the political arena move students toward empowerment. This does not mean, however, that once empowered students remain empowered. The cycle is repeated with each

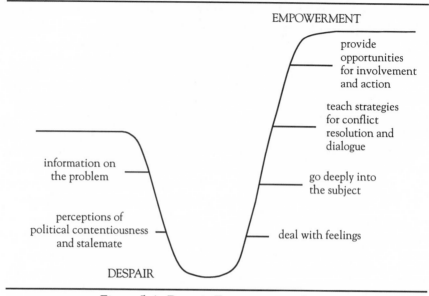

EMPOWERMENT

provide
opportunities
for involvement
and action

teach strategies
for conflict
resolution and
dialogue

information on
the problem

go deeply into
the subject

perceptions of
political contentiousness
and stalemate

deal with feelings

DESPAIR

Figure 5.1. Despair-Empowerment Curve

issue or problem. What changes as one practices these techniques with students is students' confidence that empowerment is possible (see Fig. 5.1).

Learning how to effectively manage conflict and engage in dialogue can be a powerful instructional tool. When teachers welcome conflict and controversy they are affirming its naturalness, revealing its beneficial aspects, and taking away some of the negativity and ominousness that gets attached to it. When they structure conversations that allow students to express opinions, hear divergent perspectives, and respectfully consider alternative explanations, they are teaching basic skills in coping with conflict as well as a tolerance for diversity and a respect for democratic values. When they present political conflict realistically, they are helping students become more politically aware and efficacious and decreasing some of the cynicism that comes with an emerging sense of political realism. When they focus on the basic ethical issues of justice and care raised by social and political conflict, they are helping students navigate their way toward moral commitment. And when they facilitate real engagement in conflict, whether it is around issues of school life in a democratic classroom or just community, in classroom dialogue about moral and political perspectives, or in direct engagement in real political controversy, they are teaching students the skills they will need to effectively participate in our political process. This does not mean that any conflict is appropriate or that adults should not moderate and guide these efforts, as Bardige's and Gilligan's cautions make clear. Haan, Aerts, and Cooper point out that "persistent, drastic experiences that are never mutually resolved can be harmful" (p. 66) to children. In fact, adult support is critical for young people to learn basic conflict resolution skills. The learning environment that schools and teachers create must be respectful, open, and egalitarian. Conflicts must be opportunities for self-reflection, perspective taking, transactive dialogue, consideration of alternatives, and pursuit of consensual solutions. In this context, young people may be able to acquire skills that not only help them resolve personal and public controversies but help change the political environment to one where resolving differences is done in a less contentious and destructive manner.

Participation in Decision Making and Democratic Governance

There is another aspect of the open classroom atmosphere that contributes to young people's moral and political development at both the classroom and school levels—student participation in classroom and school decision making. Pateman (1970), a political scientist who studied the relationship between workplace environment and political participation, argued that "we learn to participate by participating and . . . feelings of political efficacy are more likely to be developed in a participatory environment" (p. 105). The data, for the most part, bear her argument out. Keniston's (1968) study of activists, Edwards's (1980) review of the cross-cultural literature on moral development, and Eisenberg and Mussen's (1989) review of the prosocial literature reveal the power of a "democratic style" (Eisenberg and Mussen, 1989) of parenting for promoting political activism, higher levels of moral judgment, and prosocial behavior. This democratic style of parenting involves children in decision making, uses reasoned discussions of moral issues rather than simply resorting to punishment, and ensures fair consideration of viewpoints.

Almond and Verba (1963), in their classic study of civic culture, found that individuals in five nations who had participated in decision making in their family, school, and workplace were more likely than others to participate in politics. Across all educational levels and in all countries, they found a direct relationship between workplace decision making—

that is the ability to influence decisions, make complaints, and discuss issues—and political efficacy and active participation in voluntary associations. They also found that the effect of participation in family, school, and workplace decision making was cumulative. Those who had the opportunity to participate in all three were the most politically competent or efficacious.

Almond and Verba interviewed 1,000 adults in each country about what they *remembered* of their participation in these arenas and what they currently *believed* about their ability to participate in politics. Several other studies have taken a closer and more detailed look at the relationship between workplace decision making and political efficacy and participation. Probably the most comprehensive study was done by Karasek (1978) in a longitudinal analysis of the Swedish work force during a time when there was a great deal of experimentation in workplace decision making. After controlling for education, father's education, and income, he reported that "workers whose jobs became 'passive' also become 'passive' in their political and leisure activity. Workers with more 'active' jobs become more 'active' outside of work" (p. i). Elden (1981) studied one company's experiment in improving the quality of work life through humanizing the workplace and involving workers in decision making. He found a similar pattern, "work democracy links empirically with self-management at work and a sense of political efficacy, personal potency, and social participation beyond work" (p. 49). The aspects of worker democracy that most significantly contributed to these increases were control over one's own work and opportunities to influence organizational decisions. Corporate efforts to simply humanize the environment did not significantly contribute to increased political efficacy or participation. Elden notes that workplace decision making in the company he studied made a difference in the short term but, as the company returned to a more traditional mode of operation over the next years, political efficacy and participation diminished as well.

Not all the data are consistent, however. Greenberg (1981) studied U.S. plywood cooperatives and did not find a relationship between cooperative and egalitarian values and participation in workplace decision making. He found that workplace democracy, defined as participation in decision making, encouraged liberal individualistic values rather than communitarian ones. This was probably the case because although workers were involved in decision making, there was no effort to build a sense of community among workers. Where a sense of community is lacking, workers may tend to advocate for their own rights rather than for collective needs. Greenberg did not examine the relationship between workplace democracy and political efficacy and political participation.

The relationship between participation in one's environment and political efficacy has been a subject of research on school governance and climate as well. Ehman (1980), in his review of the relationship between schooling and political socialization, found a strong, although not conclusive, link between decision-making participation in school governance structures and democratic political attitudes. "The evidence is fairly convincing that there may be relationships between school organization and governance climate and student political attitudes and behavior. If students attend carefully to school governance patterns as cues to what the larger political world holds for them, then it is reasonable to expect some effects on students' attitudes depending on what they see going on around them in school" (pp. 111–12).

Sigel and Hoskin (1981), in their study of adolescents, found that participation in school activities and school governance was consistently and strongly related to higher levels of political knowledge and efficacy. Jennings (1974) found this same correlation between school activism and efficacy when he reanalyzed his 1965 data looking for interschool findings. Hanks and Eckland (1978), using longitudinal data from a national sample of adolescents followed up twenty-five years later, found that there was a strong and direct correlation between participation in extracurricular school activities and both membership in adult voluntary associations and increased voting. Although extracurricular participation may form habits of participation and increased efficacy, it is impossible to conclude that there is a causal relationship between the two from these studies. Students who were more active in school may have been more inclined to be socially active in general.

However, a number of studies of school governance structure and climate do confirm that there is a relationship between climate and efficacy. Rafalides and Hoy (1971) studied the relationship between school culture and alienation in forty-five high schools, giving questionnaires to 3,000 teachers and 8,000 students. They classified the schools as either custodial or humanistic. The custodial schools are rigidly structured, hierarchical, and autocratic. They emphasize order and control, with teachers and administrators having unilateral decision-making powers over students. Humanistic schools function more as educational communities where cooperative interaction between faculty and students is the norm. Self-discipline is used as a substitute for teacher control, and there is an atmosphere in which students can express opinions and have some influence in school decisions. They found a strong relationship between custodial orientation and general alienation, powerlessness, isolation, and normlessness. This relationship did not exist in humanistic schools.

Ehman and Gillespie (1975) did a similar study in thirteen Midwestern high schools looking at the relationship between the school's political system and such political variables as social trust, social integration, political interest, and political confidence. They distinguish four political systems: elite, bureaucratic, coalitional, and participant. In elite systems participation and decision making are restricted to an elite who administer the school autocratically. In bureaucratic systems participation and decision making is dependent on one's place in the hierarchy. In coalitional systems participation is open and there are competing interests. Decisions are made by coalitions achieving a majority. In participant systems participation in decision making is open and voluntary. There is constant communication between administrators, teachers, and students, and decisions are made by a rough majority or consensus. Although all the schools they studied were basically bureaucratic, there were enough differences among them to distinguish some elements of the other types. They found that students in bureaucratic and elite schools had more negative attitudes about trust, integration, interest, and confidence than students in the other two types. Students in participant schools had the most positive political attitudes.

They also examined students' views of the school's political structure using parallels to their general social attitudes. These included trust in school adults, school integration, school political interest, and school political confidence. They found a strong correlation between school attitudes and general social attitudes. They suggested that this may imply that "the student sees the school as society writ small, or the society as the school writ large" (p. 71).

Siegel (1977) replicated this study with small samples of thirty students in five Massachusetts high schools. Although this study is less rigorous than Ehman and Gillespie's, he found similar results. Students at the participant school "reflected efficacious attitudes to a substantially greater extent than did students at the other four schools" (p. 50). The bureaucratic and elite schools made students feel powerless.

There are some studies that contradict this pattern, but they are problematic in themselves. Borg (1966) studied a citizenship education program in the Davis County School District in Utah during the 1963–64 school year. The fourth, fifth, and sixth grades had city-government models of governance in their classrooms with the fifth grade as a whole having a state-government model outside the classroom and the sixth grade as a whole having a national-government model outside the classroom. Responsibilities involved making and enforcing rules, judging violators, greeting visitors, supervising the library, assuming responsibility for hall patrols, monitoring the lunchroom and playground, and planning for movies and assemblies. The governance program was closely tied to the social studies curriculum. Four schools were involved, two experimental schools and two control schools. Borg found that the students gained in political knowledge and were able to assume significant responsibilities, but they did not make any gains in democratic values relative to the control group. Jennings (1974) and Levenson (1972) also did not find a relationship between school climate and political attitudes in their reexamination of Jennings's 1965 data (Langton & Jennings, 1968). Jennings looked at the relationship between students' perceptions of influence in the school and personal efficacy. He found some relationship between efficacy and students' perceptions of being treated fairly by teachers and administrators but not between efficacy and influence in decision making. Levenson looked at the relationship between interest in political participation and the influence of students in the school. He also did not find any strong relationships. These studies are limited, however. Borg expressed a lack of confidence in the instrument he used for examining democratic values. The governance structures may also have been too formal and unnatural for upper elementary students to feel that they had serious influence in decision making. Jennings looked at personal efficacy but not political efficacy. Levenson restricted his assessment of interest in participation to whether the student mentioned participation in his or her definition of good citizenship.

Based on these studies there is a general indication that the more participatory the school, the more students experience political efficacy, trust, interest, and social integration. This conclusion must be held tentatively. The problem with the studies that explore school climate is the limited range of types of schools they assess. As Ehman and Gillespie (1975) pointed out, all the schools were basically bureaucratic. Although there were some differences in climate and decision-making structure, none were as participatory as the workplace studies. Since the time of these studies, however, there has been a growth in student participation in classroom and school governance, especially in the area of Kohlbergian experiments with just communities. It is here, in the studies of moral education efforts in classrooms and schools, that we see the most significant impact of climate on the development of social responsibility. However, moral education research rarely assesses impact on a social or political scale. Instead, most of this research demonstrates that classroom and school decision making raises levels of moral reasoning, increases prosocial behavior, diminishes negative behavior, improves conflict resolution skills, and increases a sense of personal responsibility and responsibility toward the school. Although there is no specific assessment of political efficacy or participation, all of these are basic elements of social responsibility. If, as Siegel indicates, students see the school as society writ small or society as the school writ large, then this growth may carry over to the social and political spheres.

In general, the moral education studies of student participation in decision making in classrooms and schools show that young people grow from this experience in ways that support the development of various aspects of social responsibility. McCann and Bell (1975) compared two elementary schools, one with an authoritarian governance structure and the other with a more participatory structure. They matched students for age, intelligence, sex, religion, father's occupation, number of children in family, and birth order. They found that students in the school with a participatory structure showed significantly higher levels of moral development. Clinchy, Lief, and Young (1977) compared sophomores and seniors in two high schools, one traditional and the other participatory and progressive. They found that most sophomores and seniors in the progressive school reasoned at higher moral stages than those in the traditional school. Cole and Farris (1979) compared two elementary schools in one district. The experimental school used democratic class meetings and cross-class student advisory councils at both the primary and intermediate levels. They found that students in the experimental school were more independent of adult help, more considerate of the rights of others, and less likely to use physical force to solve problems. Sullivan (1986) found that when students were involved with instructors in co-constructing a moral education course curriculum their increases in moral reasoning were far greater than when students participated in the curriculum but not in curricular decision making. Higgins (1991) reported a significant increase in moral reasoning and perspective-taking skills in her study of two just communities at Theodore Roosevelt High School in New York City. She also reported that "the RCS [Roosevelt Community School] students felt they got more from the just community than the comparison students felt they got from the parent school in the following areas, a feeling of belonging to a community, having power, knowing other students, feeling equal with teachers, helping the whole school, learning to speak up, understanding others' points of view and stopping to think before acting. . . . Moreover, when asked about what they feel they get from a just community program, the students in RCS and RCR [Roosevelt Community Renaissance] report that the just community program helps them to role take, feel efficacious and empowered, and to feel they know others in the school and are part of a human community" (p. 135). Each of the studies controlled for socioeconomic differences in the schools they studied yet together they represent a diversity of socioeconomic levels.

In addition, a number of studies have reported specific behavioral changes. Power and Reimer (1978) reported a reduction in theft. Kohlberg (1980) reported improved racial integration. Kohlberg, Lieberman, Power, and Higgins (1981) reported reductions in the use of alcohol and drugs. And Power and Higgins (1992) reported increases in attendance, participation, and educational aspirations.

In essence, what these studies show is that participation in decision making improves moral reasoning and prosocial behavior. The moral education studies of participation in decision making are stronger than the studies of school climate and closer to educational environments than studies of workplace democracy. Together they suggest that participation in decision making can promote aspects of social responsibility. It is in the just community approach recommended by Kohlberg (1985), however, that we see the clearest and most significant impact of student decision making on the development of social responsibility.

The just community, in Kohlberg's formulation, is a small political community that is based on equal political rights. Students experience direct democracy through weekly town meetings where each person, including adults, has one vote. They also experience real power in making meaningful decisions about the management, care, and direction of the school, and they experience real conflicts with other students and teachers who have different perspectives on these issues. "It is a process of 'moral communication' that involves assessing one's own interests and needs, listening to and trying to understand others, and balancing conflicting points of view in a fair and cooperative way" (Power, Higgins & Kohlberg, 1989, p. 32). Kohlberg believed that this experience with real-life moral dilemmas would be more effective in promoting moral development and moral action because the issues would be meaningful to students, and discrepancies between public judgments and actions would be apparent to and have consequences for the group. "To learn 'to understand and to feel justice,' students have to be both treated justly and called upon to act justly" (ibid., p. 25). In addition, collective decision making and shared responsibility would build a sense of community in which each of the members would have a personal sense of responsibility to the community. In this way the just community approach would not only encourage higher levels of moral reasoning but also altruism, integrity, and responsibility.

Although Kohlberg did not integrate any social or political indices into his studies of the just community, both his moral development research and his moral education interventions emerged from the commitment to help people develop the moral and political thoughtfulness and integrity that would strengthen democracy and prevent such injustices as the Holocaust. He saw the just community as an environment where young people could experience justice, feel empowered, and learn the skills and attitudes that would enable them to participate morally and effectively in the social and political arena. "Democracy in the school," he wrote, "is a necessary bridge between the family and the outside society in providing experiences of democratic participation and community leading to the development of social responsibility" (1985, p. 39). The just community is the society writ small, and young people who experience it emerge with a consciousness of their interrelatedness and a sense of collective responsibility. "Through participatory justice and democracy, a sense of the group as valuable and united, the source of altruism and solidarity, is enhanced. Through collective acts of care and responsibility for the welfare of the group and each of its members, the sense of justice is enhanced. . . . More than merely advocacy of justice and community by teachers and students, moral development also occurs in the Just Community through discovery of a small world which is in fact fair and communitarian" (ibid., p. 43).

Democracy in the just community is a dramatic change in the authority structure of the school, even from those Ehman and Gillespie labeled participatory. Students have real power to make meaningful decisions. In the just communities studied by Power, Higgins, and Kohlberg (1989), students made decisions about grading practices, course selection, racial balance in the program, rules relating to attendance, drug use and theft, and consequences for violations of community-developed rules. They participated in the hiring of faculty and in each faculty member's evaluation.

"Democracy cannot be a surface maneuver—a gesture to fairness that leaves the traditional authority structure in place. If students are asked to play at democracy while the teachers go on making the real decisions, little is gained while the good name of democracy is lost. There is a need to carefully think through how to implement a democratic process of governance that gains the acceptance and participation of both teachers and students as partners in a common endeavor" (Power et al., p. 25). Students in just communities learn that rules do not depend on the discretion of external authorities but are developed by mutual agreement and judged on the basis of their fairness to all involved. They learn about the processes that enable a group to come to agreement or consensus as well as the responsibility to preserve the rights and protect the interests of the minority. In this way students learn about democratic values and basic political processes. They also are able to break out of the egocentrism promoted by our culture and by traditional school life. "Insofar as children experience rules as imposed on them from the outside, they remain locked within the bounds of their egocentrism or subjectivity" (ibid., p. 28).

In contrast to the typical competitive or individualistic school culture, the culture of the just community is communitarian. Care, trust, and responsibility are important norms, not only in relation to other members of the community but in relation to the community as a whole. Kohlberg relied on Durkheim's (1925) work in moral education in formulating how collective norms could effectively promote moral development. The group takes on a moral role itself by creating normative expectations of its members. But members also develop an emotional attachment to others and to the group as a whole. Members of the community develop common values, common goals, and a sense of collective responsibility. Conflicts become group opportunities for ethical problem solving. The community takes on a social reality and moral force. "At the heart of the just community approach is the concern that the group view itself as a collective moral agent" (Power et al., p. 93). In Kohlberg's conception of the just community, the more authoritarian nature of Durkheim's collective expectations are balanced by the democratic structure that supports individual and minority rights.

The most comprehensive and revealing study of the impact of student participation in just communities was done by Power, Higgins, and Kohlberg (1989). They compared the moral development of students within three just communities of 100 to 200 students with the moral development of students in the larger high schools within which the just communities were situated. But, more important, they explicitly evaluated the moral culture of these institutions, the development of collective norms within the just communities, and the development of a sense of responsibility for those norms among students. Using assessments of community meetings, ethnographic moral interviews, and a standardized school dilemmas interview, the researchers constructed a means to make judgments about the moral nature of the atmosphere in an institutional setting.

Assessing a community's moral culture—that is, its shared conception of moral standards prevalent in its communication and action—is complicated. Power, Higgins, and Kohlberg used a number of measures to get at it. Their assessments involved measures of individual moral judgment, measures of the development of a sense of community, and measures of social responsibility. Although they did not find significant differences in individual moral judgment between students in the just communities and students in the parent school, they did find that the sense of community and collective interest that developed in these just communities significantly enhanced the level of students' social responsibility.

In order to assess the development of a sense of community, they charted the development of collective norms. They examined the degree to which norms developed around such issues as caring, sharing, respect for property, attendance, drug use, and racial relationships. They charted this development by observing the degree of collective responsibility the group took for these norms and the degree to which the norms had taken root or become institutionalized in the community. They also looked at the degree to which students valued the community as an end in itself. The data for these assessments came primarily from analyses of town meeting discussions around such yearly recurring issues as stealing and property damage, class attendance, racial integration, and drug use. They supplemented this with data from open-ended ethnographic interviews on students' perceptions of disciplinary practices, peer and student-teacher relationships, and the sense of community and democracy in the school. In the three just communities they studied, they found that each developed a strong sense of community. They also found that most students were able to take a collective perspective and that their community decisions reflected increasingly higher stages of moral reasoning over time.

In addition, they compared the moral culture of these communities with the culture of the parent school. Using a standardized school dilemma interview of practical dilemmas that occur in public high schools, they looked for the degree to which the student assumed responsibility for acting on behalf of other students or the community as a whole. They found that the moral culture of the just communities was significantly higher than the culture of the parent schools in spite of the fact that there was not a significant difference in individual moral reasoning. They had hypothesized that "the democratic high schools would develop different moral cultures from their parent, comparison schools" (p. 264). They found that "data from the school dilemmas interview resoundingly confirmed this hypothesis. On all of our moral culture variables students from the democratic schools rated their schools more highly than did their peers in the comparison schools" (p. 264).

In the just communities, norms were generally held collectively, justified by higher stages of reasoning, and institutionalized as part of the culture. Students tended to value the community as an end in itself and community decisions tended to be at moral levels that were congruent with or higher than the aggregate moral stage. In the traditional parent schools, norms were more often justified on the basis of individual interest, authority, or group needs rather than on collective interest and reflected lower stages of moral reasoning. Students tended to value the school instrumentally according to how it met individual needs. Decisions about school dilemmas were often at lower moral stages than the aggregate stage of individual moral judgment. They conclude that "if the results . . . point to the promise of democratic schooling, they should also call into question the approaches used in the parent schools. Although the parent high schools that we studied are recognized as being among the best in the country in terms of serving the educational needs of their respective student populations, and although they by and large are orderly schools, they fail to generate positive moral cultures" (pp. 264–65).

But even more significant than the development of a moral culture that promotes collective perspective taking and higher moral levels of group decision making is the impact these cultures had on the development of social responsibility. Using the practical school dilemmas, they assessed the degree to which students made a judgment of personal responsibility in each situation. In Kohlberg's conception of moral action, a judgment of personal responsibility—that is, the judgment that one is responsible to act in accordance with what one thinks is right—is the mediating factor between moral judgment and moral action. In analyzing the school dilemmas interviews, they found that students in the just communities more often developed a sense of personal responsibility for interceding on behalf of those that needed help. Although students in the just communities and the parent schools may have reasoned in similar ways about the right action to take in a situation, the students in the just community expressed a sense of responsibility for acting on that judgment while many in the parent schools did not. "An average of about two-thirds of the students in the democratic schools made responsibility judgments in answering school dilemmas, while less than one-fifth of the students in the traditional schools did so. The difference between each democratic and traditional school was significant on all of the dilemmas" (p. 287). They credit this increase in social responsibility to the fact that the just community develops strong interpersonal connections. Students are aware of the needs of others and are concerned about the welfare of others and the welfare of the community as a whole. In addition, "participatory democracy puts decisions in the hands of students, giving them a sense of personal efficacy and accountability" (p. 274). Haan, Aerts, and Cooper (1985) note in their study of moral action that moral judgment scores of responses to real situations tend to be lower than scores on hypothetical dilemmas. What emerges here in this study is that the just community provides the environment and the experience that enables students to act in ways that are more morally consistent with their judgments. In fact, in the communities Power, Higgins, and Kohlberg studied, stealing, cheating, and drug use declined significantly. Racial relations improved. And educational aspirations increased.

The just communities also had a powerful impact on the "politico-moral judgment" of students. The practical school dilemmas encompassed what the researchers considered as "political values."

> We have used the term 'political' to describe the values of community, democracy, fairness, and order to call attention to their implication for civics education. If the school is a transitional society between the family and the larger *polis*, then it is crucial that students develop there an understanding of these political values. It is obvious that to become citizens of any society they must develop a keen sense of fairness and appreciation for order. It is no less obvious that to become citizens of a democratic society they must learn how to live democratically. Whether coming to a better appreciation of community is important for civic virtue is rather controversial. In our view a sense of community strengthens the bonds of political association and counteracts perhaps the greatest contemporary threat to our democratic society, privatism. (p. 296)

At the beginning of their study, students' reasoning about these political values was below their moral reasoning scores. After a year in the just community their reasoning in these two areas was consistent.

No study is without problems and limitations. We do not really know how much of the communitarian culture was due to the participatory decision making, how much to the collective sense of community, and how much to the small size of the school. We also do not know if students' politico-moral development, their sense of personal responsibility, their active engagement in governance, and their understanding of collective interest are carried over into their participation in the social and political arena. The larger social and political environment lacks the cohesiveness, mutual support, and care of the just community. All of the studies reported in this section on the impact of participatory decision making examine short-term impact. We do not know if this impact is sustained over years. However, having taught in both a traditional school and one of the democratic communities these researchers studied, I believe that students' experience of democratic ideals, values, and culture and the skills they develop in political and moral decision-making bode well for their future involvement.

What all these studies reveal is that institutional structures—whether in the workplace, family, classroom, or school—that give young people the opportunity to participate in decision making about meaningful issues *can* have an impact on their sense of responsibility, their ability to take a collective perspective, their prosocial behavior, their understanding of democratic values and processes, and their personal and political efficacy. There is much more to be learned about the relationship between decision making and actual social and political participation, but these studies demonstrate that participatory and democratic school culture makes a significant difference in some of the key building blocks of social responsibility.

Classroom Communities of Care and Cooperation

A central ingredient of the just community approach articulated by Kohlberg is the creation of a community in which care, trust, and cooperation are significant norms. In Power, Higgins, and Kohlberg's (1989) study, community is so deeply enmeshed with democratic decision making that it is difficult to distinguish the impact of one from the other. However,

Lickona and Paradise (1980), in a study of experiments in democracy in elementary classrooms, reported that those classrooms where teachers explicitly helped students develop a sense of community and positive social relations were more successful than classrooms that simply stressed self-government.

> A healthy democracy means social community as well as self-government. . . . The fifth-grade teacher whose democracy was alive and well while others declined and fell had worked hard to build up a network of positive social relations in her classroom. That network, that social bonding, was the glue that seemed to hold the group together over the long winter months. For children, at least, a sense of community—a spirit of friendship, a feeling of belonging—appears to be an essential part of the democratic process. . . . When a spirit of cooperative community is missing, 'democratic' meetings can become merely a forum for pressing and defending one's narrow self-interest. 'Fairness' in such a classroom does not easily rise above a morality of looking out for Number 1. Through cooperative relationships, by contrast, children begin to feel connected to others, to develop a sense of membership in the class and a morality of concern for 'the good of the group.' The awareness dawns slowly, that every individual has a responsibility to the group, just as the group has a responsibility to every individual. (pp. 334–35)

My own experience of teaching in a just community was the same. Democracy is simply a way for a group of people to make collective decisions. It is community that gives meaning, substance, and purpose to these decisions. Community creates the bond among people that moves democratic decision making from negotiations around competing self-interests to a consideration of the common good. The experience of community also gives credibility to care solutions—solutions often endangered by the procedural justice orientation of democratic decision making—by promoting attachment, providing the opportunity and context for protest, and preventing abandonment and exit.

Classrooms and schools that emphasize community are characterized by two specific changes. First, community changes the nature of relationships between peers and between adults and young people. Relationships in the classroom are equalized, and each person becomes a resource and support to others. Peer interaction is valued. Members of the community care about and feel a commitment to the welfare of others. Adults become resources to children and to each other. Adult-child relationships are not structured along hierarchical lines but on authoritative and facilitative lines.

Second, community changes the culture of the school or classroom from an individualistic or competitive one to a collective culture (Johnson & Johnson, 1978). Although community is built on cooperative relationships and cooperative instruction, it moves beyond that as well. Children and adults are able to articulate shared values and goals and to possess a sense of collective responsibility. Members of the community are not only conscious of their own needs and interests and of the needs and interests of other members but of the needs of the community as an entity in its own right. Communities strive to live the values that its members hold dear.

Power, Higgins, and Kohlberg (1989) demonstrate at the high school level the power of community in the moral and political domain. However, theirs is not the only study to demonstrate how classrooms and schools that promote cooperation, care, and community enhance social responsibility. Studies of cooperative learning have demonstrated that cooperation can enhance such prosocial behaviors as understanding of others, interpersonal helping and sharing, distributive justice, interracial attitudes, mutual respect, concern for peers, and tendencies to cooperate with others outside the learning situation (Aronson, Bridgeman & Geffner, 1978; Battistich, Watson, Solomon, Schaps & Solomon, 1991; Blaney, Stephan, Rosenfield, Aronson & Sikes, 1977; Bryant & Crockenberg, 1974; Hertz-Lazarowitz & Sharan, 1984; Johnson, Maruyama, Johnson, Nelson & Skon, 1981; Sharan, 1980; Slavin, 1983). Cooperative learning offers students the opportunity to apply prosocial values, become conscious of how those values are applied, and learn and practice specific skills that will help them behave in ways that are consistent with those values (Solomon, Watson, Schaps, Battistich & Delucchi, 1990).

An example of this research is Hertz-Lazarowitz and Sharan's (1984) study of the impact of cooperative learning on prosocial behavior in Israeli elementary schools. They developed a Small Group Teaching (SGT) project and spent two years training second- through eighth-grade teachers from three elementary schools in cooperative learning strategies and a group investigation model. All the schools, including two control schools, were in low socioeconomic areas. The group investigation model involved students in self-directed planning and execution decisions around collaborative projects. "The unique feature of the group investigation model is the theoretical concept of *planned prosocial peer interaction*, where the students themselves serve as models, reward givers, reinforcers, role players, and a challenging support system for each other. Indeed, in this conceptualization children themselves can utilize various ways to facilitate the development of high quality helping behavior. . . ." (p. 428). Central to this strategy is cooperative peer interaction in heterogeneous groups. In their observations of classrooms over the two years of the study, they found that 30 to 40 percent of classroom time involved group investigation methods.

To examine the relationship between cooperative instruction and prosocial behavior, they constructed two experiments outside the classroom context. In both, children from the experimental and control schools were asked to complete a group task in unfamiliar groups. Children from cooperative classrooms exhibited significantly more helping behaviors than children from the control schools. "Students from small group classrooms were more altruistic and cooperative and less competitive and vengeful . . . than were students from the whole-class setting" (p. 438). This was also confirmed by teacher reports of increased prosocial behavior in the classroom and student reports that their own and others' helping behaviors were the most important aspect of the classroom to them. Cooperative learning using the group investigations model altered the social environment of the classroom so that egocentric goals were balanced by altruistic goals.

Classrooms that use cooperative learning generally emphasize prosocial peer interactions. In contrast to the helping behaviors that Dunn (1988), Zahn-Wexler and Radke-Yarrow (1982), and others observed in naturalistic observation of the family, naturalistic observation of traditional classrooms reveals few peer helping behaviors (Hertz-Lazarowitz, 1983; Jackson, 1968). In fact, there is little instructional peer interaction in tradition classrooms. Interactions are primarily teacher-student rather than student-student. Hertz-Lazarowitz and Sharan's classrooms were distinctly different. They were "peer societies" organized around learning tasks. Hertz-Lazarowitz and Sharan identified peer interaction as a central vehicle for nurturing prosocial behavior. In fact, peer interaction has been increasingly identified as a primary facilitator of development. Johnson and Johnson (1983) describe eleven significant areas in which peers have the most critical impact on the development of others. Peer interaction is central to Selman's conception of the development of interpersonal negotiations skills. In many of the most important studies that I have reviewed so far (Berkowitz and

Gibbs, 1983; Haan, Aerts, and Cooper, 1985; Kurtines and Gewirtz, 1987; Power, Higgins, and Kohlberg, 1989), peer interaction plays a dominant role in fostering development. But it is not simply peer interaction that these studies have noted as being effective in promoting development but peer interaction within a context that emphasizes cooperation and equality, that allows conflicts to be openly and effectively resolved, that promotes caring for and about others, that gives students a meaningful voice in controlling their environment, and that enlarges young people's perspectives by inviting them to consider the perspectives of others and the good of the group. Essentially, peer interaction within this context builds a sense of community.

One of the boldest experiments in classroom community building and one of the most significant studies of the relationship between classroom community and prosocial behavior has been done by the Developmental Studies Center (Battistich, Watson, Solomon, Schaps & Solomon, 1991). Initially working in three elementary schools in San Ramon, California, with three control schools in the same district, the Developmental Studies Center initiated a longitudinal intervention to create "caring community in the classroom based on a shared commitment to prosocial, democratic values" (p. 7). Their specific aim was to encourage the development of prosocial character, moral behavior, moral action, and social responsibility on the part of children. "The school may be viewed as a microcosm of the larger society in which children develop basic understandings of the self, the social world and their place in it" (p. 2). This intervention, titled the Child Development Project (CDP), combined a number of the strategies that we have already examined as supporting the development of social responsibility—an open, reflective classroom environment, participation in decision making, welcoming conflict as an opportunity for problem solving, and cooperation. In addition, they highlight prosocial values for children and involve students in helping behaviors.

> Within this general milieu of a caring and supportive environment, the CDP program attempts to promote the development of prosocial behaviors by providing children with experiences that should help them to understand and internalize values of fairness, concern and respect for others, and social responsibility. These consist of numerous opportunities to: (a) collaborate with others in the pursuit of common goals; (b) provide meaningful help to others, and to receive help when it is needed; (c) discuss and reflect

upon the experiences of others in order to gain an understanding and appreciation of others' feelings, needs, and perspectives; (d) discuss and reflect upon their own behavior and the behavior of others as it relates to prosocial values; (e) develop and practice important social skills and competencies; and (f) exercise autonomy, participate in decision making about classroom norms, rules, and activities, and otherwise occupy a responsible role in the school community. (Battistich et al., 1991, p. 8)

The program has five major components. The first is cooperative learning. There are a number of different approaches to cooperative learning but theirs "was designed primarily to promote the internalization of prosocial values and a commitment to democratic forms of social organization" (p. 9). The key difference is that teachers in the CDP program are more explicit about the norms and values that should guide group work and the skills the students need in order to function well in their groups. When problems emerge, the teacher uses a child-centered approach to solving them, that is, asking the child or the children questions that will draw out their own thinking. They spend time processing the group work as a class and discussing what could be done to improve it. They also emphasize intrinsic rather than extrinsic rewards and avoid intergroup competition. Finally, cooperative learning is integrated into a larger cooperative effort throughout the school.

The second component is an approach to classroom management they call developmental discipline because it is child-centered and adjusted to be developmentally appropriate. Children are active partners in classroom management. Through frequent class meetings they develop shared norms and values, set rules, problem-solve around issues of conflict or discipline, and initiate efforts to improve the classroom environment. The teacher's role is to establish a warm and supportive environment, help students understand the reasons for norms and rules, teach social skills, and involve students in decision making and problem solving when issues emerge. The focus of the teacher's control efforts is on problem solving rather than punishment. They rely on persuasion, reason, and guided autonomy. The goal is to help students develop self-control and internalize prosocial values. "We believe that this personal commitment to prosocial values will develop when teachers and other adults clearly communicate their expectations for prosocial behavior . . . and when they justify their requests and involve children in open discussion of the reasons for behaving in certain ways and not others. . . . The teacher should try to understand the reasons for misbehavior, attribute the best possible motive to the child that is consistent with the situation . . . , offer children alternative ways to comply with expectations, and use the *minimum* amount of pressure that is necessary to gain compliance" (pp. 13–14).

The final three strategies work in tandem. Children are involved in a variety of helping activities that put prosocial values into practice. In addition to the helping that is naturally a part of cooperative learning, students share responsibility for classroom chores, participate in peer tutoring and "buddies" programs, get involved in schoolwide maintenance and beautification projects, and participate in occasional community service activities. To complement these helping activities, teachers highlight prosocial values by specifically pointing these out in the literature the children read, the films they see, and the everyday experiences of the classroom and school they are involved in. Finally, teachers promote social understanding and perspective taking. Teachers help children become sensitive to and understanding of the feelings, needs, and perspectives of others as a basic element in the curriculum and the life of the classroom. They make extensive use of prosocial literature to enhance children's interpersonal understanding and concern for others. Books, films, class meetings, conflict situations, and events that arise spontaneously in class become the context for perspective taking and empathy development.

As in Kohlberg's just communities, perspective taking, moral discourse, and moral reflection around such values as fairness, kindness, and personal responsibility are fundamental to all five of the elements of the program. Also as in Kohlberg's just communities, the program strives to create an environment of care and solidarity that helps students to experience being a contributing member of a community and to appreciate collective interests. "Through participating in open discussion about social norms, and working collaboratively to plan activities, set goals, decide on procedures, and complete tasks, children discover that others care and are concerned about fairness, and develop feelings of trust, mutual respect, and solidarity. They feel that they are valued members of their community, are accountable to other community members for their actions, and are personally responsible for the welfare of the community" (Battistich et al., 1991, p. 18). But in a step beyond Kohlberg's work, the Child Development Program is embedded throughout the life of the school—integrated into the curriculum, the methods of instruction, and the culture of the school. In addition, the program makes a significant effort to involve parents and support them in carrying elements of the program into children's home environment.

Teachers involved in the program received extensive training and support—a week-long summer workshop, curriculum and other written materials, monthly meetings with the program staff, and frequent individual observation and coaching. Based on observations of the research staff and teacher and student reports, each of the five elements of the program has been implemented to a significant degree over the comparison schools (Battistich et al., 1991). In addition, the program was successful in creating caring communities within the classrooms as seen by the students in those classrooms (Solomon et al., 1992).

The research data come from two cohorts that they have followed longitudinally. One began the program in 1982 and the other in 1985. They used classroom and playground observations, experimental small-group activities, and student and teacher questionnaires and interviews to assess the impact of the program. Observers visited each classroom in the program and comparison school for sixteen hours each year. Although they found significant implementation of the program, the implementation for the first cohort was somewhat problematic. The teachers of the first cohort were learning the program at the same time that the students were being interviewed. By the spring of that year only a small percentage of teachers could be considered expert implementers. Most were able to implement the program moderately. A small percentage were unable or unwilling to implement it at all. In spite of this there are some strong findings from the first cohort, and these findings were replicated in the first years of follow-up with the second cohort (Battistich et al., 1991; Solomon et al., 1992).

The findings from the first five years of the first cohort show significant development of prosocial behavior and social competence. First, students in the CDP schools were observed engaging more often in such spontaneous prosocial behaviors as helpfulness, cooperation, concern for others' needs and feelings, giving of affection, support, and encouragement than students in the comparison schools. In addition, they found that "the greater the sense of community among students in a program class, the more favorable their scores on measures of the tendency to help others, reactions to transgressions, reasoning about prosocial and moral issues, conflict resolution skill, democratic values, and reading comprehension" (Solomon et al., 1992, p. 56). Using a "sense of community" questionnaire that assessed students' perceptions of whether they and their classmates care about and are supportive of one another and whether they have an important role in classroom decision making and direction, they found that students whose classes had more frequent class meetings, discussions of prosocial literature, and small group cooperative learning activities had the highest sense of community scores. Interestingly, those students in the control schools who experienced a sense of community in their classroom also showed the same benefits as those in the CDP schools. The researchers conclude that community has a powerful impact on students independent of whether it is one enhanced by the CDP program or by the inclinations and practices of the teacher.

Second, students in the CDP schools developed more effective ways of social problem solving and of resolving conflicts. The researchers presented students with hypothetical conflicts and coded their responses according to what resolution strategy was used, whose needs were considered, and who was favored. They also used dilemmas about object acquisition and peer group that were scored according to interpersonal sensitivity, ability to plan, problem resolution strategies, and ability to deal with obstacles. Students in the CDP schools demonstrated greater perspective-taking skills and showed more consideration of the other person's needs as well as their own in problem situations. They were also more likely to consider the consequences of their actions, anticipate obstacles to effective resolution, and select such prosocial and cooperative strategies as discussing the problem, explaining their position, sharing, or compromising.

Third, these students had a greater commitment to democratic values than those in the comparison schools. They operationalized democratic values as support for equal participation and representation among group members, the expression of one's opinion even when it might be unpopular, compromise as a possible solution to differences, and the right to influence group decisions and be involved in group activities. Using questionnaire measures administered in the third and fourth grades, they found that third graders in program schools scored higher than comparison children on a measure of assertion responsibility, that is, the belief that one has a responsibility to state one's position even if it seems unlikely to prevail. By the fourth grade, in addition to scoring higher on assertion responsibility, these students also had higher scores on measures of equality of representation and participation and the willingness to compromise. In addition, program students showed a greater orientation toward equality during structured small-group tasks than did students from the comparison schools.

They also observed some differences in favor of program children on assessments of interpersonal behavior in small-group activities outside the classroom. However, the researchers express disappointment at the weakness of this finding. The lack of students' application of prosocial behavior to outside of classroom settings may, in fact, be due to one element that is significantly missing in the CDP program, that is, helping children make the connection between their interpersonal, classroom, and school prosocial behavior and its value in the larger social and political arena.

Cooperative learning in general and the CDP program in particular are effective interventions in promoting prosocial behavior and democratic values. Although these researchers have not addressed political efficacy or social and political participation, the effort is grounded in the hope that these microcommunities will enable children to function more effectively and participate more actively in our democratic society. In the 1991 summary of findings of the Child Development Project, the research and project staff write that "the combination of effects produced by this program could, we hope, have a significant impact on later life—in helping youth to cope with the problems of adolescence and beyond, while becoming more committed, responsible and productive citizens" (p. 9).

Each of the cooperation and community efforts I've reviewed conceives of the school as a microsociety in which children have experiences that prepare them for responsible and participatory roles. Yet what stands out as missing in these community-building efforts as well as in Kohlberg's just community efforts is the lack of direct engagement in the larger social and political world. Educational interventions that have made this connection have had a more direct impact on students' social and political attitudes, values, and skills.

Direct Engagement in the Social and Political Arena

We know that those who are active early in life, whether in school or the community, are more likely to be active later in life (Beck & Jennings, 1982; Hanks & Eckland, 1978; Jennings & van Deth, 1990; Keniston, 1968; Merelman & King, 1986). Merelman and King found that young people who planned to be politically active at age eighteen were three times more likely to be politically active at age twenty-six. We also know that prosocial action encourages future prosocial action (Feshbach & Feshbach, 1982; Hodgkinson & Weitzman, 1992; Staub, 1975). Hodgkinson and Weitzman found that 84 percent of the young people who had participated in volunteer work in their childhood continued their volunteer activity into their teenage years. There is no longitudinal study, however, that follows students into adult life to determine if a particular educational intervention was instrumental in encouraging later participation. And we do not know if this continuity in participation is learned or is due to a deeply held predisposition. Yet, the studies of programs that involve students in active engagement in the social and political arena—whether through community service or direct political action—indicate that this involvement may, in fact, be an important stepping stone to later participation.

Those who argue for community service and direct political action begin with a different set of assumptions than many of the other research studies we've reviewed. One assumption is that young people are citizens now; they are not simply in preparation for later citizenship. Community service advocates assume that young people can contribute to the welfare of others, the welfare of the community, and the welfare of the planet by actions they take.

A second assumption is that learning requires action, and social and political learning requires social and political action. We do not learn citizenship didactically but experientially.

A third assumption is that students who are given greater responsibility develop a greater sense of responsibility (Hedin & Conrad, 1990). The impact of giving children real responsibility is evident in Whiting and Whiting's (1975) naturalistic study of child-rearing practices in six countries. They found that those children who rated significantly higher in altruistic behavior had been given significant experience in responsible helping and caretaking roles. In examining the social-contextual factors that contributed to this higher level of altruism, they found that children in the Philippines, Kenya, and Mexico were expected to help with household and family responsibilities while the parents worked outside the home to a much greater extent than children in New England, Okinawa, or India.

In spite of the current enthusiasm for community service and calls for political involvement by advocates of citizenship education (Butts, 1980; Giroux, 1988; Newmann, 1975, 1990; Reische, 1987; Shaver, 1977), research in this area is limited. Hedin and Conrad (1982, 1990) report on an extensive study of thirty experiential education programs, many of which involved community service or service learning. Seven of these programs had a matched control group of students who weren't involved in the program. The findings strongly support the value of experiential education in promoting students' social, psychological, and intellectual development. The researchers found that experiential programs enhanced self-esteem, social competence, moral reasoning, and social efficacy. Those programs that involved community service or community study/action encouraged greater development than other types of experiential programs, especially in the area of personal and social responsibility. They also found that students valued this experience and indicated that they would be likely to pursue participation in the future. In contrast, the traditional social studies classes that acted as controls showed declines in valuing community participation, in attitudes toward taking personal and social responsibility, and in complexity of thinking and empathy.

There were particular program characteristics that proved most effective. The most effective programs had a reflective component integrated as part of the experience so that students could discuss their experience, learn about the experience of others, and reflect on their own concerns and skills. Effective programs involved students in the community four to five times a week over an extended period of time. Effective programs also offered students autonomy, decision-making opportunities, and adult responsibility. "Preliminary conclusions are that the strongest predictor of change proved to be the degree to which students perceived themselves as having the freedom to develop and use their own ideas, make important decisions, and assume adult responsibility" (1990, p. 128). In terms of promoting growth in social responsibility, the most significant characteristic was a collegial relationship with adults.

The importance of autonomy, real decision-making opportunities, and responsible authority emerged in Merelman's (1985) interviews with youth activists. Those students whom he considers durables—students who were more deeply involved in political activism and who indicated that they planned on continuing this involvement in the future—were in roles that allowed them to make their own decisions, gave them autonomy and authority, and placed them in collegial relationship with adults.

Conrad and Hedin (1982) argue that their data suggest that "changes in behavior often precede rather than follow changes in attitude" (p. 66). In their study the strongest changes produced by experiential programs were toward "taking responsible action" as opposed to having more responsible attitudes. Attitude development emerged as a result of action. In contrast, in the control social studies classes where improving attitudes toward taking personal and social responsibility was a deliberate goal, there were no gains and some declines in taking responsible action and having more responsible attitudes. This corresponds to the data from the studies of activists discussed in chapter 3. Often individuals, confronted by injustice, took action after little reflection. Later they found their attitudes changing as a result of their action. Conrad and Hedin go on to suggest that "the traditional model of citizenship education, which proposes that instruction in proper attitudes about personal and social obligations will lead to responsible behavior, may need revision" (p. 66).

The power of action to influence attitude is best exemplified by Button (1974). She initiated her study because researchers had been finding that the standard civics curriculum had no effect on political attitudes and political efficacy. Believing that this was a result of how civics was taught rather than civics itself, she prepared a semester-long civics curriculum centered around political action. Eight classes in two Austin, Texas, high schools were involved in the study, four using her curriculum and four using the standard curriculum and teacher-directed discussion. The students were multicultural—one-third Anglo-American, one-third African American, and one-third Mexican American. The experimental course incorporated many of the interventions we have already reviewed—open classroom atmosphere, reflection, welcoming controversy, cooperative learning, and participation in decision making. But it added two others, critical political analysis and direct action.

There were four key elements in the curriculum. One element involved students in an analysis of their own political socialization and the key agents that had shaped their political attitudes. She placed an emphasis on introspection because "individuals who are apathetic, politically angry, or racist can liberate themselves by discovering how these orientations develop and change and how they influence and are influenced by behavior and experience" (p. 170). In addition, students examined the process of socialization of small children, racial minorities, and the poor and analyzed how the cycle of political alienation develops and might be broken.

The second element of the course involved students in an analysis of the distribution of political power in America. The students explored such questions as: Who rules America? What political linkages exist between those who hold power and those who do not? And, how does institutional racism operate in the political system? In small groups students analyzed realistic political problems in democratic societies and attempted to find just and equitable resolutions to these dilemmas.

The third element of the course focused on avenues of political involvement and change. Using the historical and current dilemmas of race and poverty, students studied the variety of strategies, both nonviolent and violent, that had been used for bringing about political and social change.

The fourth element, political fieldwork, was integrated throughout the course. Students selected a community problem that was of interest to them and worked either alone or in small groups to understand the problem and to affect change. "Thus the student could apply the concepts and skills learned in the classroom by extending the learning environment into the actual political structure" (p. 172).

Using pre- and postquestionnaires and a follow-up interview, Button examined changes in students' attitudes about political interest, cynicism, and efficacy as well as in students' knowledge. The political cynicism scale was derived from many of the earlier political socialization studies (Jennings & Niemi, 1981) and explored such issues as distrust of government, disbelief that government leaders are usually honest and competent, and disbelief that government leaders will act in the interest of the people. The political efficacy scale was an expanded ten-item version of Easton and Dennis's (1969) scale that incorporated probes of students' perceptions of their abilities to deal with local and national problems they considered pressing. Political knowledge was measured by an objective twenty-eight item test based on general civic knowledge. In addition, observers measured the degree of student-initiated discussion as a sign of active participation in the course and as a sign of more efficacious student behavior.

The findings are striking. Most of the students in the experimental group experienced marked increases in political interest and political efficacy both at the local and national level. To a lesser extent cynicism declined for the experimental group, especially at the local level and especially among Anglo-American males. In contrast, the control group experienced increases in cynicism and decreases in efficacy. The follow-up interview, which was done two months after the completion of the course, revealed a slight trend among students in the experimental group to be involved in new political activity. In addition, the experimental group showed a marked increase in student-initiated interaction during the course.

Strong cultural patterns emerged from the data as well. The influence of the course was stronger for Anglo-American and African-American females and for Mexican-American males. In addition, Button found an interesting relationship between cynicism and efficacy for students from groups that tended to have less political power. For African Americans, Anglo-American females, and Mexican-American males increased cynicism related to increased efficacy. In the interviews these students explained that they became more aware of the problems in government and less trusting that these would be taken care of without their active involvement. Their cynicism may reflect an accurate perception of the distribution of political power and makes their increase in efficacy even more significant. Mexican-American females were generally unaffected by the curriculum. In the interviews they expressed discomfort with studying about conflict and involvement in conflictual situations. Studying conflict was unpleasant and "even frightening" for them. Button suggested that this may have been due to their cultural socialization. She also reported that while the Anglo-Americans often found the fieldwork to be the most influential aspect of the course, the African Americans and Mexican Americans found the study of strategies of political change and materials that honestly addressed ethnic issues of greatest influence. As one African-American male stated in the follow-up interview, "*Now*, if I want to change something I know how to do it. Knowing keeps me from being as pessimistic as I was, and this is one of the things which brings tension and violence. If you don't know how to participate in your government, you're going to be very frustrated because the government is going to kick you around 'til you know how to use it" (p. 198).

Button concludes that the combination of reflection, political analysis, and political action produced significant changes in attitudes. In contrast to the accepted notion that student attitudes are already well formed by senior year, she demonstrated that it is possible to "teach for political efficacy" (p. 196). It demands being willing to truthfully deal with political problems and to welcome conflict as a central and vital part of our current political process. It also demands seeing students as citizens with citizenship responsibilities. "Educators must also encourage students to expand outward—to go beyond the classroom and the school, into the political structure of the community and beyond. Fieldwork, or action research, helps the student become a self-directed learner and makes political education a part of his life, rather than a preparation for life in the future" (p. 198).

Button's results have been echoed in two studies in the area of environmental education. These studies (Ramsey & Hungerford, 1988; Ramsey, Hungerford, & Tomera, 1981) examined the impact of a model action-oriented course on overt environmental behavior. The model curriculum, titled the Issue Investigation and Action Training (IIAT) model (Hungerford, Lithreland, Peyton, Ramsey & Volk, 1988), was designed for middle school students. Students examine environmental issues, explore the impact of beliefs and values on those issues, develop research questions, gather data to answer those questions, learn about environmental action strategies, and apply the knowledge and skills they learn to an environmental issue of their choice. Ramsey, Hungerford, and Tomera (1981) argue that "an environmental action training strategy could develop citizens who were not only knowledgeable and committed to solving environmental issues but who also possessed the skills and competencies necessary to address and remediate environmental problems effectively" (p. 25).

The first study of the IIAT model (Ramsey, Hungerford & Tomera, 1981) involved seven months of instruction to three heterogeneously grouped eighth-grade classes, two experimental classes and one control class. One experimental class received environmental instruction designed to increase environmental awareness using case studies of such issues as endangered species, nuclear energy, and water management. The class identified environmental issues and their causes. They then derived value positions implicit to each issue and identified potential solutions. The class was taught traditionally and was primarily teacher-directed. It utilized lectures, class discussions, demonstrations, audiovisual presentations, experiments, and guest lecturers. The second experimental class received instruction in the IIAT model with an emphasis on action training. As in the other class, students identified environmental problems and identified implicit value positions in environmental problems, but, in addition, they investigated environmental problems of their own choosing, learned environmental problem-solving skills, and took action on two local environmental problems. Unlike the teacher in the awareness class whose position was neutral, the teacher in the action group actively encouraged individual and collective involvement in environmental problems. The control group received basic science instruction in the areas of reproduction, heredity, metabolic processes, and health using a content-oriented text.

In order to determine to what extent these various treatments had an impact on overt environmental behavior, they administered a pre- and postquestionnaire about actions that were taken by students over and above school and classroom activities. In addition, they used a parental questionnaire distributed two months after the end of instruction that collected parents' observations of students' environmental behavior during and after instruction. Environmental action could be pursued through a number of avenues: trying to persuade someone to take environmental action or change their environmental values; taking consumer action by being discriminating about the goods one purchases or boycotts; taking political action aimed at persuading voters, legislators, or government agencies; taking legal action to enforce environmental laws; or taking any action aimed at "ecomanagement," that is, maintaining or improving a natural ecosystem.

They found that the action class exhibited significantly greater knowledge of environmental action and of environmental action skills and exhibited significantly more overt environmental action behaviors than either the awareness group or the control group. In fact, the action group took significantly more environmental actions over and above classroom and school activities than either group. The case study and control group did not significantly differ on either knowledge of environmental action skills or on overt environmental action. Parent reports were consistent and supportive of the student self-reports. The researchers conclude that "environmental action instruction developed a more comprehensive preparation for overt environmental action behavior by supplying: (1). the knowledge about skills needed to remediate environmental problems; and (2). practice in the use of those skills" (p. 29). They add that "environmental awareness instruction fails to develop effectively the ability to initiate environmental action" (p. 29).

Ramsey and Hungerford obtained similar results in a second study (1988). Again they examined the impact of the IIAT model on encouraging responsible environmental behavior. This study involved eight heterogeneously grouped seventh-grade classes, four classes took the IIAT course and four received regular science instruction. The classes were in both rural and urban schools in the Midwest. As in their first study, they operationalized overt environmental behavior as persuasion, political action, consumer action, and ecomanagement action.

In this study they looked at a number of other variables as well. They built upon Sia, Hungerford, and Tomera's (1986) research comparing environmentally active and inactive adults that found that there were a number of variables that were significant predictors of environmental behavior. These variables were: knowledge of environmental issues, beliefs concerning environmental issues, values related to the environment, individual and group locus of control, environmental sensitivity, knowledge of and skills in environmental action, and knowledge of ecological concepts. Of these, the ones that were the most significant predictor variables were skill in using environmental action strategies, level of environmental sensitivity, and perceived knowledge of environmental action strategies. Ramsey and Hungerford used these variables in their pre- and postquestionnaire as well.

They found that there was a significant difference in pre- and postscores for overt environmental behavior, individual locus of control, group locus of control, knowledge of environmental action skills, perceived knowledge of environmental action skills, and perceived skill in the use of environmental action skills. There was not a significant difference in environmental sensitivity. As with their first study, they conclude that the IIAT model's use of issue analysis, investigation, and action was effective in promoting responsible environmental behavior. They argue that "by providing instruction that promotes awareness and analysis of environmental issues, the knowledge and skills needed to remediate environmental issues, and practice in issue resolution, IIAT anchored students' knowledge of environmental action skills and techniques. . . . The knowledge, skills, and experiences implicit in IIAT instruction seemed to foster subjects' beliefs that they had greater control in the resolution of an issue acting both individually and collectively" (p. 32).

In both environmental studies the postquestionnaire was administered to students immediately after instruction and to parents within two months after instruction. It is impossible to say how long this behavioral change lasted. However, like Button's study, their work makes it clear that an action-oriented curriculum can have a short-term impact on students' values and behaviors.

Although the studies in this area are limited, they provide an insight into the potential of direct social and political engagement as an educational intervention. Hoehn (1983), in his study of adult activists, noted that one of the important factors that enabled political action was an "at-homeness" in the world of political action. He says that "it is one thing to know I-can-do, even that I have-done; it is another to know that 'I am at home doing' it. The potential activist needs to establish a degree of familiarity, of comfort, of 'being at home' in the world of political action" (p. 100). Because the move from noninvolvement to involvement requires a leap from the familiar to unfamiliar, he argues that "a pedagogy for social action would get people into the arenas where the action occurs so that they can overcome their fears, become at home with the world of involvement, and get some feeling that their activities contribute to a larger whole" (p. 100). If citizenship is a goal of education, then the practice of citizenship beyond the limited arena of the classroom and school must be a basic element in that education as well.

An Integration

In 1986, Educators for Social Responsibility (ESR)—a national nonprofit organization whose goal is to help schools teach social responsibility—and twelve suburban Boston school districts initiated a project titled the Educating for Living in a Nuclear Age (ELNA) Project. The goal of this project was to make social responsibility a core element of the curriculum and school program. Each district convened a team of teachers and administrators to direct its district-based efforts and to collaborate with teams from the other districts. One of the first efforts the project initiated was a curriculum assessment to identify areas of strength and weakness in each district's approach to teaching social responsibility. Because no curriculum assessment of social responsibility had ever been done, each team worked with an ESR consultant to operationalize social responsibility in the instructional program and to develop an assessment form that would then be administered to the entire district's faculty.

The assessment evolved in sophistication and depth as each district built on the earlier work of the other districts. At the conclusion of the process, the project staff took the various forms of the assessment and synthesized them into a model form. At the heart of this assessment were twenty-one items identifying core practices that teachers viewed as central aspects of teaching social responsibility. On a four-point scale with the option of "not applicable," teachers were asked how consistently they addressed these items in their classroom instruction. Although neither the ESR staff nor the teachers were familiar with much of the research reviewed in this chapter, the categories and practices they identified are virtually identical to what this research has shown to be effective (see Table 5.1). The categories that teachers felt were core to promoting social responsibility were teaching perspective-taking skills, teaching skills in managing conflict and controversy, engaging students in discussion of ethics, involving students in classroom and school decision making, building a sense of community in the classroom and school, and making the social and political world salient to young people.

What the teachers in the ELNA Project believed is that none of these individual interventions stand on their own. They work best when integrated. Battistich and his colleagues (1991) and Button (1974) found that their interventions were improved by viewing the classroom holistically and by addressing what was taught, how it was taught, and the way the classroom was structured. A theme threaded throughout many of the

Table 5.1. ELNA Curriculum Assessment Items

Perspective taking:

Helping students appreciate human differences (i.e., physical, racial, intellectual, socioeconomic, etc.).

Helping students understand and appreciate others' points of view.

Teaching about the customs of different world cultures.

Teaching about how people in different cultures view the world through their cultural, historical, and political experiences.

Teaching about the diversity of cultural experiences within the United States.

Teaching about ecological interdependence.

Welcoming conflict and controversy:

Providing direct instruction in conflict resolution, negotiation, or mediation skills.

Using conflict resolution strategies to successfully resolve classroom conflicts.

Teaching about current social and political issues in a way that is age-appropriate and fits my curriculum.

Moral development:

Teaching about the preservation of human and civil rights.

Helping students become aware of historic and current injustices.

Discussing questions of ethics and values.

Student participation in decision making:

Providing opportunities for students to make decisions about classroom and school issues.

Community building:

Providing cooperatively structured classroom activities.

Teaching about the interdependence of people within society.

Creating community within the classroom and school.

Direct engagement in the social and political world:

Helping students become self-reflective about their social and political attitudes, values, and assumptions.

Encouraging student-initiated discussion of local, national, global, or environmental concerns.

Teaching about the ways individuals and groups influence social and political change.

Helping students develop confidence in their ability to effect positive change on local and/or global issues.

Involving students in community service or some form of assisting people in need.

studies reviewed here and in the ELNA project is that the school and the classroom are microsocieties where the social lessons are taught by the way people live and work together in that setting as well as by the explicit curriculum. Battistich and his colleagues (1991), Moore, Lare, and Wagner (1985), and Button (1974) have shown us that what is taught can make a substantial difference. But in assessing the many studies reviewed here I would have to agree with Ehman's (1980) conclusion:

> The findings from this review suggest that the manifest curriculum (i.e., direct instruction involving courses and texts in civics, government, and other social studies courses) is not as important as the latent curriculum in influencing political attitudes. This latent curriculum includes *how* classes are taught, not the subject matter itself. This classroom climate is directly manipulable by teachers and represents a potentially important level in the political education of youth. The entire school governance climate, which is another aspect of the latent curriculum, is another consistent correlate of student political attitudes. (p. 113)

The social fabric of the school and the methods of instruction are the central vehicles for teaching social responsibility.

When taken together, the interventions that have been effective in fostering aspects of social responsibility create a particular kind of classroom and school. The classroom and school model that emerges from these studies is one that is open and nurturant, where personal relationships are valued and caring for others is a basic norm. The classroom and school are democratic communities where students are able to participate in decision making about matters that affect their daily lives and there is a mutual concern for the good of all in the classroom. Teachers and students are able to express divergent opinions in an atmosphere of mutual respect. Conflict and controversy—intraclassroom, school-wide and in the wider world—are treated as opportunities to learn and improve the way we live together. The curriculum integrates social and political issues in both didactic and experiential ways. All members of the school community strive to live the values they hold dear. Peer interaction and cooperation are a central teaching methodology. Adults in this school are nurturers, facilitators, and organizers. They model their commitment to prosocial values in their school roles and in their lives outside the school.

The various researchers we have reviewed make strikingly similar recommendations about the nature of education that is effective in nurturing social responsibility. Battistich and his colleagues (1991) suggest that:

> Overall, the educational implications of this perspective on sociomoral development converge on a model of the 'ideal' school as a caring community, organized and operated according to democratic principles and characterized by a clear and articulated commitment to fundamental prosocial values. . . . Under these conditions, the school becomes in many respects a microcosm of the society it represents—in social organization, norms, and values. Active participation in such a community provides children not only with the experiences necessary to develop an understanding of the basic social and moral values on which a democracy is founded, but also with opportunities to apply those values in their daily lives and to directly experience the benefits and obligations of just and caring social relationships. (p. 102)

Oliner and Oliner (1988) virtually echo this portrait:

> Schools need to become caring institutions—institutions in which students, teachers, bus drivers, principals, and all others receive positive affirmation for kindness, empathy, and concern. Participants need opportunities to work and have fun together, develop intimacies, and share successes and pain. Students also need opportunities to consider broad universal principles that relate to justice and care in matters of public concern. Discussions should focus on the logic and values, implications and consequences of public actions, as well as the philosophical heritage that underlies these principles. In short, caring schools will acknowledge diversity on the road to moral concern. They will invoke emotion and intellect in the service of responsibility and caring. (pp. 258–59)

Todd Jennings (1992) argues that there are two strategies for nurturing the connected sense of self that lies behind social and political activism:

> First, students should participate in classrooms where connection and interdependence are embedded within practice. Second, students should be engaged in curricula which are emotionally evocative and value the students' subjective experiences. Mechanisms such as cooperative learning, democratic classrooms, and an emphasis on discussion over lecture, are all pedagogical tools for

the promotion of connection because they stress relationships and community within classrooms. (p. 22)

Hoehn argues that "if the teacher talks about injustice and inequality but does not act to alleviate them in some clearly perceivable ways, the students learn that injustice and inequality are first and foremost linguistic events. They are things people talk about rather than things people do something about" (p. 119). He proposes a pedagogy for social action that includes face-to-face confrontation with suffering, taking the perspective of others and identifying with those who experience injustice, receiving help in interpreting suffering and injustice and connecting it to larger social systems, having significant role models of activism available, learning the "how" of social action until there is an at-homeness with it, and engaging directly in social action. Students would be helped "to acquire a sense of personal effectiveness by participating in successful social change events. He would learn *how to*, that he *can do*, until he felt *at home* in the world of social action. She would learn that victims can be helped, and that she can be the one who helps. Would-be activists would learn that they have a personal stake in the outcome, a personal connection with those who suffer. The pressing urgency of the suffering would help them realize that something has to be done, and that their activities can play a vital part in solving the problem" (p. 158). A pedagogy for activism would center on the school as a place for care and activism.

These researchers describe a place that is different from most schools. It is a place that helps students begin to locate themselves in the world in a meaningful way. It is a place where students experience their connection with their classmates as well as the world around them. It is a place that holds out a vision of a better society toward which each person, in his or her individual way, can contribute. It is a place that builds self-esteem and social competence at the same time that it teaches basic skills. It is a place where the ability to participate in democratic governance is seen as a central organizer of instruction and culture. But most important, it is a place where hope, responsibility, and integrity are nurtured into democratic empowerment.

Although the synthesis of the research on educational practice points in these particular directions, the interventions that have been effective in promoting aspects of social responsibility have not been studied as a single program. Kohlberg, Battistich and his colleagues, and Button have combined many of them, yet there may not be a preestablished harmony among all the interventions. There may be trade-offs and inconsistencies that we are not yet aware of. This would be a profitable area for continued experimentation and study.

CHAPTER 6

The Current State of Educating
for Social Responsibility

The society of which the child is to be a member is, in the United
States, a democratic and progressive society. The child must be
educated for leadership as well as for obedience. He must have
power of self-direction and power of directing others, power of
administration, ability to assume positions of responsibility.
(Dewey, 1909, p. 10)

I believe that the prime purpose, the highest priority, for a genuinely
public education is the political goal of empowering the whole
population to exercise its rights and to cope with the responsibilities
of a genuinely democratic citizenship. (Butts, 1980, p. 74)

Social Responsibility in Policy and Practice

The research on educational interventions that promote social responsibility
paints a very different picture than what we see in most classrooms and
schools. Yet, it isn't very different from what many educational theorists
and social studies leaders have advocated for over a century.

In the early nineteenth century, Joseph Neef (1807), an advocate of
Johann Pestalozzi's child-centered approach to education, formulated plans
for a school that intentionally encouraged moral and democratic development in young people through the recreation of a self-governing society
within the school. After some basic instruction in the rights and duties
of citizens, students would live out the processes of a democratic republic by

forming a government, drafting a constitution, and making and enforcing laws. Neef's ideas were adopted by Robert Owen's utopian community in New Harmony, Indiana.

Leaders in the Progressive Movement in education at the turn of the twentieth century articulated and put into practice many interventions that promote social responsibility. Francis Wayland Parker, one of the early progressive educators, articulated a social vision for education. He believed that a democratized school system grounded in the life of the larger community could become "the one central means by which the great problem of human liberty is to be worked out" (cited in Curti, 1959, p. 388, from N.E.A. Proceedings, 1895, p. 972). The schools could help create an ideal republic and solve such pressing social problems as war, poverty, misery, and selfishness. Altruism and democracy were the heart of his educational program. Education, for Parker, was about how to live with and for others, and this could not be taught didactically but had to be lived in the classroom. He insisted that dogmatism and authoritarianism not enter teaching and that even extrinsic rewards be ruled out so that children could experience the intrinsic value of altruism and democracy. He also welcomed conflict and controversy. He advocated for a way of teaching U.S. history that presented the truth of such injustices as our harsh treatment of Native Americans and that questioned unjust laws and practices. He was not afraid that his methods would create anarchy and nihilism as many critics who advocated law and order in the schools contended. In fact, he felt that anarchy and nihilism "are the sure and deadly products of the method of the rule of the few over the many, of the minority suppressing the rights of the majority. Let us put the blame where it belongs. Not the poor men who land upon the scaffold because oppression has made them mad, but the rulers by might, secure in palace and castle, who fatten on the vitals of the people, they and they alone are responsible for political insanity" (cited in Curti, 1959, p. 391, from Talks on Pedagogics, pp. 421-23).

John Dewey (1909, 1915, 1916) made democratic school life a centerpiece of progressive education. He believed that the way to prepare for a moral social life in the world was to engage in a moral social life in school. "The only way to prepare for social life is to engage in social life. To form habits of social usefulness and serviceableness apart from any direct social need and motive, apart from any existing social situation, is, to the letter, teaching the child to swim by going through motions outside the water" (Dewey, 1909, p. 14). Dewey believed that curriculum, teaching methods, and school culture were all part of enabling students to have social interest, social intelligence, and social power.

> In so far as the school represents, in its own spirit, a genuine community life; in so far as what are called school discipline, government, order, etc., are the expressions of this inherent social spirit; in so far as the methods used are those that appeal to the active and constructive powers, permitting the child to give out and thus to serve; in so far as the curriculum is so selected and organized as to provide the material for affording the child a consciousness of the world in which he has to play a part, and the demands he has to meet; so far as these ends are met, the school is organized on an ethical basis. (1909, pp. 43–44)

In this spirit, he advocated engaging students in meaningful cooperative activity as the primary vehicle for learning. Every subject was to be framed as a vehicle for understanding social life. He saw the school as a community in itself and yet intimately linked to the larger community. In fact, the school was to be a social center of community activity so that students could participate and experience the real life of the community and the community could benefit from the resources of the school. Learning by doing in the social arena meant involving students in actual social work. And democratic life in schools meant student participation in the making of rules, the care of the school, and social work in the community at large.

The themes of cooperative instruction, the integration of social concerns throughout the curriculum, student participation in school governance, direct student engagement in public life, and the school as a community were also articulated by such progressive theorists as George Counts, Harold Rugg, William Kilpatrick, John Childs, and Theodore Brameld throughout the first half of the twentieth century. These themes were also a central part of the National Education Association's highly influential *Cardinal Principles of Secondary Education* in 1918. The *Cardinal Principles* stressed "the assignment of projects and problems to groups of pupils for cooperative solution and the socialized recitation whereby the class as a whole develops a sense of collective responsibility. Both of these devices give training in collective thinking. Moreover, the democratic organization and administration of the school itself, as well as the cooperative relations of pupil and teacher, pupil and pupil, and teacher and teacher, are indispensable" (cited in Butts, 1980, p. 66 from National Education Association, Commission on the Reorganization of Secondary Education,

Cardinal Principles of Secondary Education, U.S. Bureau of Education, Bulletin #35 (Washington, DC: Government Printing Office, 1918), p. 14).

Educating for social responsibility was more than the rhetoric of educational philosophers and commissions. Four times in the twentieth century books have been written documenting "promising practices" that schools have initiated. In 1915, Dewey and his daughter wrote *Schools of To-morrow* to highlight how schools in Gary, Indianapolis, and other cities had implemented progressive educational philosophy. In Gary

> . . . schools do not teach civics out of a textbook. Pupils learn civics by helping to take care of their own school building, by making the rules for their own conduct in the halls and on the playgrounds, by going into the public library, and by listening to the stories of what Gary is doing as told by people who are doing it. They learn by a mock campaign, with parties, primaries, booths and ballots for the election of their own student council. Pupils who have made the furniture and the cement walks with their own hands, and who know how much it costs, are slow to destroy walks or furniture, nor are they going to be very easily fooled as to the value they get in service and improvements when they themselves become taxpayers. The health campaigns, the application work which takes them to the social agencies of the city, the auditorium periods when they learn more about their city, all give civics lessons that make their own appeal. The children can see the things with their own eyes; they are learning citizenship by being good citizens. (pp. 199–200)

The Indianapolis school had a functioning bank and a school garden tended by students, and students went on neighborhood campaigns to promote home gardens. Older students were paired with younger children to look out for their benefit and help them do well in school. The school also was a community center. Students did settlement work in the neighborhood. The school opened its shops and social rooms to the community after school. "The school comes in contact with almost all the families in a district so that community action is much easier to establish. But even more important than these economies are the far-reaching results which come from the fact that the school settlement is a democratic community, really reflecting the conditions of the community" (p. 225).

At the core of all these efforts are basic democratic principles and a desire to empower students to be effective citizens. The Deweys close *Schools of To-morrow* by affirming this central goal:

If we train our children to take orders, to do things simply because they are told to, and fail to give them confidence to act and think for themselves, we are putting an almost insurmountable obstacle in the way of overcoming the present defects of our system and of establishing the truth of democratic ideals. Our State is founded on freedom, but when we train the State of to-morrow, we allow it just as little freedom as possible. Children in school must be allowed freedom so that they will know what its use means when they become the controlling body, and they must be allowed to develop active qualities of initiative, independence, and resourcefulness, before the abuses and failures of democracy will disappear. (p. 304)

In 1940, the Educational Policies Commission of the National Education Association and the American Association of School Administrators published a case book of promising practices in civic education titled *Learning the Ways of Democracy.* This study of ninety secondary schools was probably the most extensive and encompassing review of practices. The study is framed by the concern that students need to live democracy in school in order to be effective citizens. The commission indicated that democratic values and practices need to be embedded in the course of study, the methods of teaching, and student life in the school and in the community at large. But, in addition, these values and practices need to be embedded in the administration of the school and in the evaluation of students. Set in the context of the emerging ideological threats to democracy of national socialism and communism, the commission hoped to enable students to experience the full meaning and potential of democracy.

The commission believed that democracy could be taught in every subject. They quote one art teacher as saying, "My chief interest in teaching is to help boys and girls become good American citizens. That is why I am teaching art. I know that sounds strange to you, but I chose to teach art because I believe that the art classroom can be the best laboratory of democratic living in the high school" (p. 127). They go on to say that "every classroom, laboratory, shop, and gymnasium may contribute to the development of democratic citizenship, if the teachers understand democratic principles and are skilled in their practical application to teaching. This requires something more than the rule-of-thumb learning of 'democratic teaching techniques.' It requires that teachers give careful study to the democratic ideal and its implications for life in America today; that they care deeply about the effects of their teaching on the civic behavior of young people; and that they be willing to submit their own familiar teaching practices to unsparing scrutiny in the light of the demo- cratic ideal, and to cast aside all that is inconsistent with democracy" (p. 187). If every teacher is to be involved in educating for democracy then "the implications for the professional education of teachers are far-reaching. Every teacher, in every field—not only the teachers of social studies— should have a well-grounded understanding of American democracy and thorough preservice experience with democratic classroom practices. Furthermore, every teacher should be expected to keep reasonably well informed regarding the major contemporary problems and issues of public life" (p. 187).

To demonstrate how this was implemented in the area of curriculum and instruction they point to such practices as realistic courses on con- temporary problems, discussions of controversial issues where divergent points of view are heard in an open and respectful way, contemporary issues taught across the curriculum, interdisciplinary courses on human problems, students working together cooperatively to deal with problems in and outside of school, cooperative methods of instruction replacing competitive methods, students being involved in projects of service to others, students involving themselves in "social action," and cross-age tutoring and newcomer programs. Their recommendations for community service and social action are rigorous. They point out that the programs that most effectively educate for democracy are ones where the problem is of vital interest to students, where students are able to effect real change and produce real benefits for the community, where their efforts are guided by democratic values in decision making, and where students "go beyond the immediate problem and seek to define and grapple with deeper issues" (p. 327).

In terms of school culture and student participation in decision making, they point to such efforts as democratic decision making in student organizations, students coplanning their courses with teachers, students managing their own classrooms when the teacher is absent or called away, newspapers modeling the free press, the school as a community center leading "in great social advances," cooperative management strategies that involve teachers and students in a variety of forms of shared decision making, student government that makes meaningful decisions, a student leadership course to support student government, students and teachers jointly filling out evaluation forms, and the use of student goal setting and self-evaluation. The school is seen as a community that respects the individual, addresses individual needs, but also helps students think in terms of common interests and collective needs. The nature of the democratic community they talk about is more circumscribed than the ones Kohlberg and Battistich and their colleagues have worked to develop, and the historical context of the rise of totalitarianism moves them to take a more patriotic and supportive view of U.S. policy than the early progressives. But their conception of democracy is clearly participatory and their emphasis is having students live rather than simply learn about democracy in as many aspects of school life as possible.

In 1967, promising practices in the area of social studies education were documented by the National Council for the Social Studies (NCSS) and explicitly titled *Promising Practices in Civic Education* (Robinson, 1967). Based on nominations of the best civic education programs, a four-person team visited eighty-three middle and high schools for one, two, or three days. Although focused on social studies instruction and more circumscribed than the previous two, the promising practices they identified followed the same pattern we have seen. They included such practices as realistic engagement with and open discussion of contemporary issues, consideration of opposing perspectives on issues, cultural exchange both of cultures within the United States and internationally, the development of critical thinking skills, direct engagement with local government, community service opportunities, student government with real responsibility, model experiences such as the Model U.N., student leadership conferences, and a schoolwide commitment to political participation on the part of students and faculty.

Their work, however, presaged a resurgence in interest in citizenship education moved in part by poor results on the 1969 and 1976 national assessments of educational progress. This resurgence continued into the 1980s. Many of the leaders of this movement, often past-presidents of the NCSS, took a much bolder view than that articulated by the NCSS in 1967. Byron Massialas (1972), an NCSS president and early leader in this movement, called for a "radical" program for citizenship. It included democratic school governance, integration of social and political issues throughout the curriculum, honest and penetrating discussions of pressing social issues, revision of civics and history to focus on conflict and analysis, and use of inquiry forms of instruction. Others added moral education, real-life decision making, community service, political consciousness, political action, and institutional change to this list (Berlak, 1977; Butts, 1980; Engle & Ochoa, 1988; Fenton, 1977; Mehlinger, 1977; Newmann, 1975; Reische, 1987). Taking this one step further, George Wood (1988a, 1988b, 1992), the director for the Institute of Democracy in Education, argued for the democratization of schools through direct student participation in decision making, equity in access to the curriculum, and community-building in classrooms and schools. Giroux (1988) went even further in arguing that democratic empowerment of students meant an emancipatory form of citizenship based on the principles of critique and action and grounded in the reality of the inequitable distribution of power in our society. "Citizenship . . . becomes a process of dialogue and commitment rooted in a fundamental belief in the possibility of public life and the development of forms of solidarity that allow people to reflect and organize in order to criticize and constrain the power of the state and to 'overthrow relations which inhibit and prevent the realization of humanity' " (p. 6). The 1980s saw the formation of two organizations, Educators for Social Responsibility and the Institute for Democracy in Education, that have served as resources to teachers and schools in creating these changes and as public advocates for democratic reforms in schools. Although there are many differences among these educational leaders, they would all agree with Mehlinger's (1977) statement that "it seems unlikely that a reform of civic education . . . can be achieved by the development of new curriculum materials or by in-service teacher education alone. New patterns for working with schools as total social systems must be invented and tested" (Mehlinger, 1977, p. 81).

Again in 1993, many of the successful practices that were identified by the research studies of chapter 5, documented in previous promising practices books, and called for by educational leaders were documented by Berman and LaFarge in *Promising Practices in Teaching Social Responsibility*. Emphasizing that social responsibility is developed by an integration of curriculum, teaching methods, and classroom and school culture and organization, they provide portraits of how teachers and administrators in a diverse range of classrooms and schools build social responsibility into their efforts. Again the same themes emerge: the integration of social issues throughout the curriculum, cooperative learning, community-building in the classroom and school, the teaching of conflict resolution, democratic classroom and school governance structures, and community service and political action.

The Reality of Civic Education in the Classroom: Teachers, Texts, and the Conception of Citizenship

In spite of this rich and continuous history of philosophy, policy, and practice, these classrooms and schools have always been the exception rather than the rule. In fact, the curriculum, teaching methods, and school governance and culture in most schools undermine rather than promote social responsibility. Most of the resurgence of interest in citizenship education and social responsibility was built on the acknowledgment that current efforts were failing and are still failing. The results of the most recent National Assessment of Educational Progress (Anderson et al., 1990) showed continued decline in citizenship knowledge. Ehman (1980), in his review of the literature on citizenship education, found that the current social studies curriculum had little impact on such basic political attitudes as political interest, efficacy, or participation. In 1972, Massialas declared that "what is presently offered in the school is basically obsolete, irrelevant, and has no social or political significance" (p. xii). Shaver (1977), also a past-president of the National Council for the Social Studies, concurred, "Despite the conscientious efforts of many educators, citizenship education is in disarray. There is little evidence to indicate that the school's citizenship education efforts have affected generally the quantity or quality of adult citizen participation, and social studies programs and school environments often appear to be inconsistent with the demands of 'adult citizenship' " (1977, p. vii). Ten years later Reische (1987), in a report written for the American Association of School Administrators, identified a long list of reports indicating the failure of the public schools' citizenship efforts (p. 12). Although texts have been updated and some teaching methods have changed, these statements are appropriate today.

Studies of the general patterns of teaching show that current instructional methods run counter to the strategies that are effective in promoting social responsibility. Jackson's (1968) study of fifty classrooms highlighted how coping with the crowds, praise, and power of the school's hidden curriculum fostered compliance rather than democratic participation.

> We have already seen that many features of classroom life call for patience, at best, and resignation, at worst. As he learns to live in school, our student learns to subjugate his own desires to the will of the teacher and to subdue his own actions in the interest of the common good. He learns to be passive and to acquiesce

to the network of rules, regulations, and routines in which he is embedded. He learns to tolerate petty frustrations and to accept the plans and policies of higher authorities, even when their rationale is unexplained and their meaning unclear. Like the inhabitants of most other institutions, he learns how to shrug and say, "That's the way the ball bounces." (pp. 58–59)

Twenty years later Goodlad (1984) and Sirotnik (1988) reported on observations of over 1,000 classrooms and found little change. Lecturing was the dominant form of instruction at both the elementary and secondary levels. Students working independently on assignments was the next most frequent use of class time. Group work, demonstrations, discussion, role plays, and simulations were among the rarest activities in the classroom. Students spoke 20 percent of the instructional time yet most of this was in response to questions addressed to them that demanded basic recall and comprehension skills. The study found minimal time spent on questions that asked for higher-order thinking, or comments that provided corrective feedback, guidance, praise, or encouragement. In fact, few statements had emotional content at all; most were categorized as emotionally neutral. "For whatever reasons, it seems clear that many curricular expectations established by typical arrays of common goals for American public schools enjoy little in the way of empirical support based upon what goes on in classrooms. In fact, if these expectations were aligned with typical classroom life, goal statements in the formal curriculum would read more like this: to develop in students the abilities to think linearly, depend upon authority, speak when spoken to, work alone, become socially apathetic, learn passively and nonexperientially, recall information, follow instructions, compartmentalize knowledge, and so on" (Sirotnik, 1988, p. 62).

Cuban (1984) specifically studied the impact of reform efforts to shift teaching to a more child-centered approach. In his review of data from 7,000 classrooms over the past one hundred years, he found that classrooms are now less formal and accept greater mobility, noise, and diverse grouping methods. He also found that during certain periods there have been significant changes in instructional methods, but these were not durable. Over the long term, little change has occurred in teacher-directed instruction. Only approximately 25 percent of the teacher population accepted any child-centered techniques and only 5 to 10 percent, mostly at the early elementary level, changed their teaching approach to a child-centered approach. "Drawn from a large number of varied sources in diverse settings over nearly a century, the data show striking convergence in outlining a stable core of teacher-centered instructional activities in the elementary school and, in high school classrooms, a remarkably pure and durable version of the same set of activities" (p. 238).

In terms of the promotion of social responsibility, these patterns mean that instead of an open classroom atmosphere that encourages discussion and student-initiated interaction, we see teacher-dominated classrooms with little peer interaction. Instead of cooperative learning environments that use small-group instruction and promote helping behavior, we see individualist or competitive environments that discourage prosocial behavior. Instead of nurturant, caring, and mutually supportive relationships, we see neutrality. Instead of controversy and conflict, we see discipline and obedience. Instead of participation in decision making, we see teacher control over the curriculum and the classroom environment and administrator control over the school building. Instead of learning through direct engagement in the political and social world, we see students confined to lectures, standardized texts, and written assignments. The classroom and the school are not democratic communities.

The data are even more telling when we look at the specific strategies within the social studies, which, as of the early twentieth century, assumed the major responsibility for citizenship instruction. The standard pattern of instruction, dominated by lecture, recitation, and individual written assignments and supported by a standardized text, was even clearer in the social studies (Fancett & Hawke, 1982; Lengel & Superka, 1982; Stake & Easley, 1978; Weiss, 1978). In study after study (Andrain, 1971; Cox & Massialas, 1967; Ehman, 1980; Hess & Torney, 1967; Jennings & Niemi, 1974; Moore et al., 1985; Morrissett, 1982; Torney et al., 1975), researchers have found that civic education, especially at the elementary level, has focused on compliance to rules, obedience to authority, and indoctrination of uncritical loyalty and patriotism. Instruction has emphasized patriotic symbols and rituals over meaning, offered an overly positive view of government and its leaders, avoided controversy, and promoted a highly individualistic conception of citizenship. Hess and Torney (1967), in their study of second through eighth graders, commented that:

> These rituals establish an emotional orientation toward country and flag even though an understanding of the meaning of the words and actions has not been developed. These seem to be indoctrinating acts that cue and reinforce feelings of loyalty and

patriotism. This early orientation prepares the child for later learning and stresses the importance of loyalty for citizens of all ages. . . . *Compliance to rules and authority is the major focus of civics education in elementary schools.* . . . Teachers of young children place particular stress upon citizen compliance, de-emphasizing all other political topics. The three items rated as more important than basic subjects (reading and arithmetic) by a majority of second- and third-grade teachers were *the law, the policeman,* and the child's *obligation to conform* to school rules and laws of the community. This concern with compliance is characteristic of teachers of all grades and parallels most closely the importance placed upon national symbols at these grades. . . . In summary, political social- ization at early age levels emphasizes behavior that relates the child emotionally to his country and impresses upon him the necessity for obedience and conformity. . . . The citizen's right to participate in government is not emphasized in the school curriculum. The importance placed upon the citizen's active participation (his power, right to express opinion, effectiveness, voting) shows a pattern different from the emphasis placed upon attachment to country and compliance to law. The citizen's power to influence government is stressed very little until the fourth grade and is not given equal emphasis with the citizen's duties until the seventh and eighth grades. The role of political parties and partisanship receives less attention in the elementary school than any other topic. (pp. 105–10)

Almost twenty years later, in studying the development of political consciousness in elementary school children, Moore, Lare, and Wagner (1985) also found that obedience was a central theme of civics instruction. "This relatively narrow, obedience-dominated approach to good citizenship introduced primarily by classroom teachers gives an early impetus to a model of political obligation that is more passive than it is active" (p. 162).

In spite of the fact that studies have shown that when conflict and controversy were included in the civics curriculum students gained in knowledge as well as in interest, efficacy, and participation (Button, 1974; Ehman, 1972; Hoover, 1967; Torney-Purta, 1981; Torney et al., 1975), teachers and texts have avoided issues of conflict, especially at the ele- mentary level. At the elementary level, Moore, Lare, and Wagner (1985) found that "the public school classrooms have not been very effective in introducing school children to the conflicting values that lie at the heart of a democratic process" (p. 236). Sigel (1979) found the same thing at the high school level. "The conflict aspect of democracy tends to be deemphasized in instructional materials at the elementary and secondary school levels in spite of the fact that its recognition is vital for a genuine understanding of democracy" (p. 48). Engle and Ochoa (1988), two leaders in social studies education, comment that in social studies instruction "controversial issues are usually avoided, and if they are mentioned at all, it is likely that they will be treated superficially as merely the reporting of current events or the pooling of ignorance, rather than with the depth of consideration that the serious study of social problems requires" (p. 108).

Studies of teachers in general and of social studies teachers in particular have found a strong reliance on standardized texts. The most recent National Assessment of Educational Progress in citizenship education (Anderson et al., 1990) found that "reading a textbook appears to be the most common mode of instruction by far, as 90 percent of the eighth graders and 87 percent of the twelfth graders reported being asked to read material in their textbooks either daily or weekly. . . . Nearly half of the students in each grade were expected to memorize information they had read on a daily or weekly basis" (p. 83). There have been some major changes in social studies texts in the past twenty years. They are more colorful and graphic. They deal with ethnic diversity more explicitly. They talk more about our society's shortcomings and about issues that were once thought controversial. Yet, reviews of these materials (Anyon, 1978; Beck, McKeown, & Gromoll, 1989; Carroll et al., 1989; FitzGerald, 1979; Fox & Hess, 1972; Goldstein, 1972; Litt, 1963; Patrick & Hawke, 1982; Turner, 1971; Woodward, Elliot, & Nagel, 1986) have consistently found the same patterns. In spite of the changes publishers have made, social studies texts tend to be dull collections of facts with little context to hold these facts together.

In a recent review (Carroll et al., 1989), a commission of educators and educational leaders convened by People For the American Way found that "while they [social studies texts] are impressive collections of facts, they are intellectually and pedagogically dull tools for inspiring effective participation in the democratic political process. Many of the books are largely disembodied expositions of principles and facts, lacking the passion of the conflicts that infuse politics and government with meaning and significance" (p. iv).

FitzGerald (1979) came to the same conclusion in his earlier review. The texts lacked the deeper levels of analysis of issues, problems, and underlying causes. They lack analysis of theoretical and political controversy that allows students to make sense of our current circumstances and conflicts. He used as an example the discussion of poverty in a typical text, Wood, Gabriel, and Biller's *America: Its People and Values*. "The text does not, of course, raise the profound question of whether poverty—if only relative poverty—is built into the structure of capitalism. In fact, it does not even suggest that there might be some conflict between the interests of the poor and the interests of the rich. Or that in such conflicts the richest and most powerful groups tend to have disproportionate influence over the government" (p. 113).

In fact, what stands out most significantly throughout all these reviews is the diminishing of conflict. The People For the American Way study (Carroll et al., 1989) indicated that "what is missing, in a word, is controversy. Eighty percent of civics books and half of the government books minimize conflict and compromise. The dynamic sense of government and politics—fierce debates, colorful characters, triumphs and tragedies—is lost. Controversies like school prayer and civil rights that have ignited passions at all points along the political spectrum are ignored or barely mentioned. The vitality of political involvement and the essential give and take between people and their elected officials is neglected. One text drily asserts, 'Conflicts . . . between citizens and government may be settled according to law.' Most important, the crucial role of participation is not highlighted" (p. i). FitzGerald (1979) points out that conflicts are often framed as depersonalized problems that have either been solved or will be solved. In this way no one is at fault and the problem appears adequately dealt with. He also points out that although social studies texts talk about the civil rights movement or the women's movement, the actual struggles of these groups to attain their civil rights is only mentioned in passing with little substance about the difficulties and pain these groups encountered.

> Though most books delineate the social and economic institutions that made life so hard for the nineteenth-century immigrants, they do not always do the same for the non-white Americans in modern times. The Chicano farmworkers are struggling, but some texts fail to mention the growers. The American Indians are struggling in a void, there being no mention of the historical arrangements between private corporations and the Bureau of Indian Affairs for the exploitation of natural resources on tribal lands. In regard to the civil-rights movement, there is often no discussion of institutional racism—not even that which was contained in the Southern

school systems before Little Rock. The books report at length on reform movements and reform measures but rarely take up the results, thus giving little or no indication that many of the attempts at reform have failed. This is hardly surprising, since they usually fail to explain in any detail how or why the injustices came into being in the first place. . . . Furthermore, only the most sophisticated of the inquiry books report any of the 'struggles to achieve full rights' from the point of view of the strugglers. (pp. 101–2)

Woodward, Elliot, and Nagel (1986) report a similar finding. Although many new texts deal with such contemporary problems and future challenges as civil rights, the environment, space travel, and energy resources, "this coverage was so scanty or disconnected that students find it difficult to understand the depth of passion these issues produced or their relevance to society today" (p. 51).

Some areas of conflict are specifically avoided. Social class is rarely mentioned. Equally rare is any detailed economic analysis. Anyon (1978) indicates that even the terminology used when discussing our economic system obfuscates conflict. By using phrases as the free enterprise or free market system and focusing on our freedom of choice only in the area of consumption, they ignore such issues as the inequitable distribution of economic power and wealth characteristic of the capitalist system and promote an uncritical acceptance of our economic system. In terms of political conflict and change, the texts emphasize voting and letter writing and downplay more assertive means of advocacy. In general they paint an overly positive and optimistic view that problems will be addressed and rectified by the prevailing political authorities and practices.

In 1972, Goldstein reviewed thirty commonly used texts and fifteen commonly used curriculum guides and found their portrayal of the country, government, and government officials highly favorable. He concludes that "through sins of commission and omission, it is clear that the material on the United States, the U.S. government, and citizenship and on race and social class constitutes at best a sugarcoating of history and reality and at worst a rewriting of history to eliminate unpleasant facts. . . . This type of educational approach appears unworthy of a great democracy that not infrequently boasts about its passion for truth and criticizes other countries for rewriting history to suit their own purposes" (p. 30). Although there is a more balanced approach in some current texts, most are still relatively nationalistic, positive, and simplistic in their portrayals. Texts geared to the middle-school level and those used in poor, minority, and working-class school districts are especially so (Anyon, 1978). Multiple perspectives are generally missing from all but the inquiry texts (Carroll et al., 1989; FitzGerald, 1979). And even in the inquiry texts the perspectives are severely limited to ones that are generally more acceptable.

These patterns continue. The most recent tome on what everyone should know about citizenship has been published by the Center for Citizenship Education. Like the others, *CIVITAS* (Bahmueller, 1991) provides a disconnected view of history devoid of analysis. It diminishes conflict and controversy. It often portrays the United States in a positive and noncontroversial role when, in fact, U.S. policy was quite controversial. It creates the aura of academic neutrality when its approach and content are, in fact, biased. It fails to present alternative perspectives and examine the deeper sources of problems. Its encyclopedic account of history and politics merely touches the surface of the meaning and fullness of citizenship and perpetuates the educationally destructive patterns of the previous texts.

All the studies point out the disservice this kind of text does to encouraging thoughtful democratic participation among young people. FitzGerald concludes that "to the extent that young people actually believe them, these bland fictions, propagated for the purpose of creating good citizens, may actually achieve the opposite; they give young people no warning of the real dangers ahead, and later they may well make these young people feel that their own experience of conflict or suffering is unique in history and perhaps un-American. To the extent that children can see the contrast between these fictions and the world around them, this kind of instruction can only make them cynical" (p. 218). The People For the American Way study (Carroll et al., 1989) indicates that "the result of this dry recitation of facts is texts that encourage young people to be bystanders in democracy rather than active citizens. These texts fail to instill a sense of civic responsibility, challenge students to think critically, or urge them to get involved in public life" (p. ii).

The problem may be at even a deeper level than teaching methods and texts. The very conception of citizenship that teachers and students hold and that is used to frame instruction is limited. It focuses attention primarily on being a good person rather than being actively engaged in the political process, on protecting self-interest rather than promoting the common good, and on the individual as the locus of responsibility rather than institutional, systemic, or structural aspects of our political culture.

The social studies and citizenship literature tend to define citizenship in terms of participation in political and governmental processes. For example, Farquhar and Dawson (1979), in a U.S. Office of Education publication summarizing the initiatives that need to be taken to improve citizenship education, use a definition that is common in the literature. They indicate that citizenship education involves "the development of knowledge, skills, and attitudes requisite to responsible and effective participation in civic life" (p. 1). This definition is not translated into classroom reality, however. Newmann (1975) points out that although this conception articulates a participatory intent, the underlying orientation is to have students understand, describe, or explain rather than exert an impact. What emerges in practice is that participation is not what teachers and students view as critical to citizenship. Democracy is treated as something we already have rather than an ongoing experiment and an active social movement. Dynneson and Gross (1991) surveyed students and teachers in four states and found that students and teachers generally reported a nonparticipatory and nongovernmental definition of good citizenship. They asked students to categorize a list of characteristics into what are and what are not important qualities of a good citizen. Students ranked concern for the welfare of others and the ability to make wise decisions as most important. In addition, being moral and ethical in dealings with other people ranked highly. Yet, most placed participation in community and school affairs and knowledge of government in the "what is not important" category. Fowler (1990), reporting on the *Democracy's Next Generation* study, found the same pattern. The good citizen was equated with the good person—being honest, trustworthy, or a good friend. "Their notion of a good citizen rarely had a social or political dimension, and only 12 percent believed that voting was an important part of citizenship" (p. 11). Dynneson and Gross found that social studies teachers tended to see citizenship in this personalized and nonparticipatory manner as well. In the *Democracy's Next Generation* study (Hart Research, 1989) only 26 percent of the teachers interviewed identified being involved and concerned as a defining characteristic of citizenship (p. 75).

This lack of interest in participation in political processes stands in contrast to a student's interest in helping others. The *Democracy's Next Generation* study found that the fifteen- to twenty-four-year-olds they interviewed rejected the notion that "people should take care of themselves and shouldn't expect others to do things for them" (p. 18) and described themselves as likely to engage in helping an elderly neighbor, collecting money for a needy cause, or working an hour a week on a community project. In fact, over one-third of their sample had performed some form of community or neighborhood service within the past year. The study indicates that "the emphasis by many young people on compassion, coupled with the fact that a substantial minority have indeed performed and, they report, experienced the intangible rewards of community service within the past year suggests an underlying generosity of spirit" (p. 30).

When schools are not able to make politics salient for students and when they avoid the controversy and conflict inherent in the political process, then participatory definitions become hollow and teachers and students look for other arenas in which responsibility may matter. Oliner (1983) argues that the standard conception of citizenship has focused too strongly on "the government" and not sufficiently on participatory community-building processes that are accessible to students. She points out that this focus on government encourages feelings of impotence and alienation, externalizes the locus of responsibility and minimizes personal accountability, leaves little for the citizen to do, and fails to direct students toward behaviors that build emotionally satisfying relationships and integrative community linkages. However, instead of recommending that schools bring students in closer relationship with the diverse participatory processes available in the social and political world, she too moves in the direction of personalizing citizenship efforts. She indicates that citizenship education should place primary importance on relationships among students and focus on building community.

In addition to the personalized and nonparticipatory way teachers and students tend to see citizenship, they define it in terms of protecting one's self-interest rather than promoting the common good. Sigel and Hoskin (1981) found high school seniors' notions of democracy were restricted to an emphasis on providing them with individual freedom rather than involving them in participatory responsibility. Sinatra, Beck, and McKeown (1992) found that the fifth and eighth graders they interviewed viewed freedom as a personal issue not grounded in aspects of government. The researchers note that "the right of citizens to participate in their government and the idea that the United States is a representative system were two concepts that were not evident in students' responses to a great extent" (p. 659). The *Democracy's Next Generation* study found the same pattern. Students were enchanted by our "freedom to do as we please, when we please" (Hart Research, 1989, p. 14) but did not feel any obligation to participate in governmental decision making. In Sigel and Hoskin's study, students indicated that they would enter the political arena only when their individual interests were threatened.

The emphasis on protecting one's self-interest is a classic part of most definitions of citizenship. Exemplary is Remy's (1980a) definition in his widely distributed *Handbook on Basic Citizenship Competencies*. He states that "citizenship competence refers to the quality of a person's participation individually or with others in processes related to group governance such as making decisions, protecting one's interests, or communicating effectively with group leaders. This includes the capacity to act individually in one's own behalf and the capacity to act in concert with others" (p. 15). What is missing is a consideration of collective interest and the common good. As Bellah and his coauthors argue in their studies of American political culture (1985, 1991), the focus on individualism and self-interest has undermined our sense of civic community and has destructively fragmented our political processes and identity. Newmann (1990) is even more pointed in his critique of this emphasis on self-interest, indicating that we need to move from a privatistic view of civic life to a more publicly minded view of democracy.

> The dominant conception of citizenship conveyed in media and in the teaching of civics, government and political science acts like a virus that weakens our civic culture. According to the dominant conception, the democratic citizen is a person who learns how to advance one's private interests through rational, critically-minded participation in the choosing of governing elites and who supports the essential democratic procedures and institutions (electoral politics, checks and balances, civil liberties) that presumably permit maximum freedom for others to do the same. . . . [T]his view of citizenship fails to deliver the democratic promise of empowerment of the governed, it produces vast inequalities in material opportunity, it deprives humans of critical forms of intercourse and personal growth which only participatory democracy can provide, and it threatens the very survival of the human species and the planet. (p. 77)

An additional result of defining citizenship in terms of individual self-interest is that it places the locus of responsibility for social problems on the individual rather than on institutional, systemic, or structural aspects of our political culture (Giroux, 1983a). This promotes a belief that each individual is responsible for his or her success or failure in society. It promotes a "blame-the-victim" mentality that sees poverty as the result of poor peoples' laziness, drug abuse as the result of the abuser's lack of will, teenage pregnancy as the lack of family values, and crime as a result of personal greed. Maintaining an individually focused conception of citizenship, in essence, leaves the basic nature of existing social arrangements unquestioned. Injustice is produced by individual acts that harm others rather than institutional arrangements that are, in themselves, unjust. Inequality is produced by individual incompetence or individual failure to compete within the existing structure rather than by systemic patterns and structural barriers.

This individualistic conception is even present in most of the moral education programs. The whole emphasis of Kohlberg's approach is on individual development rather than development in relationship to an existing political context. Weinreich-Haste (1986) argues that Kohlberg's approach ignores structural inequalities of the social system and perpetuates the myth of individual efficacy in making moral and political change. His approach suffers from "too much weight given to the individual as an effective political agent, too little appreciation of historical, cultural and economic factors in social change, and too great an emphasis on the analysis of *individual* behaviour. One major manifestation of this is the failure to make a distinction between democratic interaction at the interpersonal level, and democratic relations between the social group and the state" (p. 341).

The lack of awareness of institutional and structural causes of social problems and the emphasis on individual responsibility is very clear in young people's beliefs about their relationship to the social world. Merelman (1986) points out that young people in the United States internalize early a conception of steep, unjustified inequality while at the same time believing that they, as individuals, would escape the traps of this inequality and improve their condition. Sigel and Hoskin (1981), Levine (1983), and Hart Research (1989) found this a common theme in the young people they interviewed. Because the conception of citizenship is so focused on individual responsibility it deprives students of participating in the kind of social and political analysis that would enable them to reflect on their political attitudes, to establish an "ideological framework," and to make sense of their circumstances and their potential for participation.

This is not to argue for a purely collectivist notion of citizenship, a notion often embedded in the uncritically patriotic conceptions of past citizenship efforts. It is an argument for a balance between the two that illuminates both their congruence and their tensions. Individual responsibility is critical to social responsibility. Each of our actions, or our failures to act, creates the world as it is. But equally critical to social responsibility is the ability to examine larger social arrangements, to consider changes in institutions, to look for the root systemic causes of problems, to support collective interests, to see ourselves as part of a larger interdependent community, and to effectively balance the common good with the protection of individual and minority rights.

The contrast between the promising practices discussed at the beginning of this chapter and the common practices in classrooms and schools is a stark one. In actuality, only a small number of teachers and administrators integrate these practices into their instructional program. The results that Cuban found for child-centered practices in the general teaching populations are probably appropriate for practices that promote social responsibility. In fact, this is what the ELNA curriculum assessment showed in the nine relatively progressive, suburban Boston districts that used it. A small percentage of teachers used many of the strategies listed on the assessment in their classrooms. A larger percentage, probably larger than Cuban's 25 percent, had integrated a number of specific practices into their current teaching. The majority of teachers had not thought of social responsibility as an important goal in their teaching but found that they were already using some of the most general strategies on the list, such as "helping students appreciate human differences" and "helping students understand others' points of view." Interestingly, the areas that received least attention were uniform throughout these nine districts and affirm the lack of attention given to participatory conceptions of citizenship. In almost every district the item that ranked lowest was "teaching about the ways individuals and groups influence social and political change." Also low on the list were "helping students develop confidence in their ability to effect positive change on local and/or global issues," "involving students in community service or some form of assisting people in need," and "teaching about current social and political issues in a way that is age-appropriate and fits my curriculum."

Persistent Patterns

Although the overwhelming majority of school districts refer to citizenship or social responsibility in their mission statements or statements of philosophy, and although social responsibility has historically been a central purpose for public education, the data show that practices that actually facilitate social responsibility are the exception rather than the rule. Why is this the case? Why does this pattern in teaching methods, texts, and conceptions of citizenship persist?

One reason is that citizenship education has shifted from the over-arching goal of schools in the nineteenth century to the responsibility of a single discipline, social studies, in the twentieth. Even within the social studies it is one of many responsibilities. Meyer (1979), writing for the Education Commission of the States, describes a pattern of diminishing attention and priority given to citizenship education:

> Originally, in the public school concept, citizenship education was the primary focus of all education; by the mid-19th century, it had become identified with the social studies—particularly the civics class—and thus was treated more and more as a special area of study, or a 'course,' rather than a total school purpose. Then after Sputnik came a high emphasis on scientific methods, with resultant reduction of interest in the socialization processes. Even some social scientists felt that 'citizenship' was not an intellectually worthy goal of education. During the same period, the trend toward electives as well as a general broadening introduced many competing subjects and courses. Thus, from being an overall priority concern, citizenship education was gradually relegated to a single discipline—a few courses; and then those courses were submerged in the proliferation of interests and concerns taken on by the school. (p. 15)

Added to this is the fact that there is no one in the school district who is expected as part of his or her daily work to advocate for a broad conception of citizenship. As Newmann (1977) points out,

> Teachers must teach particular subjects they learned (from academicians specializing in academic disciplines, not citizenship). Curriculum developers must invent new packages to fit into a fragmented network of existing school courses; and publishers must sell those products, regardless of their relevance to a general phi-losophy of citizenship. School administrators (especially principals and superintendents) are expected perhaps more than anyone else to consider the entire schooling process. Yet they must demonstrate

their competence to the public not by building educational rationales, but by managing personnel and budgets to avoid institutional difficulties. In short, the particular roles required of teachers, academicians, curriculum developers, publishers, and administrators tend to divert attention away from the task of creating a general integrated philosophy of civic education. (p. 11)

A second reason these patterns have persisted is that teaching social responsibility means engaging students directly in controversy and politics. Controversy and politics are two areas that administrators and teachers are reticent to tackle for fear of community retribution or attacks from right-wing or back-to-basics groups. In fact, these have been historically avoided by schools. Horace Mann set this tone in the early establishment of the public schools. He was afraid that children would be harmed by entertaining issues of social conflict and parents would withdraw their children from the schools. He proposed that the schools should teach the things upon which there was common agreement and not deal with controversy. Mann wrote:

Surely, between these extremes, there must be a medium not difficult to be found. And is not this the middle course, which all sensible and judicious men, all patriots, and all genuine republicans, must approve?—namely, that those articles in the creed of republicanism, which are accepted by all, believed in by all, and which form the common basis of our political faith, shall be taught to all. But when the teacher, in the course of his lessons or lectures on the fundamental law, arrives at a controversial text, he is either to read it without comment or remark; or, at most, he is only to say that the passage is the subject of disputation, and that the schoolroom is neither the tribunal to adjudicate, nor the forum to discuss it.

Such being the rule established by common consent, and such the practice, observed with fidelity under it, it will come to be universally understood, that political proselytism is no function of the school; but that all indoctrination into matters of controversy between hostile political parties is to be elsewhere sought for, and elsewhere imparted. Thus, may all the children of the Commonwealth receive instruction in the great essentials of political knowledge,—in those elementary ideas without which they will never be able to investigate more recondite and debatable questions. (cited in Butts, 1980, p. 60–61)

Mann's approach meant that political knowledge would focus on the formal structure of governmental institutions and avoid skills related to participation. However, direct engagement in controversy and politics does not need to mean indoctrination. Many social studies educators have recommended ways to approach controversy and politics that are balanced, thorough, educative, and engaging, without being propagandistic. Although many teachers and administrators would support this kind of engagement, few have any incentive—other than good educational practice—to take the risk of exposing themselves to the criticism that these practices might incur. In fact, educators tend to shy away from political engagement themselves feeling that this kind of activity is not appropriate (Carson, Goldhammer, & Pellegrin, 1967; Hart Research, 1989; Washburn, 1986; Zeigler, 1967).

Giroux (1983a, 1988) points out that raising issues of social responsibility opens up areas to consideration that may challenge existing relationships of power and accepted belief systems. He indicates that "citizenship education's own problematic must begin with the question of whether or not this society should be changed in a particular way or be left the way it is" (1983a, p. 193). To adequately confront the vital and compelling questions posed by citizenship within a democracy means juxtaposing our political, social, and economic system against a set of ethical standards and against a vision of our collective potential. This kind of exploration raises basic questions of equality and power. It asks the question of what it means to create a democracy that lives by ethical standards. It holds out our mistreatment of others and asks how we can live in ways where we respect each other and treat each other fairly. It asks how power and wealth should be shared. It asks about what protections—economic and social as well as political—should be guaranteed to each of us by all of us. It asks how we can change social structures so that our society becomes a better place in which to live. And it asks us to look at our personal behavior by those same ethical and visionary standards and to act with integrity, responsibility, and care. Consideration of controversy and direct participation in political processes tend to open up these questions of inequality, power, and ideology and may cause some students to question or to propose changes in our political system, our social beliefs, and our international relationships. Not all students will challenge accepted notions but some will, and few educators are prepared to undertake an open examination of these issues. Giroux and other reconceptualists argue that it is not just teachers' competence and caution that inhibits this but the vested social and political interests that would find their position challenged by serious ethical examination. The current system is perpetuated so that these questions are not asked, and the inequitable distribution of wealth and power remains unchallenged.

Some teachers avoid political and social controversy for additional reasons. Not only do they feel disconnected from the world of politics but they believe that children will not be able to understand or learn from their engagement with the political world. Political and social controversies are complex and solutions unclear. It is sometimes difficult to know if one has made a difference in spite of the best of efforts. Government and government leaders seem distant and inaccessible. It is often easier not to try to create change because then one doesn't risk disappointment. These teachers reason that it is better to protect children from engagement in the political world until, as adults, they can adequately understand the complexities of social and political issues and the difficulties of creating change.

A third reason for the continuing dominance of patterns of instruction that undermine social responsibility is the demands of the existing curriculum. On the ELNA assessment, there was an open-ended question that asked teachers what their greatest obstacle was to doing more in terms of social responsibility. The overwhelming answer was time and the demands of the curriculum. The expectations for what teachers should accomplish is already extremely demanding. Their flexibility is limited by district-wide curriculum objectives and standardized tests. Their day— and, in fact, their year—is highly structured. They are often not given the time to think about significant changes in their teaching methods nor are they provided with support should they decide to initiate change.

Kohlberg found this to be the case in his work in moral education. Kohlberg (1985) trained a group of teachers to lead moral dilemma discussions in their classrooms. These teachers led discussions throughout the next year, and over half the teachers were able to have a significant impact on their students' moral reasoning. Yet, when the researchers went back the next year to see if these teachers were continuing the dilemma discussions, they found that not one did. Kohlberg wrote that "while the intervention operation was a success, the patient died; that is, we went back a year later and found not a single teacher continued to do moral discussions after the commitment to the research had ended. In other words, it didn't speak enough to the teachers' and students' needs, even though it did lead to a one-third stage change" (p. 33). Kohlberg credited this to the demands of the curriculum and claimed that the solution was to integrate moral education into existing frameworks. Schaps, in his work on the Child Development Project, also notes how difficult it is for teachers to change in spite of the extensive training offered them by the project (personal communication, 1993). Cuban (1984) agrees and suggests that the reason for stability across one hundred years of advocacy for child-centered approaches is a mix of the inhibiting effect of the current school structure and the external corporate and college demands placed on teachers and administrators.

However, probably the most significant reason that the promising qualities of the practices that foster social responsibility are not more compelling to teachers and administrators is that they demand significant changes in teaching methods and in school culture. Democratizing one's classroom or school means giving up some control, respecting points of view that one might not want to contend with, and changing one's practice in ways that may be significant. It means involving students in authentic decision making about classroom rules, structures, and procedures. Creating schools and classrooms that are democratic communities filled with care, participatory decision making, dialogue, cooperation, conflict, and action is not easy when there is little instruction in how to change and little support in making the changes. We were not taught in democratic community classrooms or schools. We are unfamiliar with their nuances and dynamics. We are often not adequately skilled in resolving conflicts or guiding a group of people to make effective decisions together. Although those who have been written about in the promising practices books have tried these methods, they too have struggled to find the right path. Change involves trial, risk, and failure until we learn what works and feel confident in taking the next step.

At the same time, these teaching strategies are difficult to pursue as an individual teacher in an otherwise authoritarian school structure. There is a need for wider acceptance of democratic classrooms as experiments in new forms of instruction. There is also a need for schoolwide and systemwide democratic, participatory changes that support the individual teacher's efforts. What we've learned about educational change from the experiments in restructuring is that it is easier to facilitate change when a whole school or whole district is intent on implementing particular strategies than it is to facilitate change in the classrooms of individual teachers who work either in isolation from or in opposition to the existing instructional patterns in the school.

There is a fifth reason that these patterns persist. In spite of the fact that we talk about U.S. society as a democratic society, democratic participation is limited. Few are actually involved in decision making in their jobs, their community, or the larger political arena. The environment that we educate students to enter does not reflect the kind of caring, ethical, participatory community that researchers advocate for schools. Although our society values these qualities in its rhetoric, the actual environment students grow up in and enter fully upon graduation is often competitive, individualistic, and hierarchical. The values of justice and care are often compromised by greed and power. A sense of national community is often only present in nationalistic campaigns for particular political ends. In order for teachers and schools to pursue educational interventions that promote social responsibility, they must hold out a vision of a more participatory, ethical, and caring society that they are preparing their students to help create. They must maintain the kinds of ideals that have moved bold political activists from Thomas Jefferson to Martin Luther King to dream of a society where all are equal, all are treated fairly, and all participate. Few are so optimistic. Few are so bold. Our day-to-day struggles focus our attention away from these larger ideals toward ensuring that we earn a living and that our students develop a saleable skill.

These five problems—the lack of any natural advocate for social responsibility, the unwillingness of educators to risk dealing with politics and controversy, the predominant demands of the existing curriculum, the difficulties inherent in changing teaching methods and school culture, and the pervasiveness of an individualistic, competitive, and hierarchical political and social culture outside the school—are powerful forces for maintaining the status quo. With current educational practices focused primarily on individual competence within a competitive society, teaching social responsibility in most school districts is a rhetorical slogan rather than a practical reality. Current methods of instruction and current classroom and school structures promote obedience and alienation rather than thoughtfulness, engagement, and commitment. We have lobotomized children, separating their social consciousness from their individual identity. As a result our schools are safe from critical attacks, but they are also dull places, isolated from the decision-making arenas that have the potential of giving young people some sense of control of their political and social future.

In spite of the forces inhibiting change, change is possible. The four promising practices books have documented classrooms and schools that have integrated practices that promote social responsibility. In some of these, participatory classroom and school communities are the norm. In my own work over the past decade with Educators for Social Responsibility (ESR), I have observed teachers and schools who hold out a different vision and create participatory communities in their classrooms and schools (Berman & LaFarge, 1993). It isn't easy work, but these individuals have persisted, not only in improving their own classrooms, but in helping others move in similar directions.

These teachers are not stopped by the persistent patterns. They do not relegate social responsibility to one curricular area but see it as embedded in all that they do. They have found ways to integrate controversy and conflict that are age-appropriate and balanced. They believe that we cannot set an arbitrary boundary between the world children experience outside the classroom and the world of the classroom. They help children negotiate their relationship with society and explore their most serious questions and concerns about the world. These teachers have found that children are far more aware of the world around them. And they have found that when students are given the opportunity, they are better able to appreciate complexity and tolerate ambiguity than many adults assume.

Also these teachers are not stopped by the demands of the curriculum or the limits of time. They build a curricular approach slowly, over time, and embed social responsibility into their existing curriculum and their classroom organization. Many have found that this integration makes teaching more compelling for students. Although it initially takes time from the curriculum, students cover material more quickly and comprehensively.

But most important, they view the current social and political environment not as a static obstacle but as an ever-changing organism that can be influenced by the actions of individuals and groups. They have a vision of what a better world might be and help students develop their own visions. They create caring communities in their classrooms as a way to give students the basic experiences and skills to deal with and possibly change the existing social reality. They empower students by having them experience a positive and constructive social environment.

These teachers are not naive idealists and their classrooms are not idyllic places. They face the conflict and tension present in all classrooms. But what they teach is that these conflicts can be handled in a way that is often caring and constructive for everyone in the class, that we each have a responsibility to those around us, and that we all can make the world a better place.

It is difficult to do this in isolation or in the context of classroom and school structures that are hierarchical and authoritarian. Yet these teachers are often not alone. Many times they work with similarly inclined teachers or in schools that strive to create this kind of culture throughout the school. In addition, they are often members of organizations that support this kind of instruction. The organizational supports of Educators for Social Responsibility and the Institute for Democracy in Education have been critical in maintaining a national focus and momentum around democracy and social responsibility in education and in providing support to teachers and schools.

Over the past decade I have observed a steady growth in the number of teachers and schools that integrate social responsibility into the curriculum. In fact, there are now whole school districts that have been able to join together to make a commitment to build social responsibility into their curriculum. It is far from a movement and far from changing the culture of education in the United States. But these efforts are making inroads. The documentation of these practices, the research programs now under way, and the organizational support provide building blocks for continued change. This does not mean that these efforts will necessarily have a long-lasting impact. There have been larger educational movements in the past, such as the progressive movement, that have been more popular but made only a small lasting impact. Whether in education or in society in general, change is slow. It is built by the efforts of individuals and groups. We can never predict whether our actions will end up creating significant change; we can only act with that intention and, if nothing else, keep a vision alive. It means living, what Sharon Welch (1990) has called, "an ethic of risk."

For the persistent patterns to be overcome and significant change to take place in education, society as a whole will have to change. To some degree this is happening. In the past decade we have seen a rapid growth in environmental consciousness, in "ethical investing," in cooperation in the workplace, in community volunteerism, and in other areas related to social responsibility. There have been many advocates for a stronger, more participatory democracy and a revitalization of our sense of community (Barber, 1984; Bellah et al., 1991; Boyte, 1989; Lappe & Du Bois, 1992). These shifts make teaching social responsibility more easily accepted. However, it is difficult to determine whether these shifts will become fundamental enough to support significant change in education.

In many ways, those who are currently struggling to integrate social responsibility into the curriculum and program of the school are recreating

Dewey's vision of democratic education after a long period of dormancy. We have lost much of the rich experience we gained in the first part of the twentieth century. But we have also learned a great deal in the interim in the small experiments that educators and researchers have pursued. Most of the early efforts in democratic community pale against the sophistication of Kohlberg's just communities or the Child Development Project's caring community classrooms or the schools that Wood (1992) documents in *Schools That Work*. Our strategies are more complex and more comprehensive. We know more about child development and about appropriate ways to respond to developmental issues. We know much more about constructive ways to negotiate conflict and about how to teach these skills to children. We have the research reported in this book that can inform practice and provide a rationale and support for particular educational interventions. Relatively new organizations like the Institute for Democracy in Education and Educators for Social Responsibility have taken steps to reestablish a knowledge base and provide professional support for educators to begin experimenting with these strategies.

Creating classrooms and schools that teach social responsibility will entail reclaiming a larger vision for education. We have come to think that the purpose of education is to ensure individual success. We have focused on making sure that students have the competencies they need to be successful in their future education and in the world of work. Even school initiatives in cooperative learning are often justified by claiming that the workplace is now structured around cooperation, and to be effective one needs to know how to work with and get along with others. We have lost a sense of how personally important a larger sense of meaning and connection is. Our survival is inextricably linked to the survival of others and of the planet as a whole. Our quality of life is inextricably linked to the welfare of others and the welfare of the planet. Our place in the world takes on meaning only in relation to making this a better world, not in relation to our personal wealth or fame. The challenge is to have the courage to claim this larger vision and to stand up for a different way of being in the classroom.

CHAPTER 7

The Courage to Teach
Social Responsibility

If Dewey and the pragmatic philosophers are correct, if indeed we learn what we experience, then the only way to guarantee a reservoir of democratic sentiment in the culture is to make public schooling a center of democratic experience. (Wood, 1988b, p. 176)

[T]he test of what you produce is in the *care* it inspires. If there is any chance at all, it is in a world more challenging, more workable, more venerable than all myths, retrospective or prospective; it is in historical reality, at last ethically cared for. (Erikson, 1965, p. 27)

A New Theoretical Framework

Over the past fifty years, the ever-increasing awareness that global events have local and personal impact has moved us to a new understanding of our relationship to the world around us. Rather than seeing ourselves as isolated individuals interacting with other isolated individuals, we have become connected. The emergence of a sense of global community has closed the circle around us. There is no escape to isolation. Our behavior has an impact on a global scale and the behavior of others, sometimes half the world away, may have a direct impact on us.

We see this most concretely in the pollution of our water, the breakdown in the ozone, and the extinction of species. We also see it in the suffering and pain perpetrated on human beings by other human beings. The Armenian genocide, the Holocaust, right-wing death squads throughout Central and South America, the Khmer Rouge's murder of millions of Cambodians, the Serbian ravages of Muslims are not distant incidents in an age of biological, chemical, and nuclear weapons. They make us all vulnerable and all aware of our ethical responsibility to stop such behavior and to prevent it in the future. And we see our new way of thinking about our relationship to the global community embodied in such collective humanitarian acts as aid to the starving in Ethiopia, the international intervention in Somalia, and aid to the victims of earthquakes and other natural disasters.

Being a responsible member of the global community demands both personal and collective action. It demands personal action in the sense of treating others as we would treat ourselves. It demands collective action in the sense of needing to work in concert with others. First, collective action to promote a more just, peaceful, and ecologically sound world through the appreciation for diversity, respect for human rights, and the peaceful resolution of conflict. Second, collective action to intervene in behalf of those in need and those suffering from oppression.

Social responsibility is the concept that communicates a commitment to live in ways that are personally and globally ethical and caring. Social responsibility means being personally invested in the well-being of others and the well-being of the planet.

For over half a century researchers have been trying various ways of understanding how social responsibility develops. They have come at it from different angles and have approached singular aspects of it. Political sociologists have explored political development and political behavior and looked for the keys to the politically conscious and politically active individual. Different schools of psychologists have researched psychosocial development, the development of prosocial behavior, and moral development to understand the motivations for helpful, caring, and ethical actions. Educational researchers have studied the impact of citizenship education to understand how young people become effective citizens. In identifying and studying individual elements that constitute social responsibility, these researchers have created the tools and strategies for studying the concept as a whole. Yet, it is only when we step out of these individual fields and examine the data holistically that we begin to answer questions about its development.

Examining the data from the perspective of the development of social responsibility gives coherence to the disparate data in citizenship education, political socialization, prosocial behavior, moral development, and psycho-social development. Social responsibility is the central theoretical construct that ties these fields together.

Social responsibility is integrative. It allows us to integrate the particu-laristic approaches of the other fields. It allows us to examine how people make sense of their relationship with society. It allows us to understand how people come to behave in ethical and caring ways on the political and social level. Finally, its multidimensionality—integrating political consciousness, prosocial behavior, moral judgment and action, and social and political participation—is a more authentic accounting of the factors influencing social and political decision making and participation.

When we use social responsibility as the central theoretical construct we see that development is relational. The development of social respon-sibility is an emotional, affiliative, and cognitive process. Throughout childhood and adolescence, young people negotiate their relationship with society. They determine if the social and political world is one that they can enter or one from which they will withdraw. They are defining their role within this society and defining the range of their moral commitments. Children, in essence, feel their way into the world—issues of safety, empathy, acceptance, attachment, fairness, and identification inform their cognitive understanding of the world around them. Cognitively, young people formulate a theory of how their society works and their place in it. The relationship they experience with society often remains implicit, visible only in off-hand comments expressing their attitudes and judgments about the world around them. The degree of connectedness they experience determines their sense of efficacy and their interest in participation.

The development of this relationship begins at an early age. The synthesis of the studies reported here reveal an early engagement—especially on an affective level—in the social and political arena. There has been a commonly accepted view in the fields of political socialization, moral development, and elementary education that children prior to age ten are egocentric, unable to take the perspective of others, morally immature, uninterested and unaware of the social and political world, and unable to think in sophisticated ways about social issues or political conflict. The research challenges these notions. Children's awareness of the social and political world emerges far earlier and their social and moral abilities are far more advanced than we thought. Such basic components of social responsibility as empathy, moral sensibilities, the understanding of social conventions, and political awareness emerge prior to the age of eight. We also see that the social and political inequalities relating to gender, race, and class have already made an impact on children's ability to enter and feel a part of the social and political world. The research indicates that in contrast to the stereotype of children as egocentric, children care about the welfare of others and care about issues of fairness on both a personal and social level. Social consciousness and social responsibility are not behaviors that we need to instill in young people but rather they are behaviors that we need to recognize emerging in them.

Social responsibility does not emerge from one's sense of efficacy or one's locus of control but from much deeper sources—the unity of one's sense of self and one's morality, the sense of connectedness to others, and the sense of meaning that one derives from contributing to something larger than oneself. This understanding dramatically shifts our focus away from concepts of internal confidence to concern with the nature of one's relationship with others and with the social and political world. It shifts our attention away from the development of self-esteem to the development of a sense of meaning, place, and commitment. The development of a positive and connected relationship with society becomes a primary contributing factor to healthy development.

There are four basic processes that nurture these deeper sources of motivation and promote social responsibility and activism (see Fig. 4.1). The first is a nurturant and caring environment, especially within the family, where reasoning is the dominant mode of discipline, children are involved in decision making and prosocial action, and warm and caring relationships are the norm. The second is modeling of prosocial and ethical behavior by parents, other adults, or peers. The third process is the development of perspective-taking skills that allow children to enter the world of another and identify with victims of injustice. The fourth process is confrontations with injustice and the development of effective ways of handling conflict situations.

A connected relationship with society emerges over time and through ongoing dialogue with others. Family and important role models play a critical role in its development. Direct experience with human suffering or injustice helps crystalize it. And it is expressed in a deep sense of connection and interdependence with humanity and one's environment.

The synthesis of the research reported here reveals that there is a far greater potential for nurturing political and social development in young people than previously thought. Researchers have found that elementary school children develop an increasing ability to apprehend the social and political world and, if engaged, can feel passionate about its dangers and its potential. Significant political development occurs in the early and middle elementary years. The social and political development of adolescents is also richer than previously thought. They are not only trying to make moral and cognitive sense of the social and political world, they are attempting to make sense of their place in it. Our conception of the child as egocentric, morally immature, uninterested in the social and political world, and unable to understand it has effectively deprived young people of the kind of contact they need to make society and politics salient. Young people's distance from politics and their lack of interest may be an effect of our misconceptions, our ignorance of their potential, and our protectiveness.

The studies of classroom interventions show that when the processes that promote social responsibility are deeply embedded within classroom and school practices, they have been effective in enhancing aspects of social responsibility. Researchers have studied such interventions as classroom climate, inclusion of controversy and conflict, participation in classroom and school decision making, democratic classroom and school governance, cooperative learning and community building, and action learning through direct engagement in the social and political arena. Because social responsibility is rarely studied holistically, these studies examine the impact of classroom practice on such variables as prosocial behavior, democratic values, sense of efficacy, interest in participation, perspective-taking abilities, and moral development. The synthesis of the research points to particular directions for practice and a cohesive vision of what this practice might look like at its best. But before articulating this vision, it is important to note two cautions. First, a vision is useful in setting directions and goals, but it may not be able to be directly realized. Although the studies point to different practices that seem consistent with one another, only rarely have they been practiced as a single program and these efforts have not been researched. There is no guarantee of preexisting harmony among these practices. There may be trade-offs and inconsistencies among the practices that only further effort and research will reveal. Second, most of the studies of educational interventions are short-term studies and do not track changes into later life. We know little about the long-term impact of these practices except as reported by activists reflecting back on their development. Therefore, this portrait of practice is only suggestive in hopes that it encourages further exploration and research.

The pedagogical model that emerges from the research affirms that classrooms and schools are microsocieties that teach children about the way the world works and about their place in it. Authoritarian classrooms and schools nurture authoritarian values. Democratic classrooms nurture democratic values. Nurturing social responsibility in young people means creating environments where children can live the challenges of a democratic society and, from an early age, learn about our civic culture.

These classrooms and schools are cooperative democratic communities where children are engaged in learning from and contributing to the social and political environment in their classroom, school, and the world outside the school. Through class meetings and schoolwide governance meetings, students participate in classroom and school decision making. They collaboratively create rules and ways of being in the classroom and school that reflect standards of fairness and care.

These classrooms and schools are also communities where people care about each other's welfare and cooperate so that all can experience success. Children learn to support and help each other. They learn the skills to resolve differences without resorting to violence. They learn to understand the perspectives of others and to appreciate the richness that having diverse cultures and perspectives offers. They also learn to step back and reflect on their own attitudes and perceptions, to hold these up to the same kind of inspection and introspection that they use in assessing the attitudes and perceptions of others. In essence, these classrooms and schools are places where the dialogue between student and student, and teacher and student is characterized by self-reflection, caring for the well-being of others, considerations of ethical standards, an entertaining of the other person's perspective, and an openness to listening to and negotiating differences.

Curricularly, these classrooms bring the world into the classroom and the classroom into the world. A central goal of the curriculum is to help students find meaningful ways to contribute to the world. As with the culture and social structure of the classroom and school, the curriculum nurtures a positive and empowered relationship with society. This relationship is positive and empowered, not in the sense of approving of current social arrangements or being accepted within those social arrangements, but in the sense of students being willing to confront inequity, injustice, and oppression in order to improve those arrangements.

Whether in science, math, social studies, reading, or other areas, the curriculum addresses social and political issues, conflicts, needs, and controversies. Although each subject area can integrate consideration of social and political issues, these issues can serve to integrate subjects themselves, such as when students study an environmental problem and use math to collect and interpret data, reading to understand the problem, science to examine possible solutions, social studies to understand how action can occur in the political arena, and writing to keep a running account of their own thoughts, reactions, and potential actions. In this way, the curriculum gives students the opportunity to engage in solving real social and political problems. And it gives them the opportunity to act and to implement solutions. Service learning and action learning are primary vehicles for engaging students' interest and teaching basic skills.

This does not mean the whole curriculum is problem-based. It is equally important to help children appreciate the beauty in the world and in themselves, understand the value of knowledge, enjoy the challenge of learning for its own sake, and feel free to play. As we saw in the studies of activists, these are not diminished by engaging in real problems and controversies. In fact, they are often enhanced. Yet, it is important to recognize that we do not always need to focus on problems. In Reindl's (1993) discussion of elementary teachers who have made social responsibility a goal in their curriculum, she describes one teacher who takes her fifth-grade children outside each day to watch and wonder at the sky. As they draw and write about what they see in their sky journals, they begin to appreciate that there is a more diverse range of skies than they had ever noticed. They begin to appreciate nature in a new way. They begin to ask questions about what accounts for these differences. And as they try to answer their questions, they also become interested in issues of air pollution, ozone depletion, and the preservation of species habitats. This teacher's approach helps children appreciate beauty, learning, and playfulness, yet it also allows them to explore questions about how that beauty is damaged and what we can do to repair the damage.

In classrooms and schools that promote social responsibility there is a congruity between content, teaching methods, and classroom or school structure. Each integrates and highlights issues related to social responsibility. Each strives to model ways of being with others and ways of being in the world that promote a unity of one's sense of self and one's morality, a sense of connectedness to others, and a sense of meaning that derives from contributing to something larger than oneself. This is not an easy task nor is there a pat "socially responsible" answer to each problem. Most issues are not simple choices between right and wrong but complex decisions between conflicting and incomplete rights. In experiencing this complexity, students learn the true difficulties of maintaining a democratic society that balances individual rights and collective well-being, individual success and the common good. It is in this environment that democracy comes to be seen as an ongoing and open-ended experiment. It is in this environment that young people begin to see that their knowledge, skills, and commitment contribute to making this experiment work.

In an earlier book (Berman & LaFarge, 1993), I and sixteen other authors studied teachers who were making social responsibility a core element in their curriculum. Although there are teachers and schools that are trying to implement many of these practices, few have brought all the elements of this pedagogy together. Each teacher we talked with and each school we observed chose what each thought was the most appropriate way to begin. Although some emphasized either content, methods, or structure, many had begun to merge these. In the vision they set for themselves, many articulated the pedagogy I've described. For them, teaching social responsibility meant teaching a way of being in the world that is deeply connected to others and respectful of the dignity of each person. It meant teaching a set of thinking skills to help students make open-minded, considered, and independent judgments. And it meant helping young people develop the vision and courage to act. Connectedness, thoughtfulness, vision, and courage were the central characteristics that echoed throughout these teachers' words. The parallels between the research findings I've reported and the practice of these teachers and principals are striking and encouraging.

This does not mean that achieving this vision is easy. The teachers we talked with described many of the forces identified in chapter 6 that maintain the persistent patterns of current instruction. The lack of any natural advocate for social responsibility, the unwillingness of educators to risk dealing with politics and controversy, the predominant demands of the existing curriculum, the difficulties inherent in changing teaching methods and school culture, and the contrast between democratic classroom practices and the social and political environment outside the classroom were powerful forces for them as well. Yet, these teachers and principals prevailed in spite of the constraints. In our conversations we realized that what kept them going was the depth of their caring both about the children they teach and about the health and welfare of the planet.

What comes out most clearly in their interviews is how deeply they care. They feel the pain of the violence, injustice, broken connection, and environmental degradation around them. They feel the pain in their students' lives and hear their concerns about the world they are expected to enter. They believe that this kind of teaching is critical for their students and the planet. They see an intimate relationship between the personal and the social and strive to help students develop both personal competence and social responsibility. In many ways teaching social responsibility has given their work a renewed sense of meaning. And this has given them the strength and courage to take on the demands of change. (Berman & LaFarge, p. 11)

The care and courage of teachers and administrators are powerful forces for change, and they encouraged my own optimism of what can be done. Yet they are not sufficient for more widespread or long-term change. There is no prescription that one can write for widespread and long-term change. However, there are important building blocks. One of these is grounding one's efforts in both theory and research. Another is providing the organizational networks that support and build on teachers' efforts.

Creating Change

The synthesizing of data related to social responsibility and the development of social responsibility as a field grounded in theory and research are vital steps in overcoming the inertia and the resistance that prevents change. To create progressive change in schools, advocates need to be able to rely on a solid base of research that supports the viability and effectiveness of their program initiatives. Currently, instead of having this research base, progressive initiatives are justified to teachers, administrators, school board members, and other policy decision makers on humanistic or ideological bases. Even more problematic is that the effectiveness of progressive programs or programs that promote social responsibility are rarely documented. Change, when it occurs, tends to be in schools where the administration and faculty of an individual school or school district are in philosophical agreement with progressive education goals. Yet the lack of research on the viability and benefits of these efforts leaves those who are involved with little to substantiate their work when it is challenged. The lack of research data also makes it more difficult to transfer successful programs to less progressive districts.

Linking research and practice, however, can produce powerful results. In fact, the research-practice link has been critical for getting a number of significant progressive innovations off the ground. There are numerous examples, but some of the most current include such efforts as cooperative learning, school restructuring, conflict resolution, and prosocial education.

The concept of cooperative learning has been around since the late 1800s. Although there have been a succession of well-known advocates, it languished due to the public's skepticism about children learning more through cooperative means than through competitive ones. However, the reception given to cooperative learning by educators and parents changed dramatically with the publication of the research findings by Roger Johnson and David Johnson (Johnson & Johnson, 1978; Johnson, Maruyama, Johnson, Nelson & Skon, 1981) and others. The Johnsons' review of the hundreds of studies comparing cooperative learning with competitive and individualistic learning showed that in two-thirds of the studies cooperative learning proved superior. These results were popularized through the Johnsons' and other researchers' books and workshops. They gave teachers and administrators a firm ground to stand on when justifying a radical change in educational methodology. Since that time there has been an explosion of interest that has touched most of the school districts in the United States.

This pattern is also the case for high school restructuring. The Coalition of Essential Schools, the organization spearheading major changes in the structure and curriculum of high schools, was launched by a research report on high schools written by Ted Sizer (1984), the initiator of the coalition. Now the coalition is working on major restructuring efforts in over 300 high schools across the country.

In the mid-1980s, the New York Metro chapter of Educators for Social Responsibility initiated a conflict resolution program in one school district with a progressive and interested administration. Working with the New York Board of Education and an independent evaluator, they produced a research report on the program that clearly demonstrated its effectiveness (Metis Associates, 1988). Based on these results ESR has been able to extend this program to other districts in New York and is replicating it in other parts of the country.

A final example is the work done by the Developmental Studies Center on prosocial education that is discussed in chapter 4. In thoroughly assessing their work with the six schools involved in the Child Development Project (CDP) they have been able to document the effectiveness of a program that combines cooperative learning, prosocial role models, opportunities for service to others, a focus on understanding the perspective of another, and a mode of discipline that helped children internalize helping values. Based on this documentation, CDP is now being funded to replicate this work in eight more districts across the country.

Each of these innovations was thought of as an idealistic pipe dream by detractors, yet became influential due to a supportive base of research. In the areas of cooperative learning and prosocial development, there was a substantial body of existing research that needed to be brought together and articulated. In the areas of high school restructuring and conflict resolution, research was needed to demonstrate the need for change in the former and the potential effectiveness of the program in the latter. In each case, administrators, school board members, and foundation decision makers were able to justify their support for or further their implementation of these efforts on the basis of the research findings. I observed this personally in my work with ESR's conflict resolution program and with numerous districts' efforts to gain acceptance of cooperative learning programs.

This book is an effort to build the link between research and practice in the area of social responsibility and to explicate a theory of social responsibility that is grounded in this research. In doing this the research can inform our practice and help improve current efforts. I hope that it will also encourage additional research that can reexamine and extend the findings reported here. Social responsibility, like moral development or higher-order thinking, is not easy to assess. Because it doesn't appear on the traditional standardized tests, teachers and schools don't chart their progress in this area. In addition, the pressures to perform in areas that are tested are often great enough to cause people to ignore or spend little time on such areas as social responsibility. With some standards by which we can measure social responsibility and with additional research that provides a base of support for interventions that promote social responsibility, we can make a credible argument for positive educational change.

The data that lead to these conclusions come from diverse fields and utilize diverse research methodologies. Yet there is a large degree of consistency in the results of studies across these fields. Each field contributes a piece to a larger understanding of the development of social responsibility. However, only a few examine social responsibility directly and none examine social responsibility holistically. Taken together they present a convincing picture of both the development of social responsibility in young people and the kinds of educational interventions that are instrumental in promoting social responsibility. There is a need for additional research to fill the gaps in the existing research and to examine the direct relationship of social responsibility and particular educational interventions. There is a need to examine some of the current interventions that may have an impact on social responsibility, such as systems thinking and multicultural education, that have not been researched from the perspective of moral development, social responsibility, or political interest, efficacy, or participation.

There are a number of research efforts that would be particularly important. One would involve taking a more in-depth look at the development of social consciousness. Currently, developmental studies have focused on cognitive aspects of political understanding or moral reasoning. We need data on the evolution of the emotional and relational aspects of social and political consciousness. Coles's (1986a) work and my own initial research in this area (1990) are starting points. The field would profit from a longitudinal study of the kind completed by Moore, Lare, and Wagner (1985) that used in-depth interviews. Rather than focusing on political knowledge, as they did, this research would pay greater attention to issues of attachment, identification, interest, efficacy, meaning, democratic values, and participation.

Another productive avenue of research would involve an examination of particular educational interventions in terms of their impact on moral integrity, sense of connectedness, meaning, and participation. Does a particular intervention have an impact on students' sense that they can make a meaningful contribution in the social and political arena? Does it encourage them to feel a sense of social responsibility and to participate in making a difference on issues of public concern in their daily lives, in their immediate environment, and in the larger society? The research tools—questionnaires, interview schedules, observational inventories—for doing this type of research are available in the various studies reported here. What needs to be done is to cull through these for the most productive questions and strategies and develop a model that can be applied in a variety of educational settings.

A third productive, although long-term, research effort would involve a longitudinal study of participation from preadolescence into adulthood. Hoehn (1983), Keniston (1968), Colby and Damon (1992), and Oliner and Oliner (1988) have given us retrospective accounts of the development of activists. None looked specifically at the educational backgrounds of these activists. Studying patterns of social and political participation among a matched sample of young people from various educational environments—democratic, participatory, authoritarian, and so on—could provide concrete data on the correlation between these environments and actual participation.

Finally, there are a number of important studies that should be replicated. Button's (1974), Haan, Aerts, and Cooper's (1985), and Power, Higgins, and Kohlberg's (1989) reveal a great deal about the kinds of interventions that promote social responsibility. Replicating these could give greater credibility to their findings. In addition, there is a great need for research similar to that reported by Conrad and Hedin (1982) that examines the impact of community service and direct political action on the development of social responsibility.

Research is an important step but not the only step in overcoming the obstacles to change. In addition, it is critical to have organizations that act as advocates of social responsibility and as support to teachers and schools that are pursuing change. Educators for Social Responsibility and the Institute for Democracy in Education are two organizations that play a critical role in this effort, yet they are small and poorly funded. There is a particular need for the funding community, both public and private, to support research in this area and the organizations that are working to create change.

It is also critical to have larger societal change that highlights socially responsible activism. In the past decade we have seen a growth in professional organizations focused on social responsibility, in investment and banking companies that use environmental and social responsibility screens in their investment practices, and in organizations promoting a renewal in democratic participation. These may be indicators of this larger social change. They set a positive climate for changes in educational practice and provide models for educators and young people to follow.

Having a research base, an organizational support network, and change in the larger society are three basic components in creating change. But more than any other factor, change will hinge on the courage of teachers and administrators who hold social responsibility as a central goal in their teaching, who challenge the accepted patterns and school structures, and who continue to experiment with ways of changing their classrooms and schools that empower students to make a difference in the world. For over a decade I have worked with educators who have the courage to teach social responsibility. They are from every region of the country and every level of education. Working individually and collectively, these people are the pioneers who are forging the renewal of participatory democracy in the United States (Berman & LaFarge, 1993). They do not experience it as an easy task. Yet, this work has often given them a renewed sense of meaning in their teaching and a revitalized commitment to young people. Research, organizational support, and social change add to their efforts by helping to make it acceptable for educators to care about the state of the world and about their students' ability to find a meaningful place in it. But it is their enduring commitment that will provide the wealth of practical experience and the results to build more long-lasting change.

A Gift of Strength and Hope

Social responsibility is more than an educational rationale or a set of educational practices. On the one hand, social responsibility is about caring. It's about the way we live with each other and treat each other. It's about touching other people's lives. On the other hand, social responsibility is about seeing a vision of our human potential and reaching for that vision. It's about bringing people together in solidarity while affirming their differences. It's about holding out standards of justice and care and creating a public dialogue about how our social and political practices can embody these standards. In essence, it's about seeing a larger sense of self that is a meaningful and contributing member of a society. Because it involves the richness of human connection, the breadth of human diversity, the complexity of human conflict, and the inspiration of human hope, social responsibility is truly a heartfelt responsiveness to the world. It's not just a tool we give to students or a skill we help them develop, it is a gift we offer them of their human birthright.

Educating for social responsibility helps young people understand that their lives are intimately connected to the well-being of others and to the social and political world around them, that they make a difference in their daily lives by their choices and values, that diversity in cultures, races, and values enriches our lives, and that they can enter the political arena and participate to create a more just, peaceful, and ecologically sound world. Educating for social responsibility is a gift of strength and hope that they can carry into the world that can enable them to live with meaning, integrity, and responsibility.

Promoting individual success is a narrow and insufficient goal for public education. Without a larger context, a context that gives social meaning to our educational efforts and that embodies a vision of a better society, education is mechanical and egocentric. Its narrow scope encourages pettiness and self-centeredness. Educating for social responsibility provides the necessary balance so that individual success can be set within the context of the public good and individualism set within a context of a local and global community. The challenge for education in the twenty-first century will be the reframing of education to integrate this larger context and the reaffirmation of our basic connection with others and the planet as a whole.

Appendix A

The Educating for Living in the Nuclear Age Project

Model Assessment

POSITION _____
(Teacher, Administrator, Specialist, Aide, etc.)

GRADE LEVEL _____ DISCIPLINE _____

NAME (optional) _____

The ELNA Project is founded on teachers coming together to share ideas and strategies about what it means to educate in the nuclear age—an age of global awareness, challenges, and responsibilities.

As part of the Educating for Living in the Nuclear Age Project, school districts around the country have joined together to develop resources and collaborative efforts to help students develop the insights and skills to make a difference in the world. The major educational objectives of the ELNA Project are to help students:

- understand the nature of social and ecological interdependence,
- develop cooperation and conflict-resolution skills,
- understand current social and political issues, and
- participate in democratic decision making about vital contemporary issues.

This questionnaire is an effort to find out:

Appendix A

- what you are doing now about these issues,
- what you would like to learn more about or do more with, and
- how you would like to learn more about your areas of interest.

We hope this questionnaire will help promote a dialogue among staff members. Are we equipping our students with the skills, attitudes and understanding to live in today's world? How can we encourage students (and ourselves) to feel that they can help create a more ecologically sound, just, and peaceful world? How can we better help students develop a sense of social responsibility—that is, a personal investment in the well-being of others and of the planet?

This project hopes to affirm the creativity and expertise of teachers and to provide you with opportunities to think and work with other educators. We welcome your participation.

We look forward to sharing the data of the survey with you and developing future plans together.

Thank you for taking the time to respond.

The _____ District Working Group

ELNA Project Assessment

Please indicate the extent to which the following are included or are not included in your classroom instruction.

A. Consistently included in my classroom instruction.
B. Often included in my classroom instruction.
C. Sometimes included in my classroom instruction (as the situation arises).
D. Not included in my classroom instruction, but I feel it should be.
E. Does not apply to my classroom.

F. Please check 3 areas you wish to explore further.

	A	B	C	D	E	F
1. Helping students appreciate human differences, i.e., physical, racial, intellectual, socio-economic, etc.						
2. Teaching about ecological interdependence.						

A. Consistently B. Often C. Sometimes D. Not included but should be
E. Does not apply F. Please check 3 areas you wish to explore further.

	A	B	C	D	E	F
3. Providing cooperatively structured classroom activities.						
4. Providing direct instruction in conflict resolution, negotiation, or mediation skills.						
5. Using conflict resolution strategies to successfully resolve classroom conflicts.						
6. Teaching about current social and political issues in a way that is age-appropriate and fits my curriculum.						
7. Helping students understand and appreciate others' points of view.						
8. Teaching about the interdependence of people within society.						
9. Teaching about the customs of different world cultures.						
10. Teaching about how people in different cultures view the world through their cultural, historical, and political experiences.						
11. Teaching about the diversity of cultural experiences within the U.S.						
12. Helping students become self-reflective about their social and political attitudes, values, and assumptions.						

A. Consistently B. Often C. Sometimes D. Not included but should be
E. Does not apply F. Please check 3 areas you wish to explore further.

	A	B	C	D	E	F
13. Encouraging student-initiated discussion of local, national, global, or environmental concerns.						
14. Teaching about the ways individuals and groups influence social and political change.						
15. Helping students develop the confidence that they can effect positive change on local and/or global issues.						
16. Providing opportunities for students to make decisions about classroom and school issues.						
17. Teaching about the preservation of human and civil rights.						
18. Discussing questions of ethics and values.						
19. Creating community within the classroom and school.						
20. Involving students in community service or some form of assisting people in need.						
21. Helping students become aware of historic injustices.						
22. Other _____						

Please answer the following questions:

23. Do you have expertise in any of the items listed above? If so, which items? (List by number.)

Would you be willing to share your expertise with other educators?

24. Going back to what you checked in the final column (F), we would like to know how you want to learn more about these areas. Here are some examples, but they are not all-inclusive. For each of the three, please elaborate on the best way for you: workshop, in-service mini-course, university course, readings, attending conferences, collaborative curriculum writing, summer course or institute, study group, peer observation, review of curricula, staff sharing, or other.

Priority 1 # _____:

Priority 2 # _____:

Priority 3 # _____:

For each of the following items, please indicate the range of your responses which most accurately reflects how important you feel it is that this school system address the following issues.

A. Very Important   D. Not Important
B. Important   E. Does Not Apply
C. Somewhat Important

	A	B	C	D	E
25. Our school system, through its curriculum, should address social and global issues (environmental pollution, racial conflict, arms control, etc.).					
26. Our school system should help students develop cooperation and conflict resolution skills.					

Appendix A

A. Very Important   B. Important   C. Somewhat Important
D. Not Important   E. Does Not Apply

	A	B	C	D	E
27. Our school system should help students investigate/understand the implications of nuclear and other advanced technologies for society and the environment.					
28. Our school system should help students develop an informed social consciousness and a sense of social responsibility.					
29. Our school system should help students develop the confidence and skills to create constructive change in the world around them.					

Please answer the following questions:

30. Are there particular social, ecological, economic, and political issues about which students express concern? If so, what are they?

31. What do you feel are the most important social, ecological, economic, and political issues that our students will be facing as adults?

32. If you could change one thing in your classroom, your curriculum, your school, or in your school system in general to more adequately help students develop a sense of social responsibility, what would that be?

33. What are the greatest obstacles you encounter in helping students develop a sense of social responsibility?

34. If you would like to receive materials (articles, reviews of new curriculum resources, etc.) to read as they become available, please sign here:

_____

35. If you would like to become more involved in the ELNA Project, please sign here:

_____

Thank you for your time!

Bibliography

Acock, A., and Scott, W. (1980). A model for predicting behavior: The effects of attitude and social class on high and low visibility political participation. *Social Psychology Quarterly, 43*(1), 59–72.

Adelson, J. (1972). The political imagination of the young adolescent. In J. Kagan and R. Coles (eds.), *Twelve to Sixteen: Early Adolescence* (pp. 106–43). New York: W. W. Norton.

Adelson, J., and O'Neil, R. P. (1966). Growth of political ideas in adolescence: The sense of community. *Journal of Personality and Social Psychology, 4*(3), 295–306.

Adler, A. (1927). *Understanding Human Nature.* London: Allen and Unwin.

Allport, G. W. (1961). *Pattern and Growth in Personality.* New York: Holt, Rinehart and Winston.

Almond, G., and Verba, S. (1963). *The Civic Culture: Political Attitudes and Democracy in Five Nations.* Boston: Little, Brown, and Co.

Anderson, L., Jenkins, L. B., Leming, J., MacDonald, W. B., Mullis, I., Turner, M. J., and Wooster, J. S. (1990). *The Civics Report Card.* Princeton, NJ: Educational Testing Service. (ERIC Document Reproduction Service No. ED 315 376).

Anderson, N. H., and Butzin, C. A. (1978). Integration theory applied to children's judgments of equity. *Developmental Psychology, 14*(6), 593–606.

Andrain, C. F. (1971). *Children and Civic Awareness: A Study in Political Education.* Columbus, OH: Charles E. Merrill.

Angyal, A. (1941). *Foundations for a Science of Personality.* Cambridge, MA: Commonwealth Fund.

Anyon, J. (1978). Elementary social studies textbooks and legitimating knowledge. *Theory and Research in Social Education*, 6(3), 40–55.

Aronson, E., Bridgeman, D. L., and Geffner, R. (1978). The effects of a cooperative classroom structure on student behavior and attitudes. In D. Bar-Tal and L. Saxe (eds.), *Social Psychology of Education* (pp. 257–72). New York: Hemisphere.

Arrendondo-Dowd, P. (1981). The psychological development and education of immigrant adolescents: A baseline study. *Adolescence*, 16(61), 175–86.

Arterton, C. F. (1974). The impact of Watergate on children's attitudes toward political authority. *Political Science Quarterly*, 89(2), 269–88.

Bahmueller, C. F. (Ed.). (1991). *Civitas: A Framework for Civic Education*. Calabasas, CA: Center for Civic Education.

Bandura, A. (1991). Social cognitive theory of moral thought and action. In W. Kurtines and J. Gewirtz (eds.), *Handbook of Moral Behavior and Development, Volume 1: Theory* (pp. 45–103). Hillsdale, NJ: Lawrence Erlbaum.

Barber, B. (1984). *Strong Democracy: Participatory Politics for a New Age*. Berkeley: University of California Press.

Bardige, B. (1988). Things so finely human: Moral sensibilities at risk in adolescence. In C. Gilligan, J. V. Ward, J. M. Taylor, and B. Bardige (eds.), *Mapping the Moral Domain* (pp. 87–110). Cambridge, MA: Harvard University Press.

Battistich, V., Schaps, E., Solomon, D., and Watson, M. (1991). The role of the school in prosocial development. In H. E. Fitzgerald, B. M. Lester, and M. W. Yogman (eds.), *Theory and Research in Behavioral Pediatrics*, vol. 5, (pp. 89–127). New York: Plenum.

Battistich, V., Watson, M., Solomon, D., Schaps, E., and Solomon, J. (1991). The child development project: Program for the development of prosocial character. In W. Kurtines and J. Gewirtz (eds.), *Handbook of Moral Behavior and Development, Volume 3: Application* (pp. 1–34). Hillsdale, NJ: Lawrence Erlbaum.

Beck, I. L., McKeown, M. G., and Gromoll, E. W. (1989). Learning from social studies texts. *Cognition and Instruction*, 62(2), 99–158.

Beck, P. A., and Jennings, M. K. (1982). Pathways to participation. *American Political Science Review*, 76(1), 94–109.

Becker, C., Chasin, L., Chasin, R., Herzig, M., and Roth, S. (1992). Fostering dialogue on abortion: A report from the Public Conversations Project. *Conscience*, 8(3), 2–9.

Belenky, M. F., Clinchy, B. M., Goldberger, N. R., and Tarule, J. M. (1986). *Women's Ways of Knowing.* New York: Basic Books.

Bellah, R. N., Madsen, R., Sullivan, W. M., Swidler, A., and Tipton, S. M. (1985). *Habits of the Heart.* New York: Harper and Row.

———. (1991). *The Good Society.* New York: Knopf.

Berkowitz, L. (1972). Social norms, feelings, and other factors affecting helping and altruism. In L. Berkowitz (ed.), *Advances in Experimental Social Psychology*, vol. 6. New York: Academic Press.

Berkowitz, L., and Lutterman, K. (1968). The traditionally socially responsible personality. *Public Opinion Quarterly*, 32(2), 169–85.

Berkowitz, M. W., and Gibbs, J. C. (1983). Measuring the developmental features of moral discussion. *Merrill-Palmer Quarterly*, 29(4), 399–410.

Berlak, H. (1977). Human consciousness, social criticism, and civic education. In J. Shaver (ed.), *Building Rationales for Citizenship Education*, Bulletin 52 (pp. 34–47). Arlington, VA: National Council for the Social Studies.

Berman, S. (1990). The real ropes course: The development of social consciousness. *ESR Journal*, 1, 1–18. Cambridge, MA: Educators for Social Responsibility.

Berman, S., and LaFarge, P. (Eds.). (1993). *Promising Practices in Teaching Social Responsibility.* Albany, NY: State University of New York Press.

Berndt, T. J. (1987). The distinctive features of conversations between friends: Theories, research, and implications for sociomoral development. In W. Kurtines and J. Gewirtz (eds.), *Moral Development through Social Interaction* (pp. 281–300). New York: Wiley.

Bernstein, E., and Gilligan, C. (1990). Unfairness and not listening. In C. Gilligan, N. Lyons, and T. Hanmer (eds.), *Making Connections: The Relational Worlds of Adolescent Girls at Emma Willard School* (pp. 147–61). Cambridge, MA: Harvard University Press.

Bettelheim, B. (1985, November). Punishment versus discipline. *Atlantic*, 256(5), 51–59.

Blaney, N. T., Stephan, S., Rosenfield, D., Aronson, E., and Sikes, J. (1977). Interdependence in the classroom: A field study. *Journal of Educational Psychology*, 69(2), 121–28.

Blasi, A. (1980). Bridging moral cognition and moral action: A critical review of the literature. *Psychological Bulletin*, 88(1), 1–45.

———. (1983). Moral cognition and moral action: A theoretical perspective. *Developmental Review*, 3(2), 178–210.

Borg, W. R. (1966). Student government and citizenship education. *Elementary School Journal, 67*(3), 154–60.

Boyte, H. (1989). *Commonwealth: A Return to Citizen Politics.* New York: Free Press.

Brabeck, M. M. (1989). Changing descriptions of the self and feminist moral visions. Paper presented at the Annual Meeting of the Association for Moral Education, Newport, CA, November 11, 1989.

Brameld, T. (1956). *Toward a Reconstructed Philosophy of Education.* New York: Holt, Rinehart and Winston.

Bronfenbrenner, U. (1979). *The Ecology of Human Development.* Cambridge, MA: Harvard University Press.

Broughton, J. M. (1986). The genesis of moral domination. In S. Modgil and C. Modgil (eds.), *Lawrence Kohlberg: Consensus and Controversy* (pp. 363–85). Philadelphia: The Falmer Press.

Browning, D. S. (1973). *Generative Man: Psychoanalytic Perspectives.* Philadelphia: Westminster.

Bruner J., and Haste H. (Eds.). (1987). *Making Sense: The Child's Construction of the World.* London: Methuen.

Bryant, B., and Crockenberg, S. (1974). Cooperative and competitive classroom environments. *JSAS Catalog of Selected Documents in Psychology, 4,* 53.

Button, C. B. (1974). Political education for minority groups. In R. Niemi (ed.), *The Politics of Future Citizens* (pp. 167–98). San Francisco: Jossey-Bass.

Butts, R. F. (1980). *The Revival of Civic Learning.* Bloomington, IN: Phi Delta Kappa.

Candee, D. (1976). Structure and choice in moral reasoning. *Journal of Personality and Social Psychology, 34*(6), 1293–301.

Carroll, J. D., Broadnax, W., Contreras, G., Mann, T., Ornstein, N., and Stiehm, J. (1989). *We the People: A Review of U.S. Government and Civics Textbooks.* Washington, DC: People for the American Way.

Carson, R. B., Goldhammer, K., and Pellegrin, R. (1967). *Teacher Participation in the Community.* Eugene: University of Oregon, Center for Advanced Study in Educational Administration.

Chasin, L., and Chasin, R. (1992). The public conversations project. A presentation at the American Association for Marriage and Family Therapy, October 17, 1992.

Chasin, R., and Herzig, M. (1994). Creating systemic interventions for the sociopolitical arena. In B. Berger-Gould and D. H. DeMuth (eds.),

The Global Family Therapist: Integrating the Personal, Professional and Political (pp. 149–92). Needham, MA: Allyn and Bacon.

Clary, E. G., and Miller, J. (1986). Socialization and situational influences on sustained altruism. *Child Development*, 57(6), 1358–1369.

Clinchy, B., Lief, J., and Young, P. (1977). Epistemological and moral development in girls from a traditional and a progressive high school. *Journal of Educational Psychology*, 69(4), 337–43.

Colby, A., and Damon, W. (1992). *Some Do Care*. New York: The Free Press.

Cole, P., and Farris, T. (1979, Summer). Building a just community at the elementary school level. *Moral Education Forum*, 4(2), 12–19.

Coles, R. (1967). *Children of Crisis, Vol. 1: A Study of Courage and Fear.* Boston: Atlantic Monthly Press.

———. (1986a). *The Moral Life of Children.* Boston: Atlantic Monthly Press.

———. (1986b). *The Political Life of Children.* Boston: Atlantic Monthly Press.

Connell, R. W. (1971). *The Child's Construction of Politics*. Melbourne, Australia: Melbourne University Press.

Conrad, D., and Hedin, D. (1977). Citizenship education through participation. In F. B. Brown (dir.), *Education for Responsible Citizenship: The Report of the National Task Force on Citizenship Education* (pp. 133–55). New York: McGraw-Hill.

———. (1982). The impact of experiential education on adolescent development. In D. Conrad and D. Hedin (eds.), *Youth Participation and Experiential Education* (pp. 57–76). New York: The Haworth Press.

Conway, M. M. (1990). Fostering group-based political participation. In O. Ichilov (ed.), *Political Socialization, Citizenship Education, and Democracy* (pp. 297–312). New York: Teachers College Press.

Conway, M. M. (1991). *Political Participation in the United States*, 2nd edition. Washington, DC: Congressional Quarterly Press.

Counts, G. S. (1932). *Dare the School Build a New Social Order?* New York: John Day.

———. (1934). *The Social Foundations of Education.* New York: Charles Scribner's Sons.

Cox, C. B., and Massialas, B. G. (eds.). (1967). *Social Studies in the United States: A Critical Appraisal.* New York: Harcourt, Brace and World.

Cuban, L. (1984). *How Teachers Taught: Constancy and Change in American Classrooms 1890–1980.* New York: Longman.

Curti, M. (1959). *The Social Ideas of American Educators.* Paterson, NJ: Littlefield, Adams & Co.

Damon, W. (1977). *The Social World of the Child.* San Francisco: Jossey-Bass.

———. (1983). *Social and Personality Development.* New York: Norton.

Damon, W., and Killen, M. (1982). Peer interaction and the process of change in children's moral reasoning. *Merrill-Palmer Quarterly, 28*(3), 347–67.

Dewey, J. (1909). *Moral Principles in Education.* Boston: Houghton Mifflin.

———. (1915). *The School and Society.* Chicago: University of Chicago Press.

———. (1916). *Democracy and Education.* New York: Macmillan.

Dewey, J., and Dewey, E. (1915). *Schools of To-morrow.* New York: Dutton.

Dowse, R. E., and Hughes, J. A. (1971). The family, the school, and the political socialization process. *Sociology, 5,* 21–45.

Dozier, M. (1974). The relative effectiveness of vicarious and experimental techniques on the development of moral judgment with groups of desegregated sixth grade pupils (Doctoral dissertation, University of Miami, 1974). *Dissertation Abstracts International, 1974, 35,* 2045A. (University Microfilms No. 74–23, 391).

Dunn, J. (1988). *The Beginnings of Social Understanding.* Cambridge, MA: Harvard University Press.

Durkheim, E. (1925/1961). *Moral Education.* New York: Free Press.

Dweck, C. S., and Goetz, T. E. (1983). Attributions and learned helplessness. In W. Damon (ed.), *Social and Personality Development* (pp. 184–203). New York: W. W. Norton.

Dweck, C. S., and Licht, B. G. (1980). Learned helplessness and intellectual achievement. In J. Garber and M. Seligman (eds.), *Human Helplessness: Theory and Applications* (pp. 197–222). New York: Academic.

Dynneson, T. L., and Gross, R. E. (1991). The educational perspective: Citizenship education in American society. In T. Dynneson and R. Gross (eds.), *Social Science Perspectives on Citizenship Education* (pp. 1–42). New York: Teachers College Press.

Easton, D., and Dennis, J. (1969). *Children in the Political System: Origins of Political Legitimacy.* New York: McGraw-Hill.

Educational Policies Commission. (1940). *Learning the Ways of Democracy: A Case Book in Civic Education.* Washington, DC: National Education Association.

Edwards, C. P. (1980). The comparative study of the development of moral judgment and reasoning. In R. L. Monroe, R. Munroe, and B. B.

Whiting (eds.), *Handbook of Cross-cultural Human Development* (pp. 501–28). New York: Garland.

Ehman, L. H. (1972). Political efficacy and the high school social studies curriculum. In B. G. Massialas (ed.), *Political Youth, Traditional Schools: National and International Perspectives* (pp. 90–102). Englewood Cliffs, NJ: Prentice-Hall.

————. (1980). The American school in the political socialization process. *Review of Educational Research, 50*(1), 99–119.

Ehman, L. H., and Gillespie, J. A. (1975, September). *The School as a Political System* (Final Report). Washington, DC: National Institute of Education. (Grant NE-G00-3-0163)

Eisenberg, N., and Mussen, P. H. (1989). *The Roots of Prosocial Behavior in Children.* Cambridge: Cambridge University Press.

Ekehammar, B., Nilsson, I., and Sidanius, J. (1987). Education and ideology: Basic aspects of education related to adolescents' sociopolitical attitudes. *Political Psychology, 8,* 395–410.

Elden, J. M. (1981). Political efficacy at work: The connection between more autonomous forms of workforce organization and a more participatory politics. *American Political Science Review, 75*(1), 43–58.

Emler, N., Renwick, S., and Malone, B. (1983). The relationship between moral reasoning and political orientation. *Journal of Personality and Social Psychology, 45*(5), 1073–86.

Engle, S. H., and Ochoa, A. S. (1988). *Education for Democratic Citizenship.* New York: Teachers College Press.

Enright, R. D., Lapsley, D. K., Harris, D. J., and Shawver, D. J. (1983). Moral development interventions in early adolescence. *Theory in Practice, 22*(2), 134–44.

Erikson, E. H. (1958). *Young Man Luther.* New York: W. W. Norton.

————. (1963). *Child and Society.* New York: W. W. Norton.

————. (1964). *Insight and Responsibility: Lectures on the Ethical Implications of Psychoanalytic Insight.* New York: W. W. Norton.

————. (1965). Youth: Fidelity and diversity. In E. Erikson (ed.), *The Challenge of Youth* (pp. 1–28). Garden City, NY: Anchor.

————. (1968). *Identity: Youth and Crisis.* New York: W. W. Norton.

Fancett, V. S., and Hawke, S. D. (1982). Instructional practices. In I. Morrissett (ed.), *Social Studies in the 1980s: A Report of Project SPAN* (pp. 61–78). Alexandria, VA: Association for Supervision and Curriculum Development.

Farquhar, E. C., and Dawson, K. S. (1979). *Citizen Education Today: Developing Civic Competencies.* Washington, DC: Office of Education.

Fenton, E. (1977). The implications of Lawrence Kohlberg's research for civic education. In F. B. Brown (dir.), *Education for Responsible Citizenship: The Report of the National Task Force on Citizenship Education* (pp. 97–132). New York: McGraw-Hill.

Feshbach, N. (1983). Learning to care: A positive approach to child training and discipline. *Journal of Clinical Child Psychology, 12*(3), 266–71.

Feshbach, N., and Feshbach, S. (1982). Empathy training and the regulation of aggression: Potentialities and limitations. *Academic Psychology Bulletin, 4*(3), 399–413.

Fisher, R., and Brown, S. (1988). *Getting Together: Building Relationship that Gets to Yes.* Boston: Houghton Mifflin.

Fisher, R., Ury, W., and Patton, B. (1991). *Getting to Yes: Negotiating Agreement Without Giving In,* 2nd ed. Boston: Houghton Mifflin.

Fishkin, J., Keniston, K., and MacKinnon, C. (1973). Moral reasoning and political ideology. *Journal of Personality and Social Psychology, 27*(1), 109–19.

FitzGerald, F. (1979). *America Revised.* Boston: Atlantic Monthly Press.

Fowler, D. (1990). Democracy's next generation. *Educational Leadership, 48*(3), 10–15.

Fox, T. E., and Hess, R. D. (1972). An analysis of social conflict in social studies textbooks. Final Report, Project No. 1-I-116, U.S. Department of Health, Education and Welfare. (ERIC Document Reproduction Service No. ED 076 493)

Furth, H. (1980). *The World of Grown-Ups.* New York: Elsevier–North Holland.

Gallatin, J., and Adelson, J. (1970). Individual rights and the public good. A cross-national study of adolescents. *Comparative Political Studies, 3*(2), 226–42.

Giarelli, J. M. (1988). Education and democratic citizenship: Toward a new public philosophy. In S. D. Franzosa (ed.), *Civic Education: Its Limits and Conditions* (pp. 50–67). Ann Arbor, MI: Prakken Publications.

Gibbs, J. C., Clark, P. M., Joseph, J. A., Green, J. L., Goodrick, T. S., and Makowski, D. G. (1986). Relations between moral judgment, moral courage, and field independence. *Child Development, 57,* 185–93.

Gilligan C. (1982). *In a Different Voice.* Cambridge, MA: Harvard University Press.

————. (1988a). Preface. In C. Gilligan, J. V. Ward, and J. M. Taylor (eds.), *Mapping the Moral Domain* (pp. i–v). Cambridge, MA: Harvard University Press.

————. (1988b). Adolescent development reconsidered. In C. Gilligan, J. V. Ward, J. M. Taylor, and B. Bardige (eds.), *Mapping the Moral Domain* (pp. vii–xxxix). Cambridge, MA: Harvard University Press.

————. (1988c). Remapping the moral domain: New images of self in relationship. In C. Gilligan, J. V. Ward, J. M. Taylor, and B. Bardige (eds.), *Mapping the Moral Domain* (pp. 3–19). Cambridge, MA: Harvard University Press.

————. (1988d). Exit-voice dilemmas in adolescent development. In C. Gilligan, J. V. Ward, J. M. Taylor, and B. Bardige (eds.), *Mapping the Moral Domain* (pp. 141–57). Cambridge, MA: Harvard University Press.

————. (1990). Teaching Shakespeare's sister: Notes from the underground of female adolescence. In C. Gilligan, N. Lyons, and T. Hanmer (eds.), *Making Connections: The Relational Worlds of Adolescent Girls at Emma Willard School* (pp. 6–29). Cambridge, MA: Harvard University Press.

Gilligan, C., and Wiggins, G. (1988). The origins of morality in early childhood relationships. In C. Gilligan, J. V. Ward, J. M. Taylor, and B. Bardige (eds.), *Mapping the Moral Domain* (pp. 111–38). Cambridge, MA: Harvard University Press.

Giroux, H. (1983a). *Theory and Resistance in Education.* South Hadley, MA: Bergin and Garvey.

————. (1983b). Critical theory and rationality in citizenship education. In H. Giroux and D. Purpel (eds.), *The Hidden Curriculum and Moral Education* (pp. 321–360). Berkeley, CA: McCutchan.

————. (1988). *Schooling and the Struggle for Public Life: Critical Pedagogy in the Modern Age.* Minneapolis: University of Minnesota Press.

Goldstein, R. J. (1972). Elementary school curriculum and political socialization. In B. G. Massialas (ed.), *Political Youth, Traditional Schools: National and International Perspectives* (pp. 14–33). Englewood Cliffs, NJ: Prentice-Hall.

Goodlad, J. (1984). *A Place Called School.* New York: McGraw-Hill.

Greenberg, E. S. (1981). Industrial self-management and political attitudes. *American Political Science Review, 75*(1), 29–42.

Greenstein, F. I. (1965). *Children and Politics.* New Haven, CT: Yale University Press.

Gurin, G., Gurin, P., and Morrison, B. M. (1978). Personal and ideological aspects of internal and external control. *Social Psychology, 41*(4), 275–96.

Haan, N. (1985). Processes of moral development: Cognitive or social disequilibrium? *Developmental Psychology, 21,* 996–1006.

———. (1991). Moral development and action from a social constructivist perspective. In W. Kurtines and J. Gewirtz (eds.), *Handbook of Moral Behavior and Development, Volume 1: Theory* (pp. 251–73). Hillsdale, NJ: Lawrence Erlbaum.

Haan, N., Aerts, E., and Cooper, B. (1985). *On Moral Grounds: The Search for Practical Morality.* New York: New York University Press.

Haan, N., Smith, M. B., and Block, J. (1968). Moral reasoning of young adults: Political-social behavior, family background, and personality correlates. *Journal of Personality and Social Psychology, 10*(3), 183–201.

Hanks, M., and Eckland, B. K. (1978). Adult voluntary associations and adolescent socialization. *Sociological Quarterly, 19*(3), 481–90.

Harris, D. B. (1957). A scale for measuring attitudes of social responsibility in children. *Journal of Abnormal and Social Psychology, 55,* 322–26.

Hart Research Associates. (1989). *Democracy's Next Generation: A Study of Youth and Teachers.* Washington, DC: People For the American Way.

Hedin, D., and Conrad, D. (1990). The impact of experiential education on youth development. In J. Kendall and Associates (eds.), *Combining Service and Learning: A Resource Book for Community and Public Service, Volume 1* (pp. 119–129). Raleigh, NC: National Society for Internships and Experiential Education.

Hertz-Lazarowitz, R. (1983). Prosocial behavior in the classroom. *Academic Psychology Bulletin, 5*(2), 319–38.

Hertz-Lazarowitz, R., and Sharan, S. (1984). Enhancing prosocial behavior through cooperative learning in the classroom. In E. Staub, D. Bar-Tal, J. Karylowski, and J. Reykowski (eds.), *Development and Maintenance of Prosocial Behavior* (pp. 423–43). New York: Plenum.

Hess, R., and Torney, J. (1967). *The Development of Political Attitudes in Children.* Chicago: Aldine.

Higgins, A. (1991). The just community approach to moral education: Evolution of the idea and recent findings. In W. Kurtines and J. Gewirtz (eds.), *Handbook of Moral Behavior and Development, Volume 3: Application* (pp. 111–41). Hillsdale, NJ: Lawrence Erlbaum.

Hodgkinson, V., and Weitzman, M. (1992). *Giving and Volunteering in the United States, 1992 Edition.* Washington, DC: The Independent Sector.

Hoehn, R. A. (1983). *Up From Apathy: A Study of Moral and Social Involvement.* Nashville, TN: Abingdon.

Hoffman, M. L. (1984). Empathy, its limitations, and its role in a comprehensive moral theory. In W. Kurtines and J. Gewirtz (eds.), *Morality, Moral Behavior, and Moral Development* (pp. 283–302). New York: Wiley.

—————. (1991). Empathy, social cognition, and moral action. In W. Kurtines and J. Gewirtz (eds.), *Handbook of Moral Behavior and Development, Volume 1: Theory* (pp. 275–301). Hillsdale, NJ: Lawrence Erlbaum.

Hoover, K. H. (1967). Using controversial issues to develop democratic values among secondary school students. *Journal of Experimental Education, 36*(2), 64–69.

Hoy, W. (1971, January). *An investigation of the relationship between characteristics of secondary schools and student alienation* (Final Report on Project No. 9-B-160 to the U.S. Office of Education). (ERIC Document Reproduction Service No. ED 046 060)

Hungerford, H. R., Lithreland, R. A., Peyton, R. B., Ramsey, J. M., and Volk, T. L. (1988). *Investigating and Evaluating Environmental Issues and Action: Skill Development Modules.* Champaign, IL: Stripes.

Jackson, P. W. (1968). *Life in Classrooms.* New York: Holt, Rinehart, and Winston.

Jennings, M. K. (1974). An aggregate analysis of home and school effects on political socialization. *Social Science Quarterly, 55*(2), 394–410.

Jennings, M. K., Ehman, L. H., and Niemi, R. G. (1974). Social studies teachers and their pupils. In M. K. Jennings and R. G. Niemi (ed.), *The Political Character of Adolescence* (pp. 207–27). Princeton, NJ: Princeton University Press.

Jennings, M. K., Langton, K. P., and Niemi, R. G. (1974). Effects of the high school civics curriculum. In M. K. Jennings and R. G. Niemi (ed.), *The Political Character of Adolescence* (pp. 181–206). Princeton, NJ: Princeton University Press.

Jennings, M. K., and Niemi, R. G. (1974). *The Political Character of Adolescents.* Princeton, NJ: Princeton University Press.

—————. (1981). *Generations and Politics.* Princeton, NJ: Princeton University Press.

Jennings, M. K., Niemi, R. G., and Sebert, S. K. (1974). The political texture of peer groups. In M. K. Jennings and R. G, Niemi (eds.), *The Political*

Character of Adolescence (pp. 229–48). Princeton, NJ: Princeton University Press.

Jennings, M. K., and van Deth, J. W. (eds.). (1990). *Continuities in Political Action: A Longitudinal Study of Political Orientations in Three Western Democracies*. New York: Walter de Gruyter.

Jennings, T. E. (1992). Self-in-connection as a component of human-rights advocacy. Unpublished manuscript.

Johnston, D. K. (1988). Adolescents' solutions to dilemmas in fables: Two moral orientations—two problem solving strategies. In C. Gilligan, J. V. Ward, J. M. Taylor, and B. Bardige (eds.), *Mapping the Moral Domain* (pp. 49–71). Cambridge, MA: Harvard University Press.

Johnson, D. W., and Johnson, R. T. (1978). Cooperative, competitive, and individualistic learning. *Journal of Research and Development in Education, 12*(1), 3–15.

———. (1983). The socialization and achievement crises: Are cooperative learning experiences the solution? In L. Bickman (ed.), *Applied Social Psychology Annual 4* (pp. 119–64). Beverly Hills, CA: Sage.

———. (1985). Classroom conflict: Controversy versus debate in learning groups. *American Educational Research Journal, 22*(2), 237–56.

Johnson, D. W., Maruyama, G., Johnson, R. T., Nelson, D., and Skon, L. (1981). Effects of cooperative, competitive, and individualistic goal structures on achievement: A meta-analysis. *Psychological Bulletin, 89*(1), 47–62.

Johnson, R. T., Johnson, D. W., Brooker, C., Stutzman, J., and Hultman, D. (1985). The effects of controversy, concurrence seeking, and individualistic learning on achievement and attitude change. *Journal of Research in Science Teaching, 22*(3), 197–205.

Kagan, J. (1987). Introduction. In J. Kagan and S. Sharon (eds.), *The Emergence of Morality in Young Children* (pp. ix–xx). Chicago: University of Chicago Press.

Karasek, R. (1978). Job socialization: A longitudinal study of work, political and leisure activity. Revised Working Paper No. 59. Stockholm: Institute for Social Research.

Katz, P. A. (1983). Developmental foundations of gender and racial attitudes. In R. L. Leahy (ed.), *The Child's Construction of Social Inequality* (pp. 41–78). New York: Academic.

Keen, C. H. (1990). Effects of a public issues program on adolescents' moral and intellectual development. In J. Kendall and Associates (eds.), *Combining Service and Learning: A Resource Book for Community and*

Public Service, Volume 1 (pp. 393–404). Raleigh, NC: National Society for Internships and Experiential Education.

Keniston, K. (1960). *The Uncommitted: Alienated Youth in American Society.* New York: Harcourt, Brace and World.

———. (1968). *Young Radicals: Notes on Committed Youth.* New York: Harcourt, Brace and World.

Killen, M. (1991). Social and moral development in early childhood. In W. Kurtines and J. Gewirtz (eds.), *Handbook of Moral Behavior and Development, Volume 2: Research* (pp. 115–38). Hillsdale, NJ: Lawrence Erlbaum.

Knutson, J. N. (1974). Prepolitical ideologies: The basis of political learning. In R. Niemi (ed.), *The Politics of Future Citizens* (pp. 7–40). San Francisco: Jossey-Bass.

Kohlberg, L. (1969). State and sequence: The cognitive-developmental approach to socialization. In D. Goslin (ed.), *Handbook of Socialization Theory and Research* (pp. 347–480). Chicago: Rand McNally.

———. (1978). The cognitive-developmental approach to moral education. In P. Scharf (ed.), *Readings in Moral Education* (pp. 36–51). Minneapolis: Winston.

———. (1980). High school democracy and educating for a just society. In R. Mosher (ed.), *Moral Education: A First Generation of Research and Development* (pp. 20–57). New York: Praeger.

———. (1984). *The Psychology of Moral Development,* vol. 2. San Francisco: Harper and Row.

———. (1985). The just community approach to moral education in theory and practice. In M. Berkowitz and F. Oser (eds.), *Moral Education: Theory and Application* (pp. 27–87). Hillsdale, NJ: Lawrence Erlbaum.

Kohlberg, L., and Candee, D. (1984a). The relation of moral judgment to moral action. In W. Kurtines and J. Gewirtz (eds.), *Morality, Moral Behavior, and Moral Development* (pp. 52–73). New York: Wiley.

———. (1984b). The relationship of moral judgment to moral action. In L. Kohlberg (ed.), *The Psychology of Moral Development,* vol. 2 (pp. 498–581). San Francisco: Harper and Row.

Kohlberg, L., Lieberman, M., Power, C., and Higgins, A. (1981). Just community and its curriculum: Implications for the future. *Moral Education Forum,* 6(4), 31–42.

Kurtines, W., and Gewirtz J. (eds.). (1987). *Moral Development Through Social Interaction.* New York: Wiley.

Lamb, S. (1991). First moral sense: Aspects of and contributors to a beginning morality in the second year of life. In W. Kurtines and J. Gewirtz (eds.), *Handbook of Moral Behavior and Development, Volume 2: Research* (pp. 171–89). Hillsdale, NJ: Lawrence Erlbaum.

Langton, K. P., and Jennings, M. K. (1968). Political socialization and the high school civics curriculum in the United States. *American Political Science Review, 62*(3), 852–67.

———. (1969). Formal environment: The school. In K. P. Langton (ed.), *Political Socialization* (pp. 84–119). New York: Oxford University Press.

Langton, K. P., and Karns, D. A. (1969). Influence of different agencies in political socialization. In K. P. Langton (ed.), *Political Socialization* (pp. 140–60). New York: Oxford University Press.

Lappe, F. M., and Du Bois, P. M. (1992). *Doing Democracy.* San Rafael, CA: Institute for the Arts of Democracy.

Lapsley, D. K., Enright, R. D., and Serlin, R. C. (1989). Moral and social education. In J. Worell and F. Dunner (eds.), *Adolescent as Decision-Maker: Applications to Development and Education* (pp. 111–41). New York: Academic.

Leming, J. S. (1981). Curriculum effectiveness in moral/values education: A review of the research. *Journal of Moral Education, 10*(3), 147–64.

———. (1992). The influence of contemporary issues curricula on school-age youth. In G. Grant (ed.), *Review of Research in Education, Vol. 18* (pp. 111–61). Washington, DC: American Educational Research Association.

Lengel, J. G., and Superka, D. P. (1982). Curriculum patterns. In I. Morrissett (ed.), *Social Studies in the 1980s: A Report of Project SPAN* (pp. 32–38). Alexandria, VA: Association for Supervision and Curriculum Development.

Levenson, G. B. (1972). The school's contribution to the learning of participatory responsibility. In B. Massialas (ed.), *Political Youth, Traditional Schools* (pp. 123–36). Englewood Cliffs, NJ: Prentice-Hall.

Levine, A. (1983). Riding first class on the Titanic: A portrait of today's college student. *NASPA Journal, 20*(4), 3–9.

Lickona, T., and Paradise, M. (1980). Democracy in the elementary school. In R. Mosher (ed.), *Moral Education: A First Generation of Research and Development* (pp. 321–38). New York: Praeger.

Lieberman, M. (1981). Facing History and Ourselves: A project evaluation. *Moral Education Forum, 6*(4), 36–41.

———. (1991). *Facing History and Ourselves: Evaluation Report 1990*. Wellesley, MA: Responsive Methodology.

Liebschutz, S. F., and Niemi, R. (1974). Political attitudes among black children. In R. Niemi (ed.), *The Politics of Future Citizens* (pp. 83–102). San Francisco: Jossey-Bass.

Light, P. (1987). Taking roles. In J. Bruner and H. Haste (eds.), *Making Sense: The Child's Construction of the World* (pp. 41–61). London: Methuen.

Litt, E. (1963). Civic education, community norms, and political indoctrination. *The American Sociological Review, 28*(1), 69–75.

Lowry, N., and Johnson, D. W. (1981). Effects of controversy on epistemic curiosity, achievement, and attitudes. *Journal of Social Psychology, 115*(1), 31–43.

Lyons, N. P., Saltonstall, J. F., and Hanmer, T. J. (1990). Competencies and visions: Emma Willard girls talk about being leaders. In C. Gilligan, N. Lyons, and T. Hanmer (eds.), *Making Connections: The Relational Worlds of Adolescent Girls at Emma Willard School* (pp. 183–214). Cambridge, MA: Harvard University Press.

Maccoby, E. E., and Martin, J. A. (1983). Socialization in the context of the family: Parent-child interaction. In E. M. Hetherington (ed.), *Handbook of Child Psychology: Volume 4. Socialization, Personality, and Social Development* (4th ed.) (pp. 1–101). New York: Wiley.

Massialas, B. G. (1972). The school and the political world of children and youth. In B. G. Massialas (ed.), *Political Youth, Traditional Schools: National and International Perspectives* (pp. 1–13). Englewood Cliffs, NJ: Prentice-Hall.

———. (1972). The inquiring activist. In B. Massialas (ed.), *Political Youth, Traditional Schools* (pp. 243–64). Englewood Cliffs, NJ: Prentice-Hall.

McCann, J. and Bell, P. (1975). Educational environment and the development of moral concepts. *Journal of Moral Education, 5*(1), 63–70.

Mead, G. H. (1934). *Mind, Self, and Society*. Chicago: University of Chicago Press.

Mehlinger, H. D. (1977). The crisis in civic education. In F. B. Brown (dir.), *Education for Responsible Citizenship: The Report of the National Task Force on Citizenship Education* (pp. 69–82). New York: McGraw-Hill.

Merelman, R. M. (1969). The development of political ideology: A framework for the analysis of political socialization. *American Political Science Review, 63*, 75–93.

————. (1971). The development of policy thinking in adolescence. *American Political Science Review, 65*, 1033–47.

————. (1985). Role and personality among adolescent political activists. *Youth and Society, 17*(1), 37–68.

————. (1986). Revitalizing political socialization. In R. Herrmann (ed.), *Political Psychology* (pp. 279–319). San Francisco: Jossey-Bass.

————. (1990). The role of conflict in children's political learning. In O. Ichilov (ed.), *Political Socialization, Citizenship Education, and Democracy* (pp. 47–65). New York: Teachers College Press.

Merelman, R. M., and King, G. (1986). The development of political activists: Toward a model of early learning. *Social Science Quarterly, 67*(3), 473–90.

Metis Associates. (1988, November). *The Resolving Conflict Creatively Program: A Summary of Significant Findings.* New York: Author.

Metzger, D. J. (1977). The impact of school political systems on selected student attitudes (Doctoral dissertation, Indiana University, 1977). *Dissertation Abstracts International,* 1977, *38*, 5385A-5386A. (University Microfilms No. 78-00, 994).

Meyer, L. (1979). *The Citizenship Education Issue: Problems and Programs.* Educational Commission of the States Report No. 123, Denver, 1979.

Midlarsky, E. (1984). Competence and helping: Notes toward a model. In E. Staub, D. Bar-Tal, J. Karylowski, and J. Reykowski (eds.), *Development and Maintenance of Prosocial Behavior* (pp. 291–308). New York: Plenum.

Milgram, S. (1974). *Obedience to Authority: An Experimental View.* New York: Harper and Row.

Minuchin, P. P., and Shapiro, E. K. (1983). The school as a context for social development. In E. M. Hetherington (ed.), *Handbook of Child Psychology: Volume 4. Socialization, Personality, and Social Development* (4th ed.) (pp. 197–274). New York: Wiley.

Moore, S. W. (1989). The need for a unified theory of political learning: Lessons from a longitudinal project. *Human Development, 32*(5), 5–13.

Moore, S. W., Lare, J., and Wagner, K. A. (1985). *The Child's Political Worlds: A Longitudinal Perspective.* New York: Praeger.

Morrison, T. R., Toews, B., and Rest, J. R. (1975). *Youth, Law and Morality.* Unpublished manuscript, Winnipeg.

Morrissett, I. (ed.). (1982). *Social Studies in the 1980s: A Report of Project SPAN.* Alexandria, VA: Association for Supervision and Curriculum Development.

Nakkula, M., and Selman, R. L. (1991). How people "treat" each other: Pair therapy as a context for the development of interpersonal ethics. In W. Kurtines and J. Gewirtz (eds.), *Handbook of Moral Behavior and Development, Volume 3: Application* (pp. 179–211). Hillsdale, NJ: Lawrence Erlbaum.

Neef, J. (1807). *A Proper System of Education for the Schools of a Free People.* Philadelphia: Author.

Newmann, F. (1975). *Education for Citizen Action.* Berkeley, CA: McCutchan.

———. (1977). Building a rationale for civic education. In J. Shaver (ed.), *Building Rationales for Citizenship Education*, Bulletin 52 (pp. 1–33). Arlington, VA: National Council for the Social Studies.

———. (1990). Reflective civic participation. In J. Kendall and Associates (eds.), *Combining Service and Learning: A Resource Book for Community and Public Service, Volume 1* (pp. 76–84). Raleigh, NC: National Society for Internships and Experiential Education.

Niles, W. J. (1986). Effects of a moral development discussion group on delinquent and predelinquent boys. *Journal of Counseling Psychology,* 33(1), 45–51.

Nucci, L. P. (1982, Spring). Conceptual development in the moral and conventional domains: Implications for values education. *Review of Educational Research,* 52(1), 93–122.

Oliner, P. (1983). Putting 'community' into citizenship education: The need for prosociality. *Theory and Research in Social Education,* 11(2), 65–81.

Oliner, S., and Oliner, P. (1988). *The Altruistic Personality.* New York: The Free Press.

Owen, D., and Dennis, J. (1987). Preadult development of political tolerance. *Political Psychology,* 8(4), 547–562.

Palonsky, S. (1987, May). Political socialization in elementary schools. *The Elementary School Journal,* 87(5), 492–505.

Pateman, C. (1970). *Participation and Democratic Theory.* Cambridge: Cambridge University Press.

Patrick, J. J. (1972). The impact of an experimental course, "American Political Behavior," on the knowledge, skills, and attitudes of secondary school students. *Social Education,* 1972, 36(2), 168–79.

Patrick, J. J., and Hawke, S. D. (1982). Curriculum materials. In I. Morrissett (ed.), *Social Studies in the 1980s: A Report of Project SPAN* (pp. 39–50). Alexandria, VA: Association for Supervision and Curriculum Development.

Patterson, J. W. (1979). Moral development and political thinking: The case of freedom of speech. *Western Political Quarterly, 32*(1), 7–20.

Perry, W. G. (1970). *Forms of Intellectual and Ethical Development in the College Years.* New York: Holt, Rinehart and Winston.

Piaget, J. (1932/1965). *The Moral Judgment of the Child.* New York: Free Press.

Power, C., and Higgins, A. (1992). The just community approach to classroom participation. In A. Garrod (ed.), *Learning for a Lifetime: Moral Education in Theory and Practice* (pp. 228–45). New York: Praeger.

Power, C., Higgins, A., and Kohlberg, L. (1989). *Lawrence Kohlberg's Approach to Moral Education.* New York: Columbia University Press.

Power, C., and Reimer, J. (1978). Moral atmosphere: An educational bridge between moral judgment and action. In W. Damon (ed.), *New Directions for Child Development, Vol. 2: Moral Development* (pp. 105–16). San Francisco: Jossey-Bass.

Radke-Yarrow, M., and Zahn-Waxler, C. (1984). Roots, motives, and patterns in children's prosocial behavior. In E. Staub, D. Bar-Tal, J. Karylowski, and J. Reykowski (eds.), *Development and Maintenance of Prosocial Behavior* (pp. 81–99). New York: Plenum.

Rafalides, M., and Hoy, W. K. (1971, December). Student sense of alienation and pupil control orientations of high schools. *High School Journal, 55*(3), 101–11.

Ramsey, J. M., and Hungerford, H. R. (1988). The effects of issue investigation and action training on environmental behavior in seventh grade students. *Journal of Environmental Education, 20*(4), 29–34.

Ramsey, J. M., Hungerford, H. R., and Tomera, A. N. (1981). The effects of environmental action and environmental case study instruction on the overt environmental behavior of eighth-grade students. *Journal of Environmental Education, 13*(1), 24–30.

Reindl, S. (1993). Bringing global awareness into elementary school classrooms. In S. Berman and P. LaFarge (eds.), *Promising Practices in Teaching Social Responsibility* (pp. 27–49). Albany: State University of New York Press.

Reische, D. L. (1987). *Citizenship Goal of Education.* Arlington, VA: American Association of School Administrators.

Remy, R. C. (1980a). *Handbook of Basic Citizenship Competencies.* Alexandria, VA: Association of Supervision and Curriculum Development.

———. (1980b, October). Criteria for judging citizenship education programs. *Educational Leadership 38*(1), 10–11.

Renshon, S. A. (1977). Assumptive frameworks in political socialization theory. In S. A. Renshon (ed.), *Handbook of Political Socialization: Theory and Research* (pp. 3–44). New York: Free Press.

Rest, J. (1975). Longitudinal study of the defining issues test of moral judgment: A strategy for analyzing developmental change. *Developmental Psychology*, 1(6), 738–48.

———. (1983). Morality. In P. Mussen (ed.), *Handbook of Child Psychology*, vol. 3 (pp. 556–629). New York: Wiley.

Rest, J. R., Ahlgren, C., and Mackey, J. (1972). *Minneapolis Police Report*. Unpublished manuscript, University of Minnesota.

Rheingold, H. L., and Emery, G. N. (1986). The nurturant acts of very young children. In D. Olwevs, J. Block, and M. Radke-Yarrow (eds.), *Development of Antisocial and Prosocial Behavior: Research, Theories, and Issues* (pp. 75–96). Orlando, FL: Academic.

Rheingold, H., and Hay, D. (1980). Prosocial behavior of the very young. In G. Stent (ed.), *Morality as a Biological Phenomenon* (pp. 93–108). Berkeley: University of California Press.

Rheingold, H. L., Hay, D. F., and West, M. J. (1976). Sharing in the second year of life. *Child Development*, 47(4), 114–25.

Robinson, D. W. (1967). *Promising Practices in Civic Education*. Washington, DC: National Council for the Social Studies.

Rosenhan, D. L. (1970). The natural socialization of altruistic autonomy. In J. Macauley and L. Berkowitz (eds.), *Altruism and Helping* (pp. 251–68). New York: Academic.

———. (1972). Learning theory and prosocial behavior. *Journal of Social Issues*, 28(3), 151–64.

Rotter, J. B. (1966). Generalized expectancies for internal versus external control of reinforcement. *Psychological Monographs: General and Applied*, 80(1), 1–28.

Sears, D. O. (1972) Development of concepts of political conflict and power by 5th and 8th graders (Final report, USOE Project No. 9-0444). August 1972. (ERIC Document Reproduction Service No. ED 071 959).

———. (1990). Whither political socialization research? The question of persistence. In O. Ichilov (ed.), *Political Socialization, Citizenship Education, and Democracy* (pp. 69–97). New York: Teachers College Press.

Seligman, M. (1991). *Learned Optimism*. New York: Knopf.

Selman, R. L. (1980). *The Growth of Interpersonal Understanding: Development and Clinical Analysis*. New York: Academic.

Sharan, S. (1980). Cooperative learning in small groups: Recent methods and effects on achievement, attitudes, and ethnic relations. *Review of Educational Reseach, 50*(2), 241–71.

Shaver, J. P. (1977). The task of rationale-building for citizenship education. In J. Shaver (ed.), *Building Rationales for Citizenship Education*, Bulletin 52 (pp. 96–116). Arlington, VA: National Council for the Social Studies.

Sia, A. P., Hungerford, H. R., and Tomera, A. N. (1986). Selected predictors of responsible environmental behavior: An analysis. *Journal of Environmental Education, 17*(2), 31–40.

Siegel, M. E. (1977). Citizenship education in five Massachusetts high schools. *Theory and Research in Social Education, 5*(2), 52–76.

Sigel, R. S. (1979). Students' comprehension of democracy and its application to conflict situations. *International Journal of Political Education, 2*(1), 47–65.

Sigel, R. S., and Hoskin, M. B. (1981). *The Political Involvement of Adolescents.* New Brunswick, NJ: Rutgers University Press.

Sinatra, G. M., Beck, I. L., and McKeown, M. G. (1992). A longitudinal characterization of young students' knowledge of their country's government. *American Educational Research Journal, 29*(3), 633–61.

Sirotnik, K. A. (1988). What goes on in classroom? Is this the way we want it? In L. E. Beyer and M. W. Apple (eds.), *The Curriculum: Problems, Politics, and Possibilities* (pp. 56–74). Albany: State University of New York Press.

Sizer, T. (1984). *Horace's Compromise: The Dilemma of the American High School.* Boston: Houghton Mifflin.

Slavin, R. E. (1983). *Cooperative Learning.* New York: Longman.

Smetana, J. (1981). Preschool children's conceptions of moral and social rules. *Child Development, 52*(5), 1333–36.

———. (1989). Toddlers' social interactions in the context of moral and conventional transgressions in the home. *Developmental Psychology, 25*(4), 499–508.

Smith, K., Johnson, D. W., and Johnson, R. T. (1981). Can conflict be constructive? Controversy versus concurrence seeking in learning groups. *Journal of Educational Psychology, 73*(5), 651–63.

Solomon, D., Schaps, E., Watson, M., and Battistich, V. (1992). Creating caring school and classroom communities for all students. In R. Villa, J. Thousand, W. Stainback, and S. Stainback (eds.), *Restructuring* for Caring and Effective Education: An Administrative Guide to Creating Heterogeneous Schools, (pp. 41–60). Baltimore: Paul H. Brookes.

Solomon, D., Watson, M., Battistich, V., Schaps, E., and Delucchi, K. (1990). Creating a caring community: A school-based program to promote children's sociomoral development. Paper presented at the International Symposium on Research on Effective and Responsible Teaching, Fribourg, Switzerland, September 4, 1990.

Solomon, D., Watson, M., Battistich, V., and Solomon, J. (1990). Cooperative learning as part of a comprehensive program designed to promote prosocial development. In S. Sharan (ed.), *Cooperative Learning: Theory and Research* (pp. 231–60). New York: Praeger.

Stake, R. E., and Easley, J. A., Jr. (1978). *Case Studies in Science Education.* Washington, DC: National Science Foundation.

Staub, E. (1975). To rear a prosocial child: Reasoning, learning by doing, and learning by teaching others. In D. DePalma and J. Folley (eds.), *Moral Development: Current Theory and Research* (pp. 113–36). Hillsdale, NJ: Lawrence Erlbaum.

———. (1988). The evolution of caring and nonaggressive persons and societies. *Journal of Social Issues, 44*(2), 81–100.

Stevens, O. (1982). *Children Talking Politics.* Oxford: Martin Robertson.

Strom, M. S., and Parsons, W. S. (1982). *Facing History and Ourselves: Holocaust and Human Behavior.* Brookline, MA: Facing History and Ourselves Foundation.

Sullivan, E. V. (1977). A study of Kohlberg's structural theory of moral development: A critique of liberal social science ideology. *Human Development, 20*(6), 352–76.

———. (1986). Kohlberg's stage theory as a progressive educationl form for value development. In S. Modgil and C. Modgil (eds.), *Lawrence Kohlberg: Consensus and Controversy* (pp. 233–44). Philadelphia: The Falmer Press.

Sullivan, E. V., and Beck, C. (1975). Moral education in a Canadian setting. *Phi Delta Kappan, 56*(10), 697–701.

Sullivan, H. (1953). *The Interpersonal Theory of Psychiatry.* New York: Norton.

Times Mirror Center for the People and the Press. (1990). *The Age of Indifference: A Study of Young Americans and How They View the News.* Washington, DC: Author.

Tjosvold, D., Johnson D. W., and Johnson, R. T. (1984). Influence strategy, perspective-taking, and relationships between high- and low-power individuals in cooperative and competitive contexts. *Journal of Psychology, 116*(2), 187–202.

Tjosvold, D., Johnson D. W., and Lerner, J. V. (1981). Effects of affirmation and acceptance on incorporation of opposing information in problem-solving. *Journal of Social Psychology, 114*(1), 103–10.

Torney-Purta, J. (1981). Recent psychological research relating to children's social cognition and its implications for social and political education. In I. Morrisett and A. M. Williams (Eds.), *Social/Political Education in Three Countries* (pp. 91–111). Boulder, CO: Social Sciences Education Consortium.

———. (1983). The development of views about the role of social institutions in redressing inequality and promoting human rights. In R. L. Leahy (ed.), *The Child's Construction of Social Inequality* (pp. 287–310). New York: Academic.

Torney, J., Oppenheim, A., and Farnen, R. (1975). *Civic Education in Ten Countries: An Empirical Study*. New York: Wiley.

Turiel, E. (1983). *The Development of Social Knowledge: Morality and Convention*. Cambridge: Cambridge University Press.

Turiel, E., Smetana, J. G., and Killen, M. (1991). Social contexts in social cognitive development. In W. Kurtines and J. Gewirtz (eds.), *Handbook of Moral Behavior and Development, Volume 2: Research* (pp. 307–32). Hillsdale, NJ: Lawrence Erlbaum.

Turner, M. J. (1971). *Materials for Civics, Government and Problems of Democracy*. Boulder, CO: Social Science Education Consortium, Inc.

Verba, S., Nie, N. H., and Kim, J. (1978). *Participation and Political Equity*. Cambridge: Cambridge University Press.

Villegas, E. (1986). Responsibility: Its definitions, characteristics and development. Doctoral Qualifying Paper, Harvard Graduate School of Education.

Volk, T. L., and Hungerford, H. R. (1981). The effects of process education on problem identification skills in environmental education. *Journal of Environmental Education, 12*(3), 36–40.

Washburn, P. C. (1986). The political role of the American school. *Theory and Research in Social Education, 14*(1), 51–65.

Weinreich-Haste, H. E. (1983). Social and moral cognition. In H. Weinreich-Haste and D. Locke (eds.), *Morality in the Making: Judgment, Action and Social Context* (pp. 87–110). Chichester: Wiley.

Weinreich-Haste, H. (1984). Morality, social meaning, and rhetoric: The social context of moral reasoning. In W. Kurtines and J. Gewirtz (eds.), *Morality, Moral Behavior, and Moral Development* (pp. 325–47). New York: Wiley.

———. (1986). Kohlberg's contribution to political psychology: A positive view. In S. Modgil and C. Modgil (eds.), *Lawrence Kohlberg: Consensus and Controversy* (pp. 337–61). Philadelphia: The Falmer Press.

Weiss, I. R. (1978). *National Survey of Science, Mathematics, and Social Studies Education.* Washington, DC: National Science Foundation.

Welch, S. D. (1990). *A Feminist Ethic of Risk.* Minneapolis: Fortress Press.

Westholm, A., Lindquist, A., and Niemi, R. (1990). Education and the making of the informed citizen: Political literacy and the outside world. In O. Ichilov (ed.), *Political Socialization, Citizenship Education, and Democracy* (pp. 177–204). New York: Teachers College Press.

White, R. W. (1981). Humanitarian Concern. In A. W. Chickering and Associates (eds.), *The Modern American College* (pp. 160–171). San Francisco: Jossey-Bass.

Whiting, B. B., and Whiting, J. W. M. (1975). *Children of Six Cultures: A Psychocultural Analysis.* Cambridge, MA: Harvard University Press.

Williams, C. B., and Minns, D. R. (1986). Agent credibility and receptivity influences on children's political learning. *Political Behavior, 8*(2), 175–200.

Wood, G. H. (1988a). Civic education for participatory democracy. In S. D. Franzosa (ed.), *Civic Education: Its Limits and Conditions* (pp. 68–98). Ann Arbor, MI: Prakken.

———. (1988b). Democracy and the curriculum. In L. E. Beyer and M. W. Apple (eds.), *The Curriculum: Problems, Politics, and Possibilities* (pp. 166–87). Albany: State University of New York Press.

———. (1992). *Schools That Work: America's Most Innovative Public Education Programs.* New York: Dutton.

Woodward, A., Elliot, D. L., and Nagel, K. C. (1986). Beyond textbooks in elementary social studies. *Social Education, 50*(1), 50–53.

Youniss, J. (1980). *Parents and Peers in Social Development.* Chicago: University of Chicago Press.

———. (1987). Social construction and moral development: Update and expansion of an idea. In W. Kurtines and J. Gewirtz (eds.), *Moral Development Through Social Interaction* (pp. 131–48). New York: Wiley.

Zahn-Waxler, C., and Radke-Yarrow, M. (1982). The development of altruism: Alternative research strategies. In N. Eisenberg-Berg (ed.),

The Development of Prosocial Behavior (pp. 109–37). New York: Academic.

Zahn-Waxler, C., Radke-Yarrow, M., and Brady-Smith, J. (1977). Perspective-taking and prosocial behavior. *Developmental Psychology, 13*(1), 87–88.

Zahn-Waxler, C., Radke-Yarrow, M., and King, R. M. (1979). Childrearing and children's prosocial initiations toward victims of distress. *Child Development, 50*(2), 319–30.

Zeigler, H. (1967). *The Political Life of American Teachers.* Englewood Cliffs, NJ: Prentice-Hall.

Subject Index

abandonment, 13–14, 118, 136

abstract: discussion, 101; thinking, 15, 32, 93

accountability, personal, 176

action, 49, 55, 68, 69, 75, 78, 94, 99–100, 116, 117, 121, 132, 146–47, 166, 179, 184, 190, 193, 195, 196; preceding reflection 197; success of, 46–47

activism, 41–83, 85–86, 114, 123, 144–58, 164, 166, 190, 192–93. See also activists; political participation

activists, 33, 193; adult, 44, 48, 51, 106, 152; diverse motivations of, 68–69

adolescence, 3, 4, 8, 20, 32, 33, 34, 35, 36, 38, 39, 44, 53, 55, 59–60, 62–63, 86, 101, 104, 106, 107, 109, 117–19, 125, 144, 145, 175, 191, 193

adult-child relationships, 25, 41, 87–88, 113, 128, 136–37, 146

adulthood, 8, 19, 32, 35, 37, 55, 61, 62, 66, 72, 76, 91, 99–100, 106, 125, 145, 151, 167, 200. See also activists, adult

adults, modeling of, 85–87. See also communication: with adults about politics; role models

alienation, 2–4, 19, 21, 34, 35, 37, 39, 42, 65, 74, 79, 110, 125, 126, 147, 176, 183, 185. See also isolation; political alienation

alternative social and political arrangements. See vision

altruism, 12, 14, 49, 53–54, 72–73, 86–89, 130, 138, 145, 160; lack of, 74. See also care; generosity; service

America. See United States

anger. See emotion

apathy, 118, 147. See also passivity

Armenian Genocide, 115–16, 190

attachment, 21, 57–59, 118, 119, 131, 136, 191, 200

attitudes, changes in, 97, 107, 109, 146–47, 149

authoritarianism, 5, 33, 108, 128, 131, 160, 184, 187, 194; anti-, 110

authority, 23, 25, 30, 31, 80, 92, 93, 95, 105, 114, 130, 133, 146, 168, 169–70; benevolence of, 33, 112, 114; political, 15, 29, 37, 49–50

autocracy, 125, 126

autonomy, 21, 63, 76, 146

beliefs, living them out, 14, 53, 57, 70–71, 73, 79, 101, 137, 155–56, 157, 160, 163, 165. See also experiential learning

benevolence, 24; of leadership, 33, 112, 114

blame, externalization of, 89

Brameld, Theodore, 161

Author Index

249